Divine Law and
Political Philosophy
in Plato's *Laws*

Divine Law and
POLITICAL PHILOSOPHY
in Plato's *Laws*

MARK J. LUTZ

NIU
PRESS

DeKalb, IL

© 2012 by Northern Illinois University Press

Published by the Northern Illinois University Press, DeKalb, Illinois   60115

Manufactured in the United States using acid-free paper.

All Rights Reserved

Design by Julia Fauci

Library of Congress Cataloging-in-Publication Data

Lutz, Mark J.

Divine law and political philosophy in Plato's Laws / Mark J. Lutz.

   p.   cm.

Includes bibliographical references and index.

ISBN 978-0-87580-445-3 (cloth: alk. paper) — ISBN 978-1-60909-048-7 (electronic)

1. Plato. Laws. 2. Political science—Philosophy. I. Title.

JC71.P264L87 2012

321'.07—dc23

2011034645

To Kelly and Andy

CONTENTS

ACKNOWLEDGMENTS

I am grateful to the College of Liberal Arts of the University of Nevada at Las Vegas for its generous financial support as I completed this book. I am pleased to thank my colleagues at UNLV Ken Fernandez, Tiffiany Howard, Michelle Kuenzi, and Rebecca Gill for their helpful consultations about this book. I am especially grateful for all the support and useful guidance that I have received from my colleagues Mehran Tamadonfar, John Tuman, and, above all, David Fott.

When I was a graduate student at the University of Toronto, I had the very good fortune to study Platonic political philosophy with Tom Pangle. I am grateful to him for his example, his learning, and his generous advice. My understanding of Plato has also benefitted greatly from many conversations with Robert Goldberg and Michael Rosano. I thank them for having read and commented on parts of the manuscript.

Most of all, I thank my wonderful wife, Kelly, and our wonderful son, Andy, for their good spirits and patient support while I was writing this book. Kelly's careful reading and thoughtful suggestions have been invaluable.

I also wish to thank my editor, Amy Farranto, at the Northern Illinois University Press and the Press's anonymous reviewers for their very useful comments and guidance.

A version of the first chapter appeared as "The *Minos* and the Socratic Examination of Law" in the *American Journal of Political Science* 54, no. 4 (2010), 988–1002, reprinted with permission of the Midwest Political Science Association (© 2010, Midwest Political Science Association).

Divine Law and
Political Philosophy
in Plato's *Laws*

INTRODUCTION

For many years, scholars have regarded the *Laws* as Plato's final proposal for practical political reform. While there is much to be learned from such an approach, it has failed to do justice to the dialogue's central concern. What leading interpretations of the dialogue fail to appreciate is that Plato's *Laws* is, first and foremost, an inquiry into divine law. It is the dialogue in which Plato directly and thematically explores what divine law is, how we come to know or believe in it, and how it shapes civic life. Moreover, it is the dialogue in which Plato demonstrates that the political philosopher has the authority to interpret or guide divine law. When read with attention to these themes and to the drama of the dialogue, the *Laws* provides an eye-opening analysis of divine law as well as a powerful defense of political rationalism.

Plato's inquiry into the relationship between political philosophy and divine law is not merely of scholarly or historical interest. Today, from North America and Europe to India and Thailand, secular rationalist governments and judicial authorities have been challenged by increasingly vigorous claims made on behalf of shari'a or divine law. As Plato knew from his own experience, the presence of divine law as a political force raises important theoretical and practical challenges to those who believe that reason should be the principal guide of politics and law. Proponents of divine law say that the law provides authoritative and comprehensive guidance because it is based on a profound wisdom regarding justice and the common good. Some of those who reflect on divine law say that the law consists solely in what is known through a prophecy that has been given to a select person or persons. Others say that divine law includes both positive revelation and what is known through a powerful religious experience that has not been experienced universally. Still others say that what is known through revelation and faith should be supplemented by what is known through the rational faculties that are available to all. But all of these believers in divine law tend to agree that even though reason may be able to recognize the wisdom that underlies divine law, reason cannot derive or disclose that wisdom on its own. Revealed law is a miracle, an uncanny sign of a divine providence that human reason cannot anticipate or elaborate by itself. Because human reason, unassisted by revelation and faith, cannot provide a complete and undistorted vision of the highest goals of politics and law, it should not be trusted to set or pursue those goals without guidance from divine law.[1]

The far-reaching claims that current defenders of divine law make about the very basis of political and legal authority have evoked few, if any, responses from contemporary theorists who would defend political rationalism. In the past, modern political philosophers did not ignore the controversy. The political philosophers who helped to found modernity pursued a common strategy as they sought to liberate both philosophy and politics from the need to rely on revelation or on any authorities that rely on religious faith. These early modern philosophers began by arguing that we cannot have genuine, rational knowledge regarding the nature of God or His purposes. They argued that we do not know the ends to which God directs nature as a whole or what happens to the soul after death (e.g., Descartes, *Meditations,* Number 4, 55; Hobbes, *Leviathan,* Chapter 31; Locke, *Essay Concerning Human Understanding,* Book IV, Chapter 3, 24, 29; Chapter 6, 11–13; Chapter 12, 10–12; Chapter 18, 7). Putting aside the quest for knowledge of these matters, they sought to turn philosophy's attention away from theological and teleological questions and to direct it instead toward the mastery of material nature for the sake of "relief of man's estate" (Bacon, *The Advancement of Learning,* Book I, V, 11; also, Hobbes, *Leviathan,* Chapter 5, 21–22). At the same time, the early modern political philosophers sought to establish an increasingly complete and consistent account of the material universe. They argued that in the past most human beings lived under the sway of superstition. Lacking knowledge of the natural causes of events and gripped by powerful fears and hopes, the vast majority of people sought help from an imaginary multitude of spiritual beings and invisible powers (Hobbes, *Leviathan,* Chapter 12; Spinoza, *Theologico-Political Treatise,* "Preface"). The early modern philosophers expected that when modern science demonstrates that it can provide most people with physical security and material well-being, it will thereby alleviate the fears and hopes that have in the past driven people to turn to spiritual authorities for safety and comfort. As modern science carries out its conquest of nature, questions about whether scripture is the product of a divine or a human mind and whether miracles or particular providence are possible will cease to be a central concern of the public. This would eventually diminish the widespread concern with and faith in the spiritual authorities that had always dominated philosophy and politics. When compelled to respond to claims made by religious authorities in moral and political matters, the early modern political philosophers argued that we can justly rely on what we learn from unassisted human reason on the grounds that reason and revelation coincide on the most important issues. Where reason and revelation seem to differ, they said, revelation should be re-interpreted so that it agrees with reason (e.g., Locke, *Two Treatises of Government*, "Second Treatise," Chapters 3 and 5 beginning; *Essay Concerning Human Understanding*, Book IV, Chapter 18, 5; Spinoza, *Theologico-Political Treatise*, 3. 79). Through this process, modern philosophy would transcend the challenges that revelation and religious faith pose to rationalism. But even as modern natural science has made great progress in mastering the forces of material nature, many have come to doubt that philosophy or science can resolve our most serious spiritual and political problems. As we continue to make dazzling technological progress, we find that we do not simultaneously acquire the moral and political guidance that we need to use it wisely. More generally, many have come to doubt that our scientific, rationalistic culture is the authoritative culture. Science, they say, is said to be but one interpretation of the world among many, and by no means is it obviously the most benign or most vital interpretation (Nietzsche, *Beyond Good and Evil*, 14). According to Richard Rorty, contemporary thinkers find it impossible to believe in the Enlightenment's teachings about nature, the self, and the truth (Rorty 1982, xiv). Viewed in this light, modern philosophy or science comes to sight as a hegemonic will or spirit rather than as a liberating insight and tool.

As doubts such as these are raised about the foundations of modern rationalism, some have observed that these doubts call into question the triumph that philosophy seemed to win over revelation. According to Leo Strauss, defenders of rationalism are now compelled to reconsider what he calls the "theological-political problem." The meaning and importance of this problem becomes clearer as we think through what seem to be irreconcilable claims made by philosophy and by revelation. The philosopher believes that human happiness comes through our own free investigation and insight. The philosopher believes that if we are able to replace our opinions about what is right and what is good with knowledge of these matters, then we may learn to do what is best (Strauss 2006, 146–48). But revelation counters that we can find fulfillment only through obedience to a god. Revelation challenges philosophy's claim to knowledge, saying that we cannot gain genuine knowledge about what is good through our own efforts but must depend on divine revelation to supply us with that knowledge. Divine revelation declares that it has what philosophy seeks: a complete and undistorted knowledge of what is good. But revelation declares that a wise god reveals his wisdom only to those whom he chooses, when he chooses, and within the limits that he chooses (Meier 2006, 6–7).

The truth of revelation is verified not by reason but by some extra-rational faculty, some spirit or faith. When revelation takes the form of divine law, it establishes a sacred and inviolable code that we must follow if we are to do what is right and if we are to escape the eternal punishment that awaits those who defy the law.

The problem for philosophy seems to be that it has no basis for answering the claims made by revelation. Insofar as philosophy lacks a rational basis for its own activity, it comes to sight as a kind of non-rational hope or commitment. The opposition between philosophy and revelation appears to be a battle of wills, a contest between one form of faith and another. The difficulty is that philosophy's faith seems more contradictory and problematic than religious faith, for the former came into existence to relieve us of the need to rely on any sort of faith that cannot be justified by reason. Yet this apparent impasse may be overcome if defenders of political rationalism would consider the possibility that there is more than one kind of rationalism and that another form of rationalism may not share the specific weaknesses of modern rationalism. If we look back to the beginnings of political rationalism, or, more precisely, to classical political rationalism, we will find that Plato offers a powerful defense of the attempt to use reason to guide politics and law, especially in light of forceful challenges leveled against it by defenders of divine law. According to Plato, classical political philosophy's original and central concern is to answer the claims made on behalf of divine law because it is only by responding to those claims that the philosopher can establish that the philosophic life is best or just or even possible. Plato's account of the life of Socrates is an attempt to show how the political philosopher responds to the charges leveled against philosophy by defenders of divine law before the bar of the city that lives under that law.

Some may question whether a pagan philosopher such as Plato can speak to issues that arise in Islamic or Jewish or Christian traditions. But the classical political philosopher's examination of law and divine law has served as a model for thinking about the relation of reason and divine law in other ages and in other religious traditions. Plato's teachings about philosophy and law had a tremendous influence on the great Islamic philosophers Al-Farabi, Avicenna, and Averroes. And they, in turn, informed the thought of thinkers such as Maimonides and Aquinas. The great Islamic philosophers wrote numerous books on Plato because they recognized that the questions that surround the relation between reason and divine law are central to Plato's thought. They placed special emphasis on the *Laws* because they recognized that this dialogue is the longest and most thematic examination of divine law in classical political philosophy.[2] It is in this dialogue that

Plato provides his most complete and most direct case that the political philosopher can provide divine law with a guidance that divine law needs in order to accomplish its goals. But in modern times, Plato's insights into the relation between reason and revelation and especially into divine law have largely been forgotten. The primary purpose of this book is to help us understand why Plato believes that the political philosopher has the authority to guide divine law and to recover Plato's insights into what divine law is and how it shapes the lives of those who live under it. By recovering these insights, we may also provide contemporary thinkers with an example of how a defender of political rationalism can engage in a fair-minded and mutually instructive dialogue with defenders of divine law.

A further reason why we should study the *Laws* concerns the common ground that Plato's Athenian Stranger finds between the political philosopher and the believer in divine law. Early in the dialogue, the Athenian Stranger takes up a conversation with two elderly statesmen who have lived their lives under revered codes of divine law. In the course of that conversation, the Athenian Stranger shows that the citizen who believes in divine law also believes that divine law has some discernable purposes or goals, and that among those goals it seeks to promote a certain way of life for those who live under the law. According to the citizen who is devoted to the law, the law instills specific virtues, certain important and laudable qualities of character and mind. In the course of the Athenian Stranger's examination, the devoted and morally serious citizen reveals that he expects divine law to bring forth the greatest virtue or rather the complete and genuine virtue of a human being. In light of this, Plato shows that if the political philosopher can demonstrate that he understands this virtue, then he will have found a common ground with the devout citizen on the basis of which he can demonstrate his knowledge of and authority to guide divine law. Because the philosopher's authority to interpret the law is grounded on his knowledge of virtue, much of the dialogue is devoted to examining what the virtues are and how they are taught. In fact, the *Laws* contains the longest and most thematic examination in classical literature of what moral education is and ought to be. The dialogue examines the virtues that law can teach as well as the virtues that it cannot promote. Its subtle exploration of how education can shape both the character and the mind makes it comparable to Locke's *Some Thoughts Concerning Education* and to Rousseau's *Emile*. This makes the *Laws* a very rich and surprisingly untapped resource for learning what the virtues are and how civic education works.

Despite the size and subject matter of the *Laws*, the dialogue has received relatively little attention from political theorists and other students of Plato. Leading works that focus on the *Laws* as a whole include Christopher

Bobonich's *Plato's Utopia Recast* (Oxford, 2002), Glenn Morrow's *Plato's Cretan City* (Princeton, 1960), Trevor Saunders's *Plato's Laws* (Penguin, 1970), and R. F. Stalley's *Plato's Laws: An Introduction* (Hackett, 1983). While each of these books sheds light on many features of the dialogue, their authors suggest that Plato assumes that the cosmos is guided by reason, that the gods are rational, and that genuine law is always rational, too. Upon reading these otherwise informative books, one would think that it never occurs to Plato—who witnessed Socrates's execution for impiety and corruption of the young—to ask where the philosopher derives the moral and spiritual authority to challenge codes of law that are said to be divinely inspired. By their accounts, Plato never paused to ask himself why devout subjects of divine law would and should abandon their faith and adopt the reason-based code of law that is outlined in the *Laws*.

Because these authors do not inquire into why Plato is confident that the political philosopher has the ability and the authority to interpret divine law, they do not recognize that much of the dialogue is written to investigate how the devout citizen experiences and knows divine law. Nor do they appreciate how the dialogue shows that the political philosopher and the devout citizen share a common ground insofar as they both claim to care about and know human virtue. Because these authors do not address the questions and controversies that surround the relation between reason and divine law, they do not observe how Plato's Athenian Stranger subtly questions whether law can teach human virtue nor how he demonstrates that divine law can pursue its goals only through the guidance of political philosophy. By contrast, this book shows that Plato raises these questions at the outset of the dialogue and examines how he pursues these questions in those subsequent passages that address them most directly. There are two older commentaries that raise questions about the relation between political philosophy and divine law. Thomas Pangle's *The Laws of Plato* (University of Chicago Press, 1988) and Leo Strauss's *The Argument and the Action of Plato's* Laws (University of Chicago Press, 1975) discuss the challenge that divine law poses to political philosophy and pay attention to the drama as well as the argument of the dialogue. But neither of these commentaries makes the relation between political philosophy and divine law its explicit and guiding theme. By contrast, this book is not a commentary on the whole dialogue but a sustained, thematic examination of the inquiry into what divine law is, the virtues that it teaches, and why Plato believes that the political philosopher has the authority to guide divine law.

This interpretation of the *Laws* is distinct from many others because it pays attention to both the substantive arguments and the drama of the dialogue. By considering the dramatic context in which the arguments take place, we can deepen our understanding of what the believer in divine law and the political philosopher each knows about divine law. In regard to the former, the drama allows devoted citizens from Crete and from Sparta to reveal what they know about divine law, even if what they know about it cannot be fully expressed in speech. And by thinking carefully about their words and actions, we are better able to recognize and perhaps even feel what is at issue for them in the dialogue. To the extent that we can enter into their understanding, the better we may understand whether or how that understanding is deficient and subject to improvement. In addition, the drama is useful for understanding what Plato's Athenian Stranger knows and learns about divine law. In the *Laws,* the Athenian Stranger says that he intends to examine not only the lawgivers of Crete and Sparta but also Kleinias, Megillus, and himself (Plato *Laws* 633a). In order that he may investigate what his interlocutors know about divine law and how they know it, the Athenian Stranger must draw them out. He must give them the opportunity to say or show what they know about divine law on their own terms. This means that the Athenian Stranger will sometimes say things that are intended more to induce his interlocutors to reveal what they know about divine law than to lay out all that he knows on the subject. Moreover, when the Athenian Stranger is asked to help Kleinias devise the best possible code of law for Crete's new colony, he agrees to do so because he wants to test whether he can produce a credible account of divine law while relying on his own, unassisted reason. In order to carry out this test, the Athenian Stranger must keep his account of divine law, its origins, and its goals within the horizon of the citizens who live under divine law. Thus, attention to the drama of the dialogue, to the context of what is said, helps us to understand and to weigh what both the believer in divine law of the cities and the political philosopher know about divine law.

Because this book follows a theme throughout the *Laws,* it is selective in the passages that it examines. While the book pursues Plato's insights into the relationship between philosophy and revelation in various parts of the dialogue, this does not mean that its scope is limited to the *Laws.* It begins its examination of the *Laws* by looking first at the *Minos,* a short, Socratic dialogue on law. This is an appropriate beginning because the *Minos* is traditionally known as the Socratic introduction to the *Laws* as a whole. In that dialogue, Socrates asks the question "what is law?" and pursues an answer to that question while conversing with an unnamed Athenian citizen. After posing the initial question, Socrates also inquires into how we come to accept the authority of the law and whether we do so through reason or some other, extra-rational faculty or art. In the course of this conversation, Socrates points to some fundamental limitations not only of law but also of his fellow citizen's understanding of law.

But in the last part of the dialogue, Socrates raises the possibility that divine law could overcome the limitations of law and indicates that it must be investigated more carefully in a conversation with those who live under divine law, such as the citizens of Crete and Sparta.

Chapters 1 through 3 show how Plato's Athenian Stranger takes up the questions that are raised in the *Minos* with a citizen from Crete and with another from Sparta in the first three books of the *Laws*. In the course of examining the origins and purposes of the laws of these cities, the Athenian Stranger finds that his Cretan and Spartan interlocutors implicitly expect divine law to aim at virtue and ultimately at the whole of human virtue. This means that the divine lawgiver's principal concern must be moral education. In the first three books of the *Laws*, the Athenian Stranger indicates that the best way to determine whether a city's laws are divine is to consider whether they provide its citizens with a correct education. It is for this reason that Book II of the *Laws* is dedicated to what the correct education of a perfect human being would be. The laws as a whole will shape the character of the citizens, but the laws that determine civic education offer the most direct and thematic account of the virtues that divine law must promote.

Chapter 4 begins by briefly examining the Athenian Stranger's remarks about divine law in Book IV. In order to clarify the kind of virtue that divine law aims to promote, it turns to the Athenian Stranger's discussion of moral education under divine law in Book VII. This chapter compares and contrasts the Athenian Stranger's account of the best possible education under divine law with what he said in Book II about the correct education of a perfect human being. Chapter 5 focuses on the discussion of festivals and erotic love in Book VIII of the *Laws*, for it is in that book that the Athenian Stranger shows how the virtues that emerge from the law-based education will emerge in civic life. It shows that the young citizens' courage is likely to spawn immoderation and that the laws that are needed to curb immoderation may bring to light the fundamental tension between the law-based, moral virtues and practical reason. This chapter calls into question whether law as such must fall short of its principal goal, which is the cultivation of complete human virtue along with the civic and individual happiness that is expected to accompany that virtue.

Chapter 6 takes up the objection that the law-based civic education is not the only source of virtue in the city that lives under divine law. That chapter explores the possibility that divine law as such, the many rules and regulations that are imposed through the rule of divine law, help to promote the virtue called "perfect justice." In discussing how the laws would inspire citizens with a love of justice, the chapter examines how the Athenian Stranger treats justice in Books II, IV, V, IX, and X. The chapter notes the great demands that perfect justice places on citizens and asks whether or how this law-based virtue leads to the happiness that is expected from the complete virtue of a human being. The chapter argues that citizens will look to divine providence to provide crucial support for justice and the law. But it also examines the kind of providence that truly just gods can be expected to exercise and asks if this providence would provide sufficient support for divine law.

The last chapter of the book focuses on the Athenian Stranger's account at the end of Book XII of the instability of the laws and on how this instability reflects a serious problem in the virtues that are taught by law. According to the Athenian Stranger, this problem threatens the laws and the city that they govern. The chapter also explores the philosophic education that the Nocturnal Council, the "guardians of the law," must receive if they are to save the laws. Paying attention to both the substance of the argument and to the dramatic context in which it takes place, this final chapter helps us to understand not simply the content of the education that the Nocturnal Council must receive if it is to save the laws but more generally the crucial role that political rationalism must play in a city that is under divine law.

The principal focus of this book is to explore why Plato believes that the political philosopher can discern the true purposes and content of divine law and how he does this without assuming what he sets out to prove. In order to carry out this investigation, we will pay close attention not only to what the Platonic political philosopher is able to learn through his conversations but also why he believes that such conversations are able to reveal what can be known about divine law.

Chapter One

THE *MINOS* AND THE SOCRATIC

EXAMINATION OF LAW

According to the classical tradition, Socrates transformed philosophy by compelling it to turn away from "the heavens" and directing it toward those things that human beings take most seriously—politics, morality, and providential gods (Cicero *Tusculan Disputations* 5.10–11; also Aristotle *Metaphysics* 987b1–2; Xenophon *Memorabilia* 1.1.11–16).[1] But the remaining, fragmentary writings of pre-Socratic philosophers such as Antiphon, Empedocles, and Heraclitus show that Socrates was not the first philosopher to investigate political, moral, and religious matters.[2] Writings such as these support the report in Plato's *Laws* that the pre-Socratic, natural philosophers looked into the non-philosophers' beliefs about politics, morality, and the gods and concluded that their beliefs about these things are based on convention rather than nature. According to such thinkers, it is natural that the strong should wish to dominate the weak: consequently, the strong always make laws that compel the weak to serve their selfish interests. But because the strong wish to conceal how they use law to dominate the weak, they call their exploitation "justice" and assert that the weak have a moral obligation to obey every law. Because different factions are strong in different places, the laws and what the laws establish as just vary from place to place and are always disputable (Plato *Laws* 889e–90a; *Republic* 358c, 359c; also Antiphon fragment 44; Aristophanes *Clouds* 94–101, 1399–1400, 1420–24; Heraclitus fragments 33, 102; Xenophanes fragment 33; also Kelly 1992, 14). Similarly, what most citizens call "noble" or "moral" is noble only by convention and does not reflect what is truly noble by nature (e.g., Plato *Gorgias* 483a). In addition, the early natural philosophers are said to have reached one of three conclusions regarding the gods: some believed that there are no gods at all, some believed that the gods are indifferent to human affairs altogether, and some believed that the gods are indifferent to justice and injustice (Plato *Laws* 885b, 889c;

Republic 362c, 364d–65a; also Heraclitus fragment 128; Thrasymachus fragment 8; Thucydides 5:105; Xenophanes fragment 23). Whatever their disagreements regarding the gods may be, many taught that the justice, nobility, and providential gods in whom most citizens believed are products not of nature but of a political art that tends to conceal and distort what is natural (Plato *Laws* 889d–90a).

The same classical tradition also tells us that Socrates breaks with his philosophic predecessors by inquiring into politics, morality, and the gods in a new way and with a new seriousness. According to Plato's *Phaedo*, Socrates's new interest in the study of justice, the noble, and the providential gods in whom the citizen believes came as a result of certain problems that emerged from his youthful pursuit of natural philosophy.[3] He says that when he was young he had a great passion for the study of nature and that he thought it was a great thing to know the causes of all the beings (Plato *Phaedo* 96a6–10). But he found that he could not find a single, comprehensive account of the causes of everything that comes into being, persists, and passes away (Plato *Phaedo* 96b5–c2; 97b1–7, 99c1–d2). Having failed to find such a decisive account, he says that he sought to learn about a different kind of cause, namely, the "look" or the "form" (*idea*) of the beings (Plato *Phaedo* 100b3–c6, 101c2–5).[4] Instead of inquiring into nature by studying atoms or elements or other causes that are ordinarily unobserved by non-philosophers, Socrates inquires into nature by considering how the beings present themselves in everyday life and what is said about them in everyday speech. Socrates examines speeches (*logoi*) because speeches reflect something of what each of the beings is (Plato *Phaedo* 99e4–100a3).[5]

Having turned away from natural philosophy in order to examine the beings through speeches, Socrates recognizes that he does not have at his disposal a comprehensive account of the whole and thus that he cannot dismiss out-of-hand what the non-philosopher says about the beings, especially about beings such as justice, nobility, and the gods (Plato *Apology* 21b–c). In order to examine these things more carefully, he asks non-philosophers questions such as "what is virtue?" and "what is piety?" Socrates's interest in these questions is not merely theoretical; in taking these matters seriously, he finds that he must give new weight to claims that he, like all human beings, has serious civic, moral, and sacred responsibilities to other people and to the gods. This is especially important because he must answer the charge that the philosophic attempt to know the causes of the beings is intrinsically impious, base, and unjust (Plato *Apology* 18b–c; *Laws* 821a; Aristophanes *Clouds* 1507–9; Hesiod *Works and Days* 54–55).[6] He recognizes that he needs to examine these claims and to consider whether he can justify his way of life in light of them (Plato *Apology* 23b). According to his fellow citizens, the highest authority regarding justice, the noble, and the gods is the law. The Socratic philosopher is thus especially concerned with examining what law is, what authority it possesses, and what it demands of him.

The Significance of the *Minos*

The *Minos* is the only dialogue in the Platonic *corpus* in which Socrates specifically asks "what is law?" Because it shows us how Socrates raises this question in conversation with one of Socrates's fellow citizens, it seems an excellent starting point for studying Plato's overall account of law. In addition, the *Minos* attracts our attention because it makes arguments that have been called the starting point for the tradition of natural law.[7] Finally, the *Minos* also appears to be the introduction to Plato's lengthier treatment of law in the *Laws* (Chroust 1947; Strauss 1987, 67).[8] But the *Minos* has fallen into relative obscurity because many classical scholars have cast doubts on whether it was written by Plato himself. This judgment on the *Minos* is relatively new. For centuries, leading Platonists such as Alexander Aphrodisiensis, Aristophanes of Byzantium, Clemens of Alexandria, Ficino, Maximus Tyrius, Plutarch, Proclus, Servius, and Stobaeus regarded the *Minos* as one of Plato's important political dialogues (Burges 1891, 447–48; Grote 1888:94–98).[9] But in the nineteenth century scholars questioned whether it, along with many of Plato's shorter dialogues, could have been written by Plato himself. Influential figures such as Beockh, Heidel, Schleiermacher, Souilhe, and Stallbaum argued that the *Minos's* style and substance are not fully consistent with those writings that are universally accepted as Plato's (Burges 1891, 447–48; Morrow 1960, 35).[10] At present, many prominent scholars still question the authenticity of the *Minos,* although recently some have treated it as a Platonic work (e.g., Benardete 2000; Best 1980; Bruell 1999; Cobb 1988; Lewis 2006; Morrow 1960; Strauss 1987). In the *Cambridge History of Greek and Roman Political Thought,* Christopher Rowe nicely summarizes the contemporary view of the *Minos* among classical scholars. Rowe allows that the dialogue is "attractive," "accomplished, and, at times, ingenious," and yet he also finds it a "strange mixture." It is strange because it "is written in a manner that strongly resembles the 'Socratic' dialogues that Plato wrote in his early period," and yet "its subject-matter is more akin to that of the *Politicus* [*Statesman*] and the *Laws*" (Rowe 2000a, 307). This unusual mixture raises numerous questions about whether it should be considered a Socratic dialogue and whether Plato would have or could have composed such an amalgamation.

According to some scholars, Plato and Xenophon wrote certain dialogues that reflect the manner and thinking of the historical Socrates (see, e.g., Guthrie 1971; Irwin 1979; Kahn 1998; Kraut 1984; Vlastos 1991). In Plato's case, these Socratic dialogues are considered by these scholars to be his "early" works and are distinguished from the "middle" and "late" dialogues that are said to reflect subsequent developments in Plato's own thought. The Socratic dialogues tend to be short and to show Socrates examining a companion regarding some aspect of virtue. Socrates typically asks a "what is?" question, such as "what is noble?" or "what is piety?" or "what is courage?" Having drawn out his companion's response, Socrates shows that it is contradictory and inadequate, and both Socrates and his companion find that they have no answer to the question (e.g., Penner 1992, 125). Because the *Minos* has these characteristics, numerous scholars have called it "Socratic" (e.g., Best 1980; Morrow 1960; Mulroy 2007; Sinclair 1952). But the Socratic dialogues are also said to be linked by the consistency of the substance of their arguments. In these dialogues, Socrates tends to argue, for example, that knowledge is virtue and that no one voluntarily harms him or herself (Penner 1992, 125–31; and 2000). But in the *Minos,* Socrates makes arguments about law that are not obviously compatible with what is said about law in Socratic dialogues like Plato's *Apology of Socrates* and *Crito.* In the *Minos,* Socrates argues that an unjust law is not a law, but in the *Apology* Socrates continues to speak of unjust Athenian laws as "laws" (Plato *Apology* 37a7–b2). And the whole tenor of the *Crito* suggests that Socrates thinks that the laws of Athens are substantial and obligatory laws even when they do Socrates a grave injustice. Similarly, Xenophon's Socrates speaks as if laws remain lawful even if they change and become unjust (Xenophon *Memorabilia* IV. 4. 12–15; but contrast Xenophon *Memorabilia* I. 2. 40–46 and Plato *Hippias Major* 284c–e). Moreover, in the *Minos,* Socrates raises questions about the limits of law that are more consistent with the arguments associated with "late" Platonic dialogues. For example, he contrasts the rule of law with the rule of an expert and questions whether law can do justice to each of the individuals whom it rules (cf. *Statesman* 294a–96c and *Minos* 316c–18d; also *Laws* 875a–d). For reasons such as these, Socrates's account of law in the *Minos* does not seem to be consistent with any simple account of law that might be found in the so-called "early" Socratic dialogues.[11]

Yet if the content of the *Minos* is not Socratic in this respect, it is Socratic in other important ways. The Socrates of the *Minos* is moved by many of the same concerns that moved Socrates to undertake the Socratic turn. He shares the Socratic philosopher's insight that philosophy must be justified before the city and the city's gods and that it must be justified using the terms that are used by the city and its gods. He asks what law is because he recognizes that he must examine the phenomenon "law" as it presents itself in everyday speech rather than in "philosophic" or "scientific" terms. He examines what a non-philosophic citizen of Athens knows about law because he wants to know if such a citizen has recognized something that eludes the grasp of the philosopher who relies solely on reason. He asks if law is known through reason or through divination because he recognizes that divine law poses the greatest challenge to reason's authority. And he ends the dialogue with an extensive praise of the laws of Minos because he recognizes that one cannot know what law is or how it is known until one has undertaken a careful and respectful examination of a divine code of law. The *Minos* is not Socratic in the sense that it helps us to distinguish what the historical Socrates thought about law from what Plato thought about it. Its discussion of law and the limits of law is not obviously consistent with what is said in the early dialogues. But the dialogue is Socratic in that it helps us to distinguish the classical political philosophy that Socrates set in motion from pre-Socratic natural philosophy and, in principle, from any form of rationalism that assumes the authority of reason and that dismisses claims made on behalf of the city and divine law. The *Minos* indicates that the same questions and insights regarding the relation between reason and divine law that led Socrates to make his famous turn continue to animate Plato and his students.

The *Minos*'s association with the late dialogues such as the *Laws* may lead one to conclude that it is also late (e.g., Cobb 1988, 188). But it is precisely this association with the *Laws* that may cause some to wonder if Plato could have written the *Minos*. Since the *Minos* refers to passages in the *Laws*, it seems unlikely that the *Minos* was written before the *Laws* (but see Morrow 1960, 37). But if the *Laws* was Plato's final work, it would seem that Plato could not have written the *Minos* after he worked on the *Laws*, either.[12] This argument would dispose of the possibility that Plato wrote the *Minos* if we knew with certainty that Plato always wrote dialogues one at a time and that he never went back to revise his earlier works. But it is possible that Plato sometimes worked on more than one dialogue at once. As Melissa Lane observes, it is difficult to establish an exact chronology for the dialogues especially since some works may have been "in progress" for years (Lane 2000, 157). Christopher Bobonich says that because the *Laws* is the longest of Plato's dialogues, "it is reasonable to think that its composition overlapped with some of his other late works" (2008, 329). Thus, Plato may have decided to take a break from the lengthy *Laws* in order to write a short dialogue like the *Minos*. Alternatively, Plato could have composed the *Minos* before writing the *Laws* but later decided to revise it, adding references to the *Laws* to underscore that it is an introduction to the longer dialogue. Far from our having evidence that Plato always published his dialogues serially and never re-edited them, we have several ancient sources who report that Plato continually reworked the *Republic*.[13] Thus, if Plato either composed more than one dialogue at a time or sometimes revised his works, it is possible that he composed or revised the *Minos* while working on the *Laws*.

At the same time, it is possible that the dialogue was written by one of Plato's students after Plato's death. But even this would not necessarily mean that the dialogue should be dismissed as unworthy of either the Platonic corpus or our attention. Some suggest that the dialogues were written for pedagogical use within the Academy rather than for publication and that some of Plato's students may have written some of them. They further suggest that some of the students' dialogues may have been of such high quality that they were included in the Academy's authoritative collection of Platonic dialogues. Since Plato's students included the likes of Aristotle, Speusippus, and Theophrastus, it is possible that such a student could write a dialogue that captures Plato's thinking on law. If such a student wrote the *Minos* prior to or after Plato's death, it would still be useful for understanding the Platonic account of law and divine law (Muller 1975, 9–44; and Phillip 1970, 296–308, quoted in Pangle 1987, 13–14).

In addition to finding the *Minos* to be a "strange mixture," Rowe also questions the authenticity of the *Minos* on the grounds that the dialogue argues that experts in the art of lawgiving would never disagree about the things they oversee and thus would issue "correct" laws that never change (Rowe 2000a, 308). But, says Rowe, Plato argues in the *Politicus* [*Statesman*] that a "constitution" is "genuine" if and only if its ruler practices the political art and knowingly gives each individual what is fitting. This means that the rule of law, whose fixed character makes it ignorant of what fits each individual, is not a genuine "constitution" (Rowe 2000b, 244 and 250). According to Rowe, "what the author of the *Minos* wants—an ideal king issuing "correct" laws, valid for all time—is actually ruled out by Plato's argument: laws can be expressions of reason without being in principle unchangeable, and indeed reason will sometimes dictate that even the most carefully framed laws may need to be changed, on the grounds suggested by the *Politicus* [*Statesman*]" (Rowe 2000a, 8). In light of how the dialogue is both "thoroughly imbued with Platonic ideas and strategies" and yet committed to the "idea of the good king" who issues correct laws,

Rowe suggests that the author of the dialogue is trying to accommodate Platonic doctrine to "Hellenic kingship theory" (Rowe 2000b, 308a).

Before we put aside the *Minos* in our effort to understand Plato's account of law, we should consider the possibility that the *Minos* is an even subtler work than Rowe and other modern scholars acknowledge. Part of the subtlety of the dialogue comes to sight when we remember that Socrates is asking the "what is" question concerning law and that one of his chief purposes is to examine what his Athenian comrade knows about law. In the course of the dialogue, Socrates affirms that his comrade respects law deeply. Consequently, Socrates wants to think through what his comrade believes law is or what law would have to be in order for it to merit his comrade's respect. He may, of course, wish to make his interlocutor aware of his ignorance regarding what law is and what authority it possesses. But he may also wish to bring his comrade's ignorance regarding law to light in a way that does not undermine his comrade's deeper respect for law. Thus, Socrates may be reluctant to make the sort of bold criticisms of law that the Eleatic Stranger makes to the young mathematician with whom he speaks in the *Statesman*. But leaving these dramatic or politic considerations aside, Socrates may also believe that the Eleatic Stranger's criticism of law is not decisive as stated. After making the case that "correct" laws never change, the Socrates of the *Minos* subtly acknowledges the very criticism of law that Rowe cites from the *Statesman*. But instead of using the *Statesman's* criticism of law to shake his comrade's respect for law and end the dialogue, the Socrates of the *Minos* responds to that criticism by suggesting that the unchanging laws that Minos established in Crete are recognizably divine and beneficial and may overcome the criticism of law that is elaborated in the *Statesman*. The discussion of Minos and his divine code of law at the end of the dialogue shows why a Socratic philosopher cannot complete his inquiry into law until he also examines what divine law is and how it presents itself in its own terms. The *Minos* does not celebrate unchanging laws as much as it helps us understand why unchanging divine laws must be examined through a respectful and probing dialogue with people who are educated by and who believe in those laws.

In the end, we do not know who wrote the dialogue or precisely when it was written. But we know that it has come down to us from antiquity as part of the body of Plato's works. We should give the *Minos* the care that we would give to any Platonic dialogue so that we might better understand the questions that it raises about law and divine law and how it came to be considered the beginning point for understanding Plato's examination of divine law in the *Laws*.

What Is Law, For Us?

The *Minos* opens with Socrates asking an unnamed Athenian comrade (*hetairos*) "what is law, for us?' The fact that Socrates's comrade is unprepared for the question suggests that Socrates raises it because he wants to learn what his fellow Athenian citizen knows or believes about law.[14] Because the comrade does not understand what Socrates is asking, he asks Socrates to clarify the sort of laws that he has in mind. Socrates explains that he wants to know the characteristics found in all laws that enable us to recognize that each of them belongs to a single class of things that we call "law." He wants to know how we are able to distinguish law from other things, like mere demands or opinions. To explain what he is looking for, Socrates says that in the same way that we are able to know how all gold is alike, so should we be able to know how all law is alike (*Minos* 313a).[15] In elaborating this point, Socrates compares law not only to gold but also to stone. But this second comparison raises an important question about law. For if law were like the element gold, then each law would be like every other law in every respect. Law might be a settled code of laws that is recognizable everywhere as law. But if law were like stone, then there would be many different laws or legal codes that would still be recognizable as laws even though the particular laws or codes differed markedly among themselves.

In response to Socrates's question, the comrade says that laws are those things that are "believed in" or recognized (*nomizomena*), by which he seems to mean that laws are those public decrees that we citizens customarily respect and believe to be lawful. Having initially compared law to gold and stone, Socrates drops his own claim that laws are external objects like gold or stones and adopts his comrade's suggestion that law is rooted in our ability to believe in or recognize that some things are lawful. Law is not found in books or written codes but within those who respect and follow the law.[16] In order to explore this latter suggestion, Socrates points out that there is a distinction between things that are seen and the power of sight. Having called our attention to the faculty of sight that enables us to see what is seen, Socrates asks if there is some special faculty that allows us to "believe in" or recognize that certain rules are morally binding; if so, this would be the special faculty through which one could recognize law (*Minos* 314a; Best 1980, 102). In asking his comrade about this faculty, Socrates compares it not only to the power of sight but also to the powers of hearing and reasoned speech (logos). In asking whether law is a power like seeing, hearing, and reasoned speech, he is asking if our ability to recognize law is grounded in something other than the senses and the faculty of reasoned speech through which we see, hear, and reason about all other things. By suggesting that law might be believed in or recognized through something other than reason and sense perception, Socrates raises the possibility that we believe in law not through rational knowledge but through ignorance or perhaps through the "power" of opinion (cf. *Republic* 477a–b). But this is not the only possibility that he raises. By suggesting that one might recognize law through something other than reason, Socrates is also raising the possibility that some have a special "legal faculty" that enables them to discern laws that are beyond reason but nonetheless substantial, authoritative, and true. If there were such a supra-rational faculty, then those who possess it would have a supra-rational experience or knowledge of law while those who lack it might be simply and unfortunately blind, deaf, and speechless in respect to what is lawful and what is not. If laws came to light only through such a faculty, then the philosopher who sought to understand law relying solely on his own reason and perception might find law unfathomable.

If, on the other hand, law can be recognized on the basis of some kind of rational knowledge, there are two alternatives. Socrates says that law might be scientific knowledge (*episteme*) or an art (*techne*) like medicine which, he says, discovers what brings health or sickness to bodies (*Minos* 314b3–4). The difference between a science and an art seems to be that the former is a kind of rational knowledge that reveals what things are while the latter is a kind of rational knowledge that reveals how things become better or worse. If law simply reveals what is permitted or forbidden, then the faculty that makes it might be a kind of scientific knowledge. If, however, law reveals what is beneficial or harmful, then the faculty that makes the law might be an art. In addition to these possibilities, Socrates asks if law is akin to the art of divination. Unlike arts such as medicine, the art of divination does not necessarily show what benefits or harms something but instead reveals "what the gods have in mind" (*Minos* 314b4). In addition, the art of divination seems to differ from scientific knowledge because of the role that the gods play in divination. If one can practice the art of divination only through the cooperation of gods who disclose things that are otherwise unknown to us, then the art of divination is a kind of revelation rather than a body of rational knowledge that can be passed on from person to person, like either scientific knowledge or the art of medicine.[17] If the gods reveal what they have in mind to the experts in the art of divination through something other than reasoned speech and the ordinary senses, then the law that comes through such an art may prove to be mysterious to the Socratic philosopher who studies the beings through speeches.

The Content of Law

Having revised his initial "what is" question in this way, Socrates's examination of his comrade now has several discernable ends: He wants to learn what law is and also whether law can be known at all. He will pursue these questions by finding out whether his comrade knows what the "legal faculty" might be and also whether his comrade possesses this faculty. In order to pursue these questions further, Socrates presses his comrade to say what sort of discovery law is. The comrade says that laws are the opinions of the city that are voted on by the citizens (*Minos* 314b10–c1). Socrates says that this may be nobly spoken, but it is necessary to explore his comrade's account of the content of the city's opinions. In the subsequent exchange, Socrates brings out the comrade's deep respect for law and clarifies what he respects about law. Socrates begins by asking about those people whom the comrade considers lawful or law-abiding. The comrade agrees that those people who are law-abiding are law-abiding because they have the law within them. The comrade also believes that law is just and that law and justice together are good or useful, on the grounds that they "save cities and everything else" (*Minos* 314d). Socrates is not content to define law simply as whatever rules are made by the authoritative element in the city. Much like John Finnis (1980), he would define law as it is understood by a morally serious citizen and, after a few questions, he finds that his companion regards law as something that is intrinsically just and good. Whatever else law may be, it is a morally binding rule.

After agreeing to the sweeping claim that law and justice save cities and everything else, Socrates's comrade also affirms that those without law are base and destructive (*Minos* 314e2–5). Having brought this respect for law to light, Socrates probes more deeply into its implications. Up to this point, the comrade has mentioned two features of law: He has said that law is whatever the city recognizes or opines and that law is just, noble, and good or at least not unjust, base, and ruinous. When Socrates confronts him with a conflict between these two principles, the comrade finds that he is more strongly convinced of the latter than of the former. He agrees that whatever else the law may be, it cannot be unjust, base, and ruinous. So therefore, an evil law is not a law (*Minos* 314e2–6; cf. *Hippias Major* 284e). If an evil decree is passed by the majority of the citizens, that decree will not have the full moral authority of law for the serious citizen. This apparent discovery of an intelligible standard for distinguishing genuine laws from false ones has been said to mark the beginning of the natural law tradition.[18]

Socrates follows up the conclusion that an evil decree cannot be a law by winning his comrade's agreement that since law is a useful (*chrestos*) opinion it must also be a true opinion and a kind of discovery (*Minos* 315a1–2). It is important to note, however, that Socrates does not challenge his comrade's earlier claim that an opinion must be affirmed by the ruling part of the city in order for it to become lawful. Useful and true opinions are not lawful until they partake of the city's authority. However useful and true an opinion might be, it evidently needs to have the additional dignity and force of the city in order for it to be law. In addition, because laws must always have been voted on by a particular city, laws will always bear the stamp of the particular city that enacts them. Because opinions will inevitably vary from city to city, law is bound to appear in a variety of forms even if it is based on a true opinion.[19]

Changing Laws

Immediately after declaring that law is a true opinion and a kind of discovery, Socrates immediately qualifies this by saying that law is a true opinion that "wishes" (*bouletai*) to discover "what is " (*tou ontos; Minos* 315a3, 315b1). It is not immediately clear what Socrates means when he says that law wishes to discover "what is." How does a law regulating how fast we drive a car or what sort of license we need to sell insurance reveal to us "what is?" In one respect, at least, laws tell us what is forbidden and what is permitted. But beyond this, law also tells us what is just and what is unjust and what is respectable and what is base. In this way, law makes authoritative claims about the most serious things. In light of Socrates's remark, one wonders not only why law must only wish to discover what is but also how one can distinguish genuine laws from evil decrees if law merely wants to discover "what is." The comrade does not notice Socrates's qualification regarding the law's ability to discover "what is" and understands Socrates to mean that law succeeds in discovering it. Consequently, the comrade objects that if law were truly a discovery of "what is," then law would not constantly change (*Minos* 315a). He questions Socrates's claim because he, like Socrates, wants a coherent account of law. Socrates says that law wishes to discover "what is" but the human beings who make the laws are not always able to discover what the law wishes to discover and thus make different laws at different times. But Socrates pauses to ask if laws really change over time and whether different peoples really use different laws (*Minos* 315b2–5). He suggests that law itself never changes, but those who try to legislate make mistakes and unintentionally produce a wide variety of decrees that are not laws, strictly speaking.

The comrade, however, does not seem to grasp the distinction between the law that does not change and the variety of mistaken statutes that are made by fallible human beings. Surprised at Socrates's apparent naiveté, the comrade says that it is easy to show that different peoples use different laws and that the same people change their laws over time. He points out that while Athenians no longer practice human sacrifices, some barbarian cities continue to do so, sacrificing even their own sons to honor Kronos (*Minos* 315b8–c2). Socrates's comrade does not seem to be especially disturbed by the discrepancy between Athenian and barbarian laws. He expects the laws of Greek cities to be comparatively civilized. What troubles him is that he knows of Greek cities that follow the same barbaric laws regarding human sacrifices "even though they are Greek" (*Minos* 315c4–5). Even civilized Athens once obeyed laws that seem crude by the comrade's contemporary standards. He points out that years ago in Athens, animals were sacrificed before funerals and bodies were buried inside their homes (*Minos* 315c5–d5). What is particularly disturbing is that "we" Athenians change even the laws that regulate how we worship the gods and honor the dead, laws that are supposed to originate from the gods themselves (Fustel de Coulanges 1984, 220–22). But if even sacred laws can be uncivilized or subject to change, then these laws do not seem to reflect the elevated and presumably unwavering wishes of the immortal gods. The comrade's respect for the law is bound up with his belief that the legislators are supposed to know or to have divined "what the gods have in mind" (*Minos* 314b4) regarding the honor that we owe them and the honor that we owe to those human beings who have perished.

It is at this point that Socrates decides to examine his comrade's conviction that law should be stable. He asks his comrade if he recognizes or considers (*nomizeis*) that the just things are unjust and the unjust things are just or if the just things are just and the unjust, unjust. In asking if the just things are unjust or just, Socrates seems to be asking if the just things are altogether just. If they are, then every just decree, action, and speech would be just in every circumstance and would involve no injustice to any party. The comrade answers that "for me" the just things are just (*Minos* 315e9–10a1), meaning that the just things are purely just in every circumstance for everyone involved. He agrees that the just things are recognized (*nomizetai*) as being just not only in Athens but also in Persia (*Minos* 316a1). Justice does not vary according to circumstance any more than does weight. If something is heavier in Athens it is also heavier in Persia (*Minos* 316a4–7). Similarly, the noble things are recognized (*nomizetai*) as noble everywhere, just as the base things are recognized (*nomizetai*) as base (316b). Speaking "universally," Socrates says that the "things that are"

are recognized (*nomizetai*) by everyone, while "the things that are not" are not so recognized. He concludes by saying that those who mistake "what is" are making mistakes in regard to law (*Minos* 316b5). Recognition, in other words, seems to be a knowledge of beings that are the same under all conditions. The comrade accepts that in the same way that we are able to recognize what is just and noble everywhere we should also always be able to recognize what is lawful everywhere, and thus that the law should be the same for everyone (*Minos* 316b6–7). But here the comrade objects that "we" keep changing laws and says that he therefore cannot be persuaded (*Minos* 316b7–c2). Again, the comrade wants a coherent account of law and is disturbed that he does not have one. Based on the previous argument, Socrates's Athenian comrade could have concluded that since "we" keep changing the laws, "we" must not be able to recognize "what is" because of some deficiency in our power to recognize it. Instead, Socrates's comrade doubts whether law itself is ever constant and true. His reluctance to question his ability to recognize "what is" prevents him from entertaining the possibility that others might be able to know and believe in the stable laws that he seeks.

Expert Knowledge and Law

Wishing to help his comrade discover a stable basis for law, Socrates argues that some laws do not change because they are grounded in a kind of rational knowledge. Socrates compares laws to the writings of experts in various arts. Focusing on the example of doctors who know how to heal the sick, Socrates wins his comrade's full agreement that those who know medicine always recognize (*nomizousin*) the same things in regard to the same things, at all times and in all places, regardless if they are Greeks or barbarians. Being grounded in an art, these experts' recognition seems to be based on rational knowledge. Furthermore, when these experts write down what they recognize regarding sickness and health, these writings may be called the "laws" of medicine. In fact, those who are experts in a whole range of productive arts such as medicine, farming, gardening, and cooking compose writings that could be considered the "laws" of each of those arts (*Minos* 316c–e). Socrates's association of the legal faculty with an art follows from his comrade's earlier affirmation that law is just and useful for "saving cities and everything else." At the start of the dialogue Socrates indicates that the knowledge that reveals what benefits or harms us is an art. When his comrade affirms that law is both just and useful, it makes sense to speak of the faculty that makes laws as an art.

The comrade agrees that if there is knowledge of how to manage a city, then the writings of those kings and statesmen (or good men) who possess that knowledge are what people ordinarily call "laws" (*Minos* 317a5–b1). Socrates argues that since those who know an art will always agree about the same things, these experts would never change their laws. Consequently, those who change their laws are not experts. Socrates next introduces the standard of "correctness" to law: He says that those writings that are "correct" regarding justice and injustice and regarding the management of cities are "kingly laws." Moreover, what is not "correct" is not law even though it seems to be law to those who do not know (*Minos* 317c2–7). Socrates now retracts his earlier qualification that law merely wishes to discover what is and asserts that they were correct in agreeing that law is the discovery of what is (*Minos* 317d1–2). Socrates seems to have satisfied his comrade by saying that expertise in the kingly art gives laws genuine stability and produces laws that are intelligibly correct. By accepting that there are experts in every art who can make stable laws, the comrade becomes willing to accept that "we Athenians" might not know enough to recognize what is lawful and what is not. Socrates also seems to have satisfied his own quest for a legal faculty that can recognize morally binding rules, for those who have this kingly art would have this faculty.

Just Distributions and the Problem of Law

As soon as his companion agrees to this argument, however, Socrates suggests that they consider it further and offers a more precise account of what it means to say that law is the discovery of what is. He says that the expert farmer knows how to distribute (*dianeimai*) the seeds that are "fitting" to "each" piece of land and that this farmer's laws and distributions are correct (*Minos* 317d3–5). They agree that this is also true in the other comparable arts such as medicine, music, and athletic training and that this is also true of those who know the kingly art (*Minos* 317a–18a). And as we apply this standard of expertise to the kingly art, we find that the expert in the kingly art would have to distribute what is fitting to each individual in the city. Using the arts of medicine, music, and athletic training as models for this kingly art, we see that the expert in the art not only pays attention to the particular needs and abilities of each individual for whom he cares but also looks to some constant standard of health or excellence toward which he wants to lead the individual. Socrates does not discuss the constant standard of health or excellence that the expert in the kingly art would bear in mind. But it is something like the goal to which Socrates referred at the start of the current discussion, where he says that the legislator who keeps changing the laws might be similar to those who keeps moving pieces in a board game (*Minos* 316c; cf. *Laws* 621c–e, 628e).

Yet this model of the king who is able to make correct laws and distributions raises a grave problem for law. Because law is not only intrinsically difficult to change but also intrinsically broad, it cannot discriminate among different individuals and cannot be "correct" in the way that the experts in the kingly art's distributions are correct. Socrates's use of this model alludes to how those who know an art like medicine or farming cannot formulate a rule that covers every case (Best 1980, 108). Thus, in raising this new standard for the correctness of an art, Socrates subtly introduces the criticism of law that is elaborated by the Eleatic Stranger in the *Statesman*. According to the Eleatic Stranger's well-known analysis, law does not care adequately for particular individuals because it always tries to formulate a rule that covers every individual under every circumstance. But human beings are so diverse and changeable that such rules cannot account for every need and exigency. Nonetheless, law rules like a "stubborn and ignorant man" who will not allow anything to be done contrary to his command or any question to be asked even when circumstances change (*Statesman* 294c1–4).[20] It may happen, under some circumstances, that a particular law benefits a given individual. But the correctness of that law for that individual depends on potentially changing circumstances that may render the law unfit. In any case, the kingly art cannot make laws that fit every individual. At best, the kingly art makes laws that govern the generality of citizens. The king who rules a city through law is like the shepherd who rules over a herd rather than one who cares for individual sheep (*Minos* 318a; also *Statesman* 261d–e).

Socrates's reconsideration of what it means to say that law discovers "what is" has important implications for his quest to discover a legal faculty that recognizes that certain statutes or decrees are morally binding. Socrates has raised the possibility that the expert in the art of the king or statesman (*Minos* 317a6) might write laws and thus that those who know the kingly art could have the faculty to recognize that some rules are "correct" and thus morally binding. But we now see that the expert in the kingly art cannot recognize that a given law is correct unless he also considers whether it fits a particular individual. Consequently, such an expert cannot look at a law or at a decree all by itself and recognize that it is morally binding (Bruell 1999, 13). This means that the kingly art is not the faculty by which one can recognize that certain rules are always binding for everyone. In fact, it is precisely knowledge of how the kingly art gives what is fitting to different individuals that reveals that fixed laws cannot be based on the same knowledge that underlies the kingly art. The expert in the kingly art understands that there may not be a law that is correct "for us." This problem with law suggests that the class character of law is different from that of both gold and a stone, for unlike gold or a stone, what counts as a law in one city or nation might cease to be a law in another. In this discussion, law comes to sight not as a being that persists on its own but as a relation that may or may not exist between a particular decree and a particular individual. Unchanging laws wish to discover what is fitting, that is to say, what is just and good for the individual, but this changes according to circumstance. Thus, it appears that the dialogue that has been said to mark the beginning of the natural law tradition (e.g., Crowe 1977, 17; Cairns 1949, 38n22) is also a dialogue that succinctly calls into question whether one can rationally conceive of an unchanging law that is always binding.

The problem with law emerges from a conflict that is implicit in Socrates's comrade's beliefs about law. The comrade believes that law is always just and that what is just is the same everywhere and never changes. At the same time, he also thinks that what is just involves giving each person what is fitting. This would require that what is just and what is lawful change in different circumstances. But Socrates's comrade emphatically denies that what is just can vary from place to place. The comrade's confusion in this regard is due to the fact that he believes that what is just is always lasting and universal. From the point of view of the expert in distributing what is fitting to individual citizens, the comrade errs by taking the particular "distribution" or rule that fits the individual case to be a universal rule and by disregarding the constant standard of health or excellence to which the expert looks in determining what is best for the individual. The comrade's manifest confusion regarding both justice and law shows that he does not possess a legal faculty that enables him to know what a law is. Even though the Athenian comrade expects law to be just, noble, and useful, his own belief in the law is not based in knowledge of any science or art but is, as he said at first, grounded in the fact that he and his city customarily believe that some things are lawful and some are not.

Minos and the Art of Divine Legislation

By alluding to how experts in arts that give what is correct to each thing like farming do not issue laws when they give what is fitting to the things that they oversee, Socrates subtly calls into question the authority of law itself. But instead of elaborating this problem, Socrates quickly raises the possibility that the kingly art is not simply identical to "correct" arts like the art of farming and the art of medicine but is also related to a kind of art whose "laws" are recognizably excellent and authoritative even though they do not change. In order to introduce us to this kind of art, Socrates begins by speaking about the art of flute music. According to Socrates, the art of flute music was perfected by the satyr Marsyas and his beloved Olympus. Socrates says that their compositions should be called the "laws" of flute music and that their music is "most divine" (*Minos* 318b). Their art of flute music differs from a "correct" art like medicine because it does not distribute different things to different people but always broadcasts the same music to everyone. For this reason, it may seem to lack the discretion that characterizes correct arts. Yet for many centuries, listeners could discern its divine beauty. And, what is most important, at any given time, some of the listeners have been deeply moved by it. Socrates says that the music of Marsyas and Olympus is the only music that reveals those who are "in need of the gods" (*Minos* 318b4–c3). Thus, even though the same music is always played for everyone and therefore seems to be unselective, the music, in fact, reaches out and selects those individuals who need or who especially long for the gods. Marsyas's and Olympus's flute music seems to be able to divine those who are in need of gods, perhaps because the music has hit upon some insight or principle regarding the needs of such people. The fact that their ancient music's divine beauty has been celebrated for centuries and has always awakened pious longings suggests that Marsyas and Olympus have an insight into some deep and lasting human need.[21]

After alluding to this divine musical art, Socrates suggests that certain kings might possess a similar kind of divine legislative art. But how is divine law like the flute music of Marsyas and Olympus? One possibility is that when those who take law seriously look to divine law, they expect it to be altogether just and good (*Minos* 314b). But because the fundamental limitations of law prevent the law from achieving these ends, those who take law seriously tend to look to the gods to bring about those ends. In this way, both divine music and divine law would reveal those who are "in need of gods" (*Minos* 318b). Yet we should also be open to the possibility that divine law, like divine music, may be grounded in some sort of art through which the law is able to benefit those who live under it. The Athenian Stranger says that Minos learned the "whole kingly art" through speaking (or reasoning) with Zeus and that he used this art to make divine laws that teach virtue and bring happiness to those who live under the laws (*Minos* 320b1–c2). Much like Marsyas's and Olympus's divine music, the longevity of the laws of Minos shows that the laws are divine and that Minos had some insight into "the truth" about how to manage the city (*Minos* 321b1–4). If Minos did make a code of laws that can be known at any time or place to be lawful and morally binding, such a code might be like gold. Recalling Socrates's implicit criticism of law in the previous section of the dialogue, we wonder precisely how divine law could overcome the manifest limitations of law. If experts in the kingly art would not make unchanging laws, and if those who believe in such laws do so only out of mere belief, how can the unchanging laws of Minos not only last but also bring virtue and happiness to those who live under them? One possibility is that Minos found a way to use laws that do not perfectly fit each individual but that nonetheless instills a kind of virtue in each of them. But how is this possible, and what kind of virtue would it produce? And how can the laws bring happiness if they do not give what is fitting?[22] It is also possible that Minos, like Marsyas and Olympus, had some insight into the needs of a certain kind of human being and made laws that will always appeal to or even fit that kind of person. But what sort of person would these laws affect, and how would they do so?

Rather than discuss these possibilities and questions directly, Socrates must reply to his comrade's objection that Minos is said to be savage, harsh, and unjust (*Minos* 318d9–10). It was the comrade's lack of respect for Minos that made him initially reluctant to acknowledge that the laws of Crete are said to be oldest and divine (*Minos* 318e4–7). Faced with a challenge to his claim that Minos made divine laws, Socrates mounts a demonstration that Minos and his laws are divine. Socrates begins by reminding his comrade that Minos is a son of Zeus and by saying that a divine man like Minos deserves to be spoken of with respect (*Minos* 318e–19a). According to Socrates's procedure, the best way to understand a divine matter is to approach it with appropriate respect. Socrates further supports Minos's reputation and authority by citing the authority of Homer and Hesiod. Based on his reading of Homer, Socrates says that Zeus is a sophist who taught Minos the "whole kingly art" and that this art is "altogether noble" (*Minos* 319c3–4). He says that Homer tells us that Minos would confer with Zeus through reasoned speeches (*logoi*) and show Zeus what he had learned every ninth year (*Minos* 319c4). Socrates's most important evidence for the divinity of Minos and his laws lies in his exegesis of a particular passage from the *Odyssey*. The passage says that Minos was the king of Knossos and the confidant (*oaristes*) of great Zeus (*Minos* 319b5–6; Homer *Odyssey* XI 568–72). But, as Socrates himself points out, the meaning of the passage that he quotes is disputed because the word *oaristes* could mean either a "partner in conversation" or else a "drinking partner" and "fellow reveler." Consequently, some have interpreted the passage to mean that Minos did not learn from Zeus but merely drank and caroused with him (*Minos* 319e6–7). Socrates resolves this dispute by approaching the text and its subject matter with the greatest respect. He reasons that since Minos is a divine man, he would not believe one thing and do another, as would a worthless man. He did not "believe in" (*enomizen*) laws that forbid drinking wine and then "believe in" (*enomizen*) drinking wine himself (*Minos* 320a1–b8). Socrates concludes that Minos's communion with Zeus came through "reasoned speeches" (*dia logon*) about being educated in virtue (*Minos* 320b2–4). On the basis of that communion, Minos set up the laws that have brought happiness to the citizens of Crete (*Minos* 320b4–7). Socrates also mentions that this same communion also brought happiness to Sparta (*Minos* 320b6–7). This raises the possibility that the laws' principles and goals are sufficiently intelligible to human reason that Lycurgus was able to apprehend them and successfully apply them to Sparta.

Despite Socrates's interpretation of such lines from Hesiod, Socrates's comrade makes a further objection to Socrates's claim that Minos is a divine man. He does not dispute Socrates's evidence that Minos was just. But he calls out Socrates's name as if to stop him and challenges him to explain how Minos acquired his reputation for being savage and harsh (*Minos* 320d8–e1). Socrates explains that Minos is blamed for being savage and harsh by Athens's tragic poets. Socrates cannot simply dismiss the authority of these poets. Like Homer, they too are said to be divine (cf. Plato *Apology* 22c; *Laws* 719c). Confronted with a conflict between two such authorities, Socrates cannot resolve it by approaching both authorities with respect. Such a dispute, he implies, can be settled only by giving an account of how the one authority came to be mistaken along with another account that demonstrates why the other is correct. As for the first of these, Socrates claims that Minos provoked the Athenian poets' anger by waging a mistaken war against Athens and by imposing a harsh penalty on her (*Minos* 321a1–b1). As for the second account, Socrates points to the longevity of the laws as proof that Minos discovered the truth about managing cities (*Minos* 321b1–4). In response to this evidence, Socrates's comrade says that Socrates seems to have discovered a likely account (*logos*) of the matter (*Minos* 321b5). The comrade's pious respect for a divine man like Minos and his respect for Socrates's reasoning has overcome his Athenian prejudice against Minos.

But Socrates is not satisfied with his comrade's acquiescence. He points out that someone else might still not be satisfied and might ask how the unchanging laws of Minos benefit the souls of those who live under them (*Minos* 321d1). In order to satisfy this unnamed questioner, Socrates asks for an account of how the laws improve the soul. He asks his comrade whether he knows that physical trainers distribute food and toil to those whom they train so that their bodies become stronger and more developed (*Minos* 321c4–8). After the comrade affirms that he does, Socrates asks his comrade what the good legislator gives to the citizens to make their souls better, but his comrade cannot say. Socrates concludes by declaring that it is most shameful for "the soul" of both the comrade and Socrates himself if they know what benefits the body but do not know "what it is in the soul that becomes good or bad" (*Minos* 321d6–10). If they do not know how law improves "the soul," they do not know in what respect a soul is better or worse. At this impasse, the dialogue ends. But numerous implications and questions follow from the argument and the impasse. Socrates's closing statement assumes that we know that law improves the soul. But Socrates inquires into how the laws of Minos improve the soul in order to answer the unnamed questioner at 321d1 who still doubts that Minos and his laws are divine. Because they have not been able to say how the laws of Minos benefit the soul, they have still not been able to show decisively that Minos is not savage and unjust. In fact, their failure to say how the laws of Minos bring some good to the soul calls into question whether Minos was educated by Zeus and whether Minos knew the kingly art. Despite Socrates's efforts to persuade his comrade that Minos and his laws are divine, he has not demonstrated that Minos conversed with Zeus through reasoned speeches or that he used what he learned to teach virtue and bring happiness to Crete. In fact, he has not proven that reasoned speech is the medium through which Zeus would establish his laws. He has not demonstrated that it is possible to know divine law through reasoned speech alone.

The *Minos* and the Laws

The *Minos* shows Socrates examining one of his fellow Athenians about what law is and about how we come to believe in it. Behind Socrates's questions lies a deeper concern: he wants to know if we come to respect the law through rational knowledge or through some other faculty. In the course of the conversation, Socrates finds that his comrade does not have a coherent account of law. Based on what he says about law, our ever-changing laws do not seem to be grounded in rational knowledge of how to care for human beings. Socrates does not, however, conclude from his fellow citizen's confusion that law is not a serious thing. Instead, he leads his comrade to consider the possibility that even if we keep changing laws without knowing what is truly lawful and just, a god or a divine human being might know the whole kingly art and might use it to make a code of laws that are recognizably beneficial and divine. The last section of the *Minos* raises the possibility that Zeus used reason to teach Minos how to make unchanging laws that both "save cities" and bring virtue and happiness to the citizens (*Minos* 320b2–4) In the end, however, Socrates does not demonstrate that the laws of Minos can accomplish these goals. Moreover, he has not shown that Zeus reasoned with Minos or that Zeus teaches a ruling art that can be understood by reason. He has not proven that he knows either the source or the full purposes of the laws of Minos. In short, his conversation with his Athenian comrade shows that he needs to continue his examination of law by examining divine law. As he indicates by his treatment of Minos and Homer at the end of the dialogue, he will examine divine law as it presents itself. He will need to examine those who have been educated by the laws and who believe in their authority. Only then might he learn whether they know something that he does not know about the origins and purposes of divine law. Only then might he learn whether and what sort of knowledge was conveyed by Zeus to Minos and specifically whether divine law is fully knowable through human reason.

Chapter Two

THE RATIONAL INTERPRETATION

OF DIVINE LAW

No one is more closely associated with the birth and growth of rationalism than Plato. Across two millennia, he has been credited with lending dignity and legitimacy to many sciences including astronomy, theology, and philosophy itself.[1] Contemporary thinkers regard him as the "iconic rationalist" (Nelson 2005, xv). But modern scholars have begun to question whether the trust in reason that Plato displays in the *Laws* is well founded. It is useful for those who want to understand Plato's thinking about reason and revealed law to consider the kinds of questions that these scholars now raise.

While it is generally agreed that Plato remained a thoroughgoing rationalist to the end of his life, there has been some dispute about how he understood the relationship between philosophy and politics in his later years. According to a long-standing tradition, Plato eventually grew disappointed and embittered by philosophy's inability to reform politics. Abandoning his youthful hope that philosophers might rule in an actual city, Plato instead uses the *Laws* to urge that philosophy should rule the city indirectly, in the guise of a fixed code of religious law (Jowett 1908, 156; Klosko 1986, 198–99; Sabine 1961, 75). More recently, however, this older reading has been challenged by scholars who find evidence in the *Laws* shows that Plato has become even more hopeful than ever that reason can come to guide politics and morality. According to this more recent view, the mature Plato believed that reason can inform law in a way that enlightens and liberates the ordinary citizen. By this account, the *Laws* introduces the notion that law need not rule citizens with blunt commands but can instead converse with them so that they might think through the principles behind the laws and accept them willingly as their own. When they come to embrace the reasoning behind the law, these citizens not only feel as if they give the laws to themselves but also begin to develop virtues and to find a happiness that Plato had earlier believed was available only to philosophers. In light of this, scholars such as Christopher Bobonich say the *Laws* shows that the mature Plato is "far more optimistic than Aristotle about the capacity of human beings to attain a good and flourishing state of soul" (Bobonich 2002, 179; also Cohen 1993). Andre Laks agrees that Plato wishes to make politics as rational as possible, but Laks also observes signs that Plato thinks that the laws will sometimes fall short of this goal and that the laws will sometimes need to rely on rhetoric to persuade the citizens to do what is best (Laks 1990, 1991, and 2005; Diamond 2002, 3–4).

According to most contemporary scholars, the mature Plato is hopeful about the power of law because he believes that law, in its correct form, is the expression or embodiment of "reason" (Bobonich 2002, 95; Stalley 1983, 28; also Barker 1960, 302).[2] Believing that law is derived from the intellect, Plato does not doubt that law can be known through and through. He is thus confident that it is an "object of knowledge" rather than an object of mere opinion or faith (Stalley 1983, 28).[3] Beyond this, Plato is also said to believe that the reason that guides law is intrinsically benign. According to Bobonich, Plato maintains that reason "has an inherent tendency both to grasp what is best and to order things so as to bring them into the best condition" (2002, 95). In addition to believing that reason has god-like benevolence, Plato is also said to believe that the gods are "supremely rational" (Stalley 1983, 28, 176). Bobonich says that Plato believes that there is a god who "perfectly instantiates reason and orders both bodies and souls so that, as far as possible, their best condition is attained" (Bobonich 2002, 94–95; also Stalley 1983, 28). The key evidence that either reason itself or a rational god superintends the entire cosmos is said to lie in the natural theology elaborated in Book X of the *Laws* as well as in the more general study of the motions of the heavenly beings (Bobonich 2002, 94–95; Cairns 1949, 47–48; Stalley 1983, 175; Weinreb 1987, 30–33). Plato is said to believe that the gods take part in a rational order in the heavens and that they also issue divine laws to the sublunar world so that cities and human beings can share in the great and rational order of the cosmos. These divine laws benefit cities by leading them to happiness and individuals by leading them to virtue in both body and soul (Bobonich 2002, 95). According to Bobonich, Plato thinks that "law can be an especially good expression of reason insofar as it helps bring to order human beings, beings who come to possess reason within themselves and are not always subject to external direction" (2002, 96). In light of this, the *Laws* as a whole comes to sight as a powerful expression of Plato's confidence that reason can and should guide law. By showing that reason can unite and guide all things in the cosmos, it is said to stand as a refutation of the sophistic view that nature and law are fundamentally at odds (Stalley 1983, 29).

While agreeing that Plato places great faith in rationalism, some of these same scholars question the validity and practicality of Plato's rationalism. In regard to the *Laws,* they say that Plato's attempt to derive law from reason is based on numerous and unwarranted assumptions about reason, nature, and law. Despite its "aesthetic appeal," says Stalley, "the parallel between the order apparent in the visible heavens does not solve any fundamental problems in the theory of law." The "order of the heavens," he says, "tells us nothing whatever about what we, as human beings, ought or ought not to do" (Stalley 1983, 29, 34). But that is not the only problem with the Platonic account of law. Like other "ethical rationalists," Plato's attempt to derive concrete moral and legal rules from "self-evident principles of reason" yields little substantial guidance; since he needs to provide some positive content to his laws, he is forced to make numerous assumptions about what is rational, moral, and lawful. According to Stalley, Plato's primary supposition is that whatever preserves the state is good (Stalley 1983, 29, 34). Beyond this, he "generally assumes that existing systems of law and morality reflect the divine law of reason and thus raises them to the status of eternal truths" (Stalley 1983, 34). Left empty-handed by reason, Plato is forced to rely on "the accumulated experience of mankind rather than on any kind of specialist knowledge" when he devises his code of law. Plato's dependence on Greek moral and legal conventions is especially evident in his deference to Cretan and Spartan law and in his general respect for the authority of old age (Stalley 1983, 29–30). According to Stalley and other scholars such as Trevor Saunders, Plato's attempt to ground law in what is universally knowable, orderly, and permanent merely shows the futility of using reason by itself to develop law.[4]

While these scholars criticize Plato for making these unwarranted assumptions, they seem to overlook an even more fundamental supposition in any attempt to base law on sciences such as cosmology and astronomy. According to their accounts, Plato trusts that the same rational gods who guide the cosmos also make laws to guide cities and individual human beings. But how can the philosopher know that the gods who make laws for human beings and cities are guided solely by reason? Or that those human beings who are guided solely by reason can discern all the gods' purposes? According to Stalley, Plato recounts his thinking about the cosmic foundations of law in Book X of the *Laws,* where the Athenian Stranger argues that "the order of the universe" is governed by reason and on the basis of this claim concludes that the gods are "supremely rational deities" (Stalley 1983, 28). But we must wonder whether either Plato or his Athenian Stranger expects Book X by itself to prove that all the gods are moved solely by reason and that human beings are able to use reason to comprehend all the gods' thoughts and purposes. The argument in Book X regarding the gods consists of three parts. In the first, the Athenian Stranger establishes the existence of the gods by refuting the pre-Socratic philosophers who claim that chance is prior to nature and to art and that body is prior to soul. In response, the Athenian Stranger presents reasons why soul is prior to body and why intelligence guides the motions of the heavenly beings (*Laws* 891e, 899b).[5] On the basis of this reasoning, we could deduce that some sort of god exists but we cannot yet come to the conclusion that the gods exercise providence over human beings. For this reason, it is necessary for the Athenian Stranger to prove in the next part of Book X that the gods care about and for human beings. His proof is based on the postulates that human beings are the possessions of the gods and that the gods are courageous and prudent. He reasons that if the gods have these virtues, they will surely care for their possessions conscientiously, in the same way that pilots, generals, household managers, and stonemasons care for the things that they supervise (*Laws* 901–2). Yet we must note that the Athenian Stranger does not prove that the gods have all the same virtues as do human beings. We can wonder whether the gods own human beings in the same way that human craftsmen own their possessions and whether even the most conscientious owners are always concerned with the well-being of each of their many possessions. We might grant that the gods would have all the virtues that human beings may possess (*Laws* 896d–e, 987c, 898e, and 900d–e). But this does not prove that the gods could not have additional, supra-human virtues or other divine qualities that are not readily known to human beings. Nowhere in Book X does the Athenian Stranger demonstrate that gods cannot possibly be moved by unfathomable purposes or act in mysterious ways. Nowhere does he prove that every god must be permanently and completely knowable to human beings. There is nothing in Book X that forecloses the possibility that at some time in past or present or future a god could select some individual and, through inspiration rather than reason, bestow on him a miraculous code of divine law. Plato's apparent failure in Book X and elsewhere to question whether all the gods are fully knowable is especially significant since the gods who are said to have established the venerable codes of law in ancient Greece are the Olympian gods, and these are gods who are sometimes said to be beyond the full comprehension of human knowledge (e.g., Euripides *Bachae,* ll. 200 ff; Sophocles *Oedipus Tyrannus,* ll. 598–602). If we do not know with certainty why the gods act, we cannot know with certainty that the laws that they make are always objects of rational knowledge.

In light of this, it appears that Plato assumes not merely that cosmology and astronomy provide substantive legal and moral guidance but also that the way that the gods manifest themselves in the heavens accurately reflects all the gods' thoughts, intentions, and commandments. As presented by leading contemporary Platonists, the *Laws* seems to confirm in its own way Nietzsche's claim that Plato merely assumes that reason can illuminate the whole and that the gods aim solely at what reason shows us to be good (Nietzsche, *Beyond Good and Evil,* 190–91). Plato seems to be responsible indeed for the dogmatism regarding reason that has overhung Western religion, politics, and morality for two millennia (Nietzsche, *Beyond Good and Evil,* "Preface").

Yet there are reasons to wonder whether Plato would make such assumptions about reason and the gods. We know from Plato's other dialogues that the Socratic or Platonic philosopher does not simply assume that human beings can know what all the gods think or what all of them will. In the *Apology,* Socrates takes seriously the possibility that there is another kind of wisdom that differs from and is superior to his human wisdom. In that dialogue, he says that he has led his distinctive way of life in order to examine the meaning of an obscure statement made by the Oracle at Delphi (Plato *Apology of Socrates* 20e–23c). Socrates interrogates those of his fellow citizens who are considered wise in the hope that one of them possesses some wisdom that he lacks about what is noble and good (*Apology* 21b–c, 20b1). Far from assuming that all human beings need and want to have a rational account of how they live, Socrates not only tests other people to learn if they can give a rational account of what is noble and good but also watches to see whether they are content or dissatisfied with their failure to give a coherent, rational account of the greatest things (*Apology* 21c–d). In the *Euthyphro,* too, he says that he is willing to learn some wisdom regarding the gods from Euthyphro, who claims to have access to a divine wisdom that is not accessible to Socrates or to ordinary Athenian citizens (*Euthyphro* 3b–c, 6c–d).

One might grant that a Socratic political philosopher would not assume that the gods are supremely rational and that such a philosopher would not assume that we can derive substantive human laws from cosmology and astronomy. But one might still contend that the Athenian Stranger is not a Socratic precisely on the grounds that he assumes that the heavenly gods are the only gods who must be consulted regarding the content of divine law. There is, however, ample evidence that the Athenian Stranger himself wishes to avoid making any assumptions about reason's capacity or authority in understanding divine law. If we take a close look at the start of the *Laws,* we find that the dialogue begins with the Athenian Stranger asking one elderly statesman from Sparta and another from Crete about what they know about the origin and purpose of their cities' laws. And if we consider how the drama of the dialogue unfolds, we find that the Athenian Stranger does not brush aside or debunk what they say about their cities' laws but patiently and respectfully examines what they know about those laws and how they know those laws. Contrary to most contemporary interpretations of the *Laws,* Plato does not assume that philosophers have the authority to interpret or guide divine law but instead opens the dialogue with an extensive exploration of how the serious citizen comes to recognize or believe in divine law. His goal, he says, is to test not only what he and his interlocutors know about divine law but also how they come to know it (*Laws* 633a, 635b). Far from assuming that philosophy ought to reform politics and law, Plato's Athenian Stranger devotes the first three books of the dialogue to a careful examination of the claim that the laws of Crete and Sparta are divine and sacrosanct. It is only by looking carefully at what the Athenian Stranger and his interlocutors say and do that we can determine whether Plato makes unwarranted assumptions regarding reason and divine law.

The Inquiry into the Origin and Purpose of Divine Law

The *Laws* opens with the Athenian Stranger asking Kleinias, who is from Crete, and Megillus, who is from Sparta, if a god or a human being is the source of their cities' laws. It is true that this question asks Kleinias to supply a reason for these laws, thus inviting some to draw the conclusion that the dialogue takes place on the assumption that there are intelligible purposes behind divine laws (Stalley 1983, 25). But the dialogue form leaves open the possibility that Kleinias will say that he does not know about the purposes behind the laws. The Athenian Stranger's first questions give Kleinias the opportunity to say that he cannot identify the purposes behind the law because he possesses a kind of inner knowledge of divine law that cannot be expressed through reasoned speech. But the dialogue shows us that Kleinias quickly embraces the opportunity to explain the reasons behind these laws. Rather than claim that the purpose behind these laws is unknowable or inexpressible, Kleinias claims that they are easy for anyone to understand (*Laws* 625c9–10). He adds that in order to understand the purpose behind the laws, one must recognize something that most people overlook. Kleinias says that the lawgiver recognized that by nature every city is at war with every other city. The lawgiver also perceived that it is only through victory in war that all other goods are useful, since those who lose in wars thereby lose all good things (*Laws* 625e5–26b4). As a result of these insights, he sought to make laws that would lead Crete to victory in war. Moreover, the legislator recognized what is distinctive about Crete's terrain and made laws that are suitable to its particular nature (*Laws* 625c6). Once we understand how the lawgiver perceives the city's natural needs and its particular, natural attributes, we will recognize that practical reason or intellect has been guiding the law (*Laws* 625e5–7). This beginning shows not only that Kleinias wants to answer the Athenian Stranger's question but also that he has thought about it at some length himself. He admires the lawgiver's prudence in recognizing the city's natural needs and in taking into consideration the city's natural attributes. The beginning shows that the serious citizen who lives under divine law not only believes that the law provides what is good but also is willing to give reasons why it is good. In fact, his forethought regarding these questions indicates that he is inclined to seek out reasons why it is good.

Without challenging this account, the Athenian Stranger asks about the purpose of the laws that regulate relations within the city itself. Kleinias indicates that the laws that pertain to neighborhoods and households also enable those neighborhoods and households that follow the law to win victories over those that do not. Finally, the Athenian Stranger asks about laws that regulate the individual. Kleinias says emphatically that these enable one to triumph over oneself and thereby to achieve the first and best victory (*Laws* 626e–3). This shows us that when Kleinias is asked to explain the purpose of laws that he has not yet considered, he turns immediately to reasoned argument to find the purpose and quickly draws an analogy that he finds apt. His reasoning alerts him to a ranking among the laws, and in finding himself able to reason about these laws, he expresses even more admiration for the lawgiver. Indeed, Kleinias so closely associates reasoning about the laws with the divinity of the laws that he identifies the Athenian Stranger's incisive questions about the purposes of the laws with the wisdom of the goddess Athena (*Laws* 626d3–9).

Having established that the serious citizen believes that divine laws bring forth important goods that are intelligible to the citizen, the Athenian Stranger asks Kleinias to consider more closely the purpose of the laws that regulate the city's internal affairs. When the Athenian Stranger asks if the laws intend for the city to triumph over itself, much as they intend for the individual to triumph over himself, Kleinias agrees. With this agreement, Kleinias concedes that divine law does not aim at victory as such but at the victory that establishes a certain order in the city, namely, the rule of the just over the unjust. The lawgiver seems to want those who care for the good of the whole city to have authority over those who do not (*Laws* 627a–b). But how should they exercise that authority? Pursuing this question, the Athenian Stranger asks Kleinias to consider a household that is made up of brothers, some of whom are just and most of whom are not. The Athenian asks Kleinias if it would be best for the better brothers to eliminate the worse or for the better to rule the worse or for someone to establish a law that rules all the brothers in peace and friendship (*Laws* 627c–28a). The Athenian Stranger adds that this last alternative would be "third in respect to virtue," meaning that the other options would allow for the unfettered rule of virtue in the household (*Laws* 627c3–4). Despite this addition, Kleinias says that the best of these alternatives would be for all the brothers to submit to the rule of law (*Laws* 628a4–5). By removing any superiority or subordination within the family, the rule of law establishes the basis of friendship among the brothers. At the same time, the rule of law obscures differences in justice or virtue among the brothers. Consequently, it seems that Kleinias's desire to promote the spirit of fraternity in the household is in tension with or even outweighs his concern with justice or virtue (Benardete 2000, 15; Pangle 1988, 384).

In order to clarify what kind of harmony Kleinias would expect to prevail in a city under divine law, the Athenian Stranger learns that Kleinias would prefer that it come through peaceful reconciliation rather than through war. They agree that this is in keeping with the principle that the lawgiver always makes law for the sake of what is best (*Laws* 628c6–7). And as a result of this agreement, they also accept that the laws of the city ought to aim not simply at overcoming conflict within the city but more importantly at introducing to it peace, goodwill, and happiness (*Laws* 628d3–7). By comparing the city that undergoes domestic conflict to a body that suffers from a disease (*Laws* 628d2–3), the Athenian Stranger suggests that the city in which the citizens live harmoniously would be like a body whose parts work together, producing a positive, glowing health in the body as a whole. And the corresponding aim of divine law would be to bring this sort of health or well-being to the civic body.

While Kleinias does not try to refute the argument that divine law aims at peace rather than at war, neither does he fully accept it. He says "in all seriousness" that his city's laws aim at war (*Laws* 628e). Recognizing that he has at least partly shaken Kleinias's confidence that the current laws of Crete aim at the goal at which divine law aims, the Athenian Stranger probes more deeply into Kleinias's beliefs about the relation between divine law and virtue. Kleinias has already indicated that he thinks that divine law is concerned with virtue when he says that divine law regards self-overcoming as the noblest and best victory and that the law seeks the triumph of the just over the unjust (*Laws* 627a–c). In order to clarify

Kleinias's beliefs about the kind of virtue that divine law supports and promotes, the Athenian Stranger asks about the poetry that is most admired in Crete. Kleinias agrees that the poet Tyrtaeus, who is "most serious about these matters" (*Laws* 629a2–3), strongly praises the courage that is displayed by warriors who fight against foreign enemies (*Laws* 629a–b, 629d–e). But the Athenian Stranger argues that the poet Theognis offers even greater praise to the man who proves to be trustworthy in a civil war. He says that such a man must have not only courage but also justice, moderation, and practical reason. He would never be trustworthy and sound in a civil war without "virtue as a whole" (*Laws* 630b3). The surpassing virtue that shines forth even in a civil war is not reducible to a willingness to do whatever is good for the city or to patriotism.[6]

In fact, the virtue that Theognis praises and that Kleinias most admires shines forth during the very breakdown of political society, when the law itself has lost its hold on the city. The goal of divine law is not simply civic virtue but "the greatest virtue" or "virtue as a whole" (*Laws* 630c3–4). The Athenian Stranger concludes from this that a truly worthwhile lawgiver would not make laws for the sake of anything but the greatest virtue, which some call "perfect justice." Yet Tyrtaeus, who is revered in Crete, praises only courage, the least of the four virtues (*Laws* 629a3–b4, 630c6–d1).

In response to this argument, Kleinias again objects that it denigrates his lawgiver. But this time, and for the first time, he associates himself with the argument, saying that he fears that "we" are denigrating him (*Laws* 630d2–3). Having consulted his own beliefs about the virtue at which divine law must aim and having reasoned about those beliefs, Kleinias now recognizes that he expects divine law to bring forth the greatest or most complete virtue of a human being. Whatever else Kleinias may know about the gods, whatever attributes he may or may not ascribe to them, he knows that they want to lead citizens to the whole of human virtue.

According to Kleinias's implicit understanding of virtue, some virtues like courage can stand alone and are admirable in their own right. But he also believes that it is far better to develop and exercise all the particular virtues. And he agrees that the best man is he whose many virtues culminate in some form of human excellence that is greater than courage alone. According to Kleinias, the different particular virtues neither conflict with nor undermine one another. His life is not tragic. It is not marked by inner contradiction. At its peak, a virtue such as courage does not lead one to be immoderate or unjust or imprudent. Rather, all the virtues work together in a beautiful harmony that leads to or is at least consistent with the happiness of both the city and the individual. Earlier, Kleinias says that the rule of law is better than the direct rule of the virtuous over the vicious on the grounds that the former promotes fraternity. Now, Kleinias is willing to judge the validity of his city's laws by considering whether they bring forth the greatest or most complete form of virtue. Instead of being torn between a concern with virtue and a concern with fraternity, Kleinias now shows that his deepest and most strongly held conviction regarding divine law is that it aims at complete human virtue. At the heart of his piety lies a great seriousness regarding the virtues of character and mind. And at the heart of this moral seriousness lies a strong belief that the person who has the greatest virtue possesses a multitude of different virtues that somehow work together or constitute virtue as a whole.

The Athenian Stranger replies to Kleinias's objection that they are denigrating the lawgiver by saying that they would be giving themselves a low rank if they thought that Minos and Lycurgus truly aimed their laws at war alone (*Laws* 630d4–7). Precisely because divine law must aim at complete virtue and because Minos is a "divine man," the laws that Minos established in Crete must have become corrupted. Upon hearing this argument, Kleinias is persuaded that the laws of Crete did not come from a god or from a divine human being. He says that he would like to hear what should be said about the goal of divine law. In light of these considerations, the opening of the dialogue suggests that the Athenian Stranger's account of divine law is grounded on the serious citizen's beliefs about the purposes of divine law. In addition, it comes to light that this citizen relies on reason to resolve questions that arise in regard to those beliefs. When confronted with two alternative accounts of divine law, Kleinias relies on his own reasoning to determine which of the two is truly divine. In this case, his reasoning persuades him that the laws, which he has believed to be divine up until now, are not in fact divine. By rejecting the current laws of Crete and wanting to hear more from the Athenian Stranger, Kleinias becomes open to a deeper and more strongly held form of piety.

Ordinarily, contemporary scholars place little weight on Kleinias's thinking at the opening of the *Laws*. According to Bobonich, the opening of the *Laws* shows that Kleinias is "morally limited" and that he suffers from "grave ethical shortcomings" (2002, 122). He says that the opening exchange between Kleinias and the Athenian Stranger shows that the "best products of Crete and Sparta think that goods other than virtue are much more important than virtue itself and may well think that virtue is worthwhile only insofar as it produces these goods" (Bobonich 2002, 122). In saying this, Bobonich suggests that neither Kleinias nor the reticent Megillus have much to contribute to the subsequent elaboration of divine law. The account of divine law that is developed throughout the *Laws* is attributed to the thinking of Plato the philosopher, but not to the non-philosophic citizen of Crete. There are, however, two problems with this approach. The first is that in sketching the Cretan account of divine law, Bobonich overlooks the Athenian Stranger's paraphrase of Crete's and Sparta's favorite poet Tyrtaeus at the start of the discussion of virtue. Tyrtaeus explicitly says that he does not consider wealth or any external good to be worthy of any praise unless it is also accompanied by the ability to win victories in war, an ability which reflects courage (*Laws* 629b). According to this thinking, which both Kleinias and Megillus affirm reflects the beliefs of their cities, courage is not a mere means to other goods but is the one good that is worthy of praise in itself. But there is a more general problem with Bobonich's account of Kleinias's character and of Kleinias's understanding of law. By identifying Kleinias's understanding of law with his initial account of the purpose of divine law, Bobonich ignores how Kleinias participates in and joins the subsequent argument about the genuine purpose of divine law. If Kleinias's understanding of divine law were limited to what the laws of Crete declare, then Kleinias would have dismissed the Athenian Stranger's probing questions with anger or contempt or indifference. Instead, Kleinias's belief that divine laws aim at what is best and at virtue as a whole leads him to accept a fuller and better account of what is best and of what that virtue is. In the end, the Athenian Stranger's examination of Kleinias leads him to accept an account of divine law that is more in keeping with his own implicit yet unrecognized expectations of divine law. To be sure, in the course of the exchange, the Athenian Stranger may have been expecting Kleinias to answer as he does (*Laws* 631d). But that does not diminish the importance of Kleinias's responses. For Kleinias's willingness to answer the Athenian Stranger's questions and his own reasoning about the goal of divine law show that Kleinias himself is able to draw on a knowledge of divine law that is "written in his heart." The dialogue shows that it is reasoned argument that enables Kleinias to read and interpret what is "written" there.

By showing that Kleinias's understanding of divine law is rooted in his knowledge of virtue, the Athenian Stranger provides an answer to the question that Socrates posed in the *Minos*. In the *Minos,* Socrates asks if one recognizes or believes in divine law through reason or through some other, extra-rational faculty. In the last part of that dialogue, he hypothesizes that one can know divine law through reason and that Minos relied on reason and the kingly art to devise the laws of Crete. In the opening of the *Laws,* the Athenian Stranger shows that Kleinias, at least, relies on reason to understand and explain that law. Kleinias does not hesitate to offer an account of the goal of divine law. When challenged to say which of two alternative codes is divine, he uses reason to weigh which of his beliefs seems truest. In the end, he relies on reason to recognize the divinity of the law. By showing that Kleinias trusts reason when he tries to sound out what he knows about divine law and virtue, the Athenian Stranger shows that the serious citizen shares some common ground with the philosopher. If the Athenian Stranger can show that he has a satisfactory, rational account of virtue, then he may be able to show that the philosopher who relies on reason rather than divination or revelation can provide a complete or satisfactory account of divine law.

Correct Law and Its Goals

There are, however, numerous objections to this conclusion. The first comes to sight as soon as the Athenian Stranger begins to give his own, fuller account of the aims of divine law. After Kleinias says that he wants to hear what should be said about the goals of divine law, the Athenian Stranger says that "correct law" would provide "all good things." These good things include not only the virtues but also happiness for those who live under the law (*Laws* 631b3–7). The Athenian Stranger says that correct law brings forth two kinds of goods. The first are the "human goods," which seem to be external goods and goods of the body. He says that health is the leader of these goods and that it is followed, in descending order, by beauty in second place, bodily strength in third, and wealth (combined with practical reason) in fourth (*Laws* 631c–d). These human goods result directly from the possession of four particular virtues, which he calls "divine goods." According to the Athenian Stranger, the leader of the divine goods is practical reason (*phronesis*). In second place is moderation, which is said to follow intellect (*nous*). In third place is justice, which is said to include the other three parts of virtue. In fourth place is courage, which is again asserted to be the least of the virtues. The Athenian Stranger says that "by nature" the divine goods are "placed prior in rank" to the human goods and that the legislator should follow that ranking. Because it is the legislator's task to promote virtue, he should use praise and blame and other rewards and punishments to shape each citizen's character from birth until death (*Laws* 631d–32b).[7]

The Athenian Stranger's description of the goals of correct law goes beyond what Kleinias has said regarding both happiness and the virtues at which divine law aims. While Kleinias has agreed that in addition to particular virtues such as courage and moderation there is also a complete or perfect form of virtue, which is more important to the lawgiver than the particular virtues, he has not said anything that implies that the law aims at only four particular virtues or that they have a particular "leader."

This may seem to indicate that the Athenian Stranger is now imposing his own beliefs onto the conversation rather than drawing out implications of Kleinias's thinking. This may appear to be the point in the dialogue where the Athenian Stranger begins to import the philosopher's rational vision into onto divine law. But instead of regarding this account of correct law as evidence that Plato assumes that reason should guide the city, one might also regard his description of correct law as a proposition that is to be demonstrated in the course of the whole dialogue. The Athenian Stranger must provide his own description of correct law because even though Kleinias now accepts that divine law must aim at virtue as a whole and happiness, he has never reflected on what that virtue might be nor on how it is related to happiness nor on how these things could come into being through law. The Athenian Stranger, on the other hand, indicates that he has thought through what "virtue as a whole" would possibly mean and how it would be related to the happiness of both the city and of the individual citizen. In addition, he indicates that he has carefully considered the kinds of virtues that can be taught by law. His discussion of the goods at which correct law must aim reflects his belief that if there is something that can be called "virtue as a whole" and that this virtue leads to happiness, then it would have to have these parts and they would have to be ranked in the way that he now indicates.

When the Athenian Stranger speaks of correct law in Book I, it is not immediately clear what he means by ranking the particular virtues or what he means when he says that one virtue leads and that others follow. Some light is shed on these questions by considering an analogy between the human and the divine goods. The lowest of the human goods, wealth, is an external good that is truly good only when it is linked with practical reason. In itself, wealth is neither good nor bad but is good only when it serves as a means to some other end. The other three goods are goods of the body. But precisely why would the Athenian Stranger say that health is the leader of these goods, ranking ahead of presumably more impressive goods such as beauty and strength? Benardete characterizes health as a mere precondition of those higher goods (Benardete 2000, 23). Nonetheless, a prudent human being would take special care to acquire and attain health, for we believe that it would be very imprudent to risk our health in order to acquire strength or beauty. Any steps we took to gain strength or beauty that ultimately cost us our health would not be considered good. If we draw an analogy between the two sets of goods, practical reason comes to sight as the health of the soul, as the virtue that is indispensable and in light of which the other virtues become good. But there is ambiguity concerning whether or how practical reason is the leader of the divine goods.

At first, the Athenian Stranger says that practical reason leads the other goods (*Laws* 631c5). A few lines later, however, he says that intellect (*nous*) is the leader of all the goods (*Laws* 631c7). Still later, he says that some citizens will be guided by practical reason and others by true opinion while intellect binds everything together (*Laws* 632c). What, then, is the relation between practical reason and intellect, and which is the leader?[8] The two faculties do not seem to be interchangeable, for the Athenian Stranger says that the former leads the divine goods while the latter is said to lead all the goods, both divine and human (*Laws* 632c6–7). It seems that practical reason must be led by intellect. But if this is so, it is not yet clear why intellect leads the goods in general and how it is related to practical reason in particular. Later, in Book IV, the Athenian Stranger will argue that the divine mind is characterized as intellect and that this intellect is the source of divine law (*Laws* 714a). In Book XII, he will argue that intellect is needed to discern and guide the different laws regarding virtue to make sure that they work together or that they aim at a single goal (*Laws* 957c–e, 963a–b, 965a). His thinking seems to be that if the gods want citizens to possess a certain order of virtues, then the gods will use intellect to distinguish each of the particular virtues and to make laws that put them in the order that the gods seek to promote. In this respect, intellect must lead the other virtues if, as Kleinias has agreed, the many, particular virtues must work together or come together in some virtue as a whole that is compatible with civic and individual happiness.

Immediately after identifying the goods at which divine law aims, the Athenian Stranger indicates in rough outline what the legislator would have to do in order to accomplish those aims. Because divine law aims at what is best for both the city and the individual citizen, the legislator must direct the citizen's life from birth until death. Because the legislator aims primarily at promoting virtue, he will focus on moral education. In order to instill moderation, the legislator will blame the incorrect kind of pleasures and pains and praise the correct kind. In order to promote courage, he will define what is noble and what is not noble regarding anger and fear (*Laws* 632a). And in regard to justice, the Athenian Stranger speaks of justice not as the whole of virtue but as one of the particular virtues. Instead of identifying justice with the trustworthiness of the citizen, the Athenian Stranger says that the legislator must observe what is just and what is unjust in the citizens' dealings with property and with one another. Regarding this particular form of justice, the legislator should identify justice with obedience to the law and should honor those who obey the law and penalize those who break it (*Laws* 632b). Looking beyond the virtues of character, the Athenian Stranger says that the legislator will also appoint guardians of all the laws, some of whom will be guided by practical reason, others by true opinion. Intellect, having bound all things together, will order them toward justice and moderation rather than to wealth and ambition (*Laws* 632c). In these ways, the legislator will concern himself with each of the four particular virtues identified at *Laws* 631c–d along with intellect. One might expect that the Athenian Stranger will now say something in regard to how these particular virtues constitute virtue as a whole and how they bring about or contribute to the happiness of both the city and of the individual citizen. But the Athenian Stranger instead says that the goal of the whole regime is to make sure that those who have died receive their full honor (*Laws* 632c). By alluding to the importance of posthumous honor, the Athenian Stranger makes us wonder why the virtuous and happy citizen would be deeply concerned with them. Evidently, there is something in the life and death of the virtuous citizen that is incomplete without such honors.

The Athenian Stranger and Socratic Philosophy

While it would appear that the Athenian Stranger is able to bring to light Kleinias's most strongly held beliefs about the origin and aims of divine law, there remain some doubts whether the Athenian Stranger's concerns and methods reflect those of the Platonic Socrates. Catherine Zuckert notes that many scholars begin their interpretations of the *Laws* with the hypothesis that the Athenian Stranger is Socrates. According to this view, the *Laws* is a thought experiment in which Socrates is somehow transported to Crete "to converse with practicing statesmen from the reputedly best-governed regimes in ancient Greece" (Zuckert 2009, 52). But Zuckert says that those who simply identify the Athenian Stranger with Socrates fail to explain why no one in the *Laws* ever mentions the Peloponnesian War or any of the persons and events associated with it. It is not likely, she says, that Plato would have "given his own, final political understanding or practical proposals for constitutional reform without even mentioning the war in which his own city had been defeated and subjected to a series of unstable regimes" (Zuckert 2009, 53). Would, she asks, an "Athenian politician try to convince Dorian politicians to introduce a series of institutions drawn from prewar Athens without giving an explanation of that defeat?" Zuckert grants that a tactful Athenian may wish to avoid contentious topics while conversing with a Cretan and Spartan statesman (Zuckert 2009, 54). But, she suggests, an Athenian politician could never persuade Dorians to adopt Athenian political institutions or practices without discussing Athens's ostensible shortcomings, including its ordeal with the plague and its notorious leaders, such as Pericles, Cleon, and Alcibiades. But since no one in the *Laws* ever mentions either a person or an event that became either famous or infamous during the Peloponnesian War, Zuckert concludes that the dialogue must have taken place before 450 B.C.E., which is before both the start of the Peloponnesian War and the date on which Socrates initiated his decisive turn away from pre-Socratic philosophy toward Socratic political philosophy (Zuckert 2009, 8).

Zuckert begins by arguing that Plato's chief purpose in writing the *Laws* is to lay out his own, final political understanding and practical proposals for constitutional reform. But we need to consider the possibility that Plato wrote the *Laws* with the additional purpose of examining what divine law is and how it is known. For if the Athenian Stranger is a Socratic philosopher, his guiding concern would be that he can understand the goals and principles of divine law on the basis of his own rational knowledge.

While it is true that there is nothing in the *Laws* that links it to people or events that are directly associated with Athenian politics during the Peloponnesian War, there are indications that the dialogue took place some years after the end of the Persian War. For instance, the Athenian Stranger alludes to the general corruption of Athenian politics and morals that took place at some time after the end of "the Persian danger," which means that the dialogue must have taken place well after 479 BCE. There is at least one reference to an event that took place in 447 BCE.[9] Most importantly, there is no reference in the dialogue that ties it to a specific date before the Socratic revolution, which Zuckert estimates took place in 450 BCE (Zuckert 2009, 8). If the interlocutors were tactful enough to put aside discussions of contemporary politics, the conversation could have taken place anytime after 450 BCE.

Turning to the substance of the Athenian Stranger's arguments, Zuckert notes that he sometimes says things about himself that suggest that he is not the Socrates whom we know from Plato's dialogues. In Book VII, the Athenian Stranger says that he has only recently discovered that certain lines and figures are not commensurable with others (Zuckert 2009, 55). This, says Zuckert, indicates that he lacks Socrates's presumably long-standing familiarity with mathematics (Zuckert 2009, 55n13). Putting aside the possibility that the Athenian Stranger speaks of his ignorance of mathematics with Socratic irony, we could conclude from this that the Athenian Stranger is not the Socrates whom we know from Plato's other dialogues; he may be an Athenian philosopher who has understood the need to turn from pre-Socratic natural philosophy to the political philosophy originated by Socrates.

Yet, as Zuckert notes, there seem to be important differences between the way that the Platonic Socrates ordinarily conducts himself and the way that the Athenian Stranger acts in the *Laws*. She points out that while Socrates is famous for asking his "what is?" questions of his interlocutors, the Athenian Stranger never asks either Kleinias or Megillus the "what is law?" question. As she also observes, these "what is?" questions often lead Socrates's interlocutors to become angry when they find that they are incapable of answering them on their own (Zuckert 2009, 62, 65). And the question "what is law?" may prove to be an especially controversial question. As we see in the *Minos*, Socrates's inquiry into the "what is law?" question leads to the suggestion that no law is ever truly fitting or just and that law can never be what it always claims to be (*Minos* 317a–e). Indeed, the question "what is law?" is so controversial that Xenophon does not put the question into the mouth of Socrates but allows it to be asked by Socrates's erstwhile follower Alcibiades (Xenophon *Memorabilia* 1. 2. 40–46). Yet the fact that the Athenian Stranger does not raise this question directly does not mean that it is not on his mind. If he is following up on the sort of questions that Socrates raises in the *Minos*, then he is inquiring into divine law in order to learn what law is and how we come to know or believe in it (Benardete 2000; Morrow 1960; Strauss 1975). And the fact that he does not anger Kleinias or Megillus by asking them disturbing questions about law itself does not prevent the Athenian Stranger from testing their knowledge of divine law or even from making them aware of their ignorance regarding it. After Zuckert correctly observes that Socrates's usual practice is to make his interlocutors aware of their ignorance and of their need for further self-examination in regard to the matter under discussion, she notes that the Athenian Stranger never makes his interlocutors aware of what they do not know and of their need to take care in regard to themselves (Zuckert 2009, 62–65). While it is true that the Athenian Stranger does not follow Socrates's usual practice in the *Laws*, it is not true that Socrates always shows his interlocutors that they are ignorant about the subject under discussion. In the *Republic*, for example, Socrates does not subject Glaucon and Adeimantus to a rigorous cross-examination before he begins his elaboration of the city in speech. Moreover, the Athenian Stranger's decision not to compel his interlocutors to confront their aporia in regard to divine law does not mean that he is not carrying out an important part of the Socratic inquiry into law. After all, the Athenian Stranger says at the start of the dialogue that his purpose in this opening conversation is to test not only Kleinias but also Megillus and himself (*Laws* 633a; compare 637d). Rather than try to lead Kleinias and Megillus to abandon their reliance on law, the Athenian Stranger wants to learn what such men know about divine law and how they know it. To that end, he does not seek merely to show that such men do not know what they claim to know. Instead, he also wants to demonstrate to them and to himself that when devout citizens come to doubt that their laws aim at the best things, they will abandon their trust in their old laws and will become open to a more complete or more adequate version of divine law. By showing that he can transform his interlocutors' beliefs about divine law, the Athenian Stranger is able to demonstrate that he understands important principles and goals of divine law. Moreover, this helps to show that the morally serious citizens with whom he speaks become open to the possibility that a political philosopher is able to discern and illuminate divine law. Consequently, it is important that he present his criticisms of Dorian law in ways that do not provoke such anger that his interlocutors will not listen to his own account of divine law and will not assent to it. By the end of the dialogue, the Athenian Stranger's attempt to win his interlocutors' assent to his code of law appears to be a great success (*Laws* 965c7–8, 968b2–3, 968b10–c2, 969c4–d2).

Wishing to delineate the differences between Socrates and the Athenian Stranger, Zuckert questions whether some of the Athenian Stranger's positive teachings are consistent with those of Socrates. Most notably, she says, Plato's Socrates never tries to demonstrate the existence of a god or to describe a code of divine law (Zuckert 2009, 61). The project that the Athenian Stranger undertakes is very ambitious, to say the least. In this regard, it does not seem to be in keeping with Socrates's well-known modesty, especially regarding divine matters. But Socrates is not always unable or unwilling to provide an account of the gods' attributes (*Republic* 377d–383c). Moreover, Socrates is sometimes willing to elaborate extensive and ambitious projects of his own, such as the city in speech in the *Republic* as well as his accounts of the ideas. If the Athenian Stranger's extensive theological arguments and teachings about divine law go beyond anything that Socrates says about divine law, his project is not inconsistent with Socrates's own endeavor to learn what law is and how it is known. In fact, it seems to be a necessary stage in that endeavor.

Beyond this, Zuckert points out that the Athenian Stranger attempts to ground his account of virtue in an account of the cosmos that is problematic. According to Zuckert, the Athenian Stranger teaches that the whole is not guided by order but is characterized by a cosmic war. She says that this "pious" belief in strife is incompatible with the possibility that there are unchanging ideas or "eternally unchanging intelligible entities" (Zuckert 2009, 33, 126–27; see also, Zuckert 2004, 394). Indeed, the Athenian Stranger alludes to a cosmic conflict between the gods and injustice, insolence, and imprudence in order to argue that the gods would never allow the unjust to go unpunished because this would amount to abandoning their posts in that great conflict (*Laws* 906a–b). Now, this allusion to a war between the gods and forces of disorder is not consistent with other things that the Athenian Stranger says about the rational order of the whole. Only a few pages before he mentions the conflict between the gods and the forces of disorder, he refers to a great god who oversees the whole and who establishes order throughout the entire cosmos (*Laws* 904a–c). In order to weigh the full meaning of each of these arguments about the cosmos, we would need to consider the context in which each of them is made. Yet even if we look in isolation at the Athenian Stranger's claim that there is a great cosmic war between the gods and the forces of cosmic disorder, this, by itself, may not exclude the possibility that such a war could take place in light of another, higher order in which the ideas dwell. In the *Euthyphro*, Euthyphro and Socrates raise the possibility of a similar conflict (*Euthyphro* 7b2–7e6, cf. 5d, 6d–e, 10d).[10]

For most of the dialogue, the Athenian Stranger keeps the conversation within the moral horizon of Kleinias and Megillus. Because the Athenian Stranger does not direct his interlocutors' attention away from their everyday understanding of virtue toward the ideas, the argument has been called "sub-Socratic" (Strauss 1975, 17, 27, 61, 182). According to Malcolm Schofield, "issues are at crucial junctures not pushed back to first principles." "Yet," says Schofield, the "need for a more searching inquiry is kept in view" (Schofield 2003, 7). Schofield tends to attribute this limitation on the scope of the conversation to the relative naiveté that marks the character of both Kleinias and Megillus. But we must also consider the possibility that the Athenian Stranger chooses to talk to men from a very traditional background because he wants to examine the belief in divine law as it presents itself to those whose understanding has been formed entirely by divine law. The Athenian Stranger's persistent interest in how his Dorian companions understand the laws indicates that he is not a typical pre-Socratic natural philosopher. For the natural philosophers who preceded Socrates were not known for their piety or for their respect for piety by the non-philosophers who encountered their teachings.[11] While some of the pre-Socratics seem to have used religious language in their writings, they were widely regarded as atheists or as heretics (e.g., *Laws* 967c–d). According to Cicero, Socrates was the first to compel philosophy to turn from the study of the heavenly or supra-human things and to force it to take up the study of the human things, which include the anthropomorphic and providential gods whom citizens take seriously (*Tusculan Disputations* V. 10; also *Brutus* 31). Unlike the pre-Socratics, the Athenian Stranger asks the non-philosopher about the origins and purposes of their laws and acknowledges that he cannot proceed unless he confirms that they accept what he is saying. Rather than taking his bearings from doctrines about the first principles of the cosmos, the Athenian Stranger spends most of the dialogue listening to citizens who speak in the language of everyday life, and clarifying and supplementing their beliefs in that same language. Rather than dismiss out of hand the possibility of providential gods who establish and support divine law, the Athenian Stranger has reflected deeply about the gods and their concern with human virtue and especially with the virtue justice.

The drama of the dialogue suggests that the conversation took place either as soon as or sometime after Socrates originated classical political philosophy. The ambiguity about the precise date of the dialogue indicates that it could have taken place at any time after Socrates set political philosophy in motion. While it could have taken place at any time, it, or a similar examination of divine law, must have taken place at some time in order to justify the political philosopher's enterprise. For Plato recognizes that divine law poses a great challenge to those who believe that reason should hold the highest authority in politics and in law. The *Laws* shows how a Platonic political philosopher would engage believers in divine law in conversation in order to show that those who believe in divine law also, implicitly, believe that the law should be guided by political philosophy.

Conclusion

Plato is said to assume that reason is the source of all religious, moral, and legal standards. In the *Laws,* he is said to teach that cosmology or astronomy reveals what is lawful and what is not for human beings and for cities. His unblinking faith in reason's power to discern what is just and good would seem to be grounded on the ungrounded hopes that the gods are thoroughly rational beings and that human reason can fully understand the gods' minds and purposes. But if we take seriously what the Athenian Stranger says and does at the outset of the *Laws*, we find that he makes no such assumptions. Instead, he begins by inquiring into how divine law is understood by the serious citizen. On the basis of his careful examination of the citizen's beliefs, the Athenian Stranger shows that when the citizen is pressed to explain the goals of divine law, he tries to provide a coherent account of those goals. Believing that divine law aims at what is best, the citizen thinks that it aims at the greatest goods for human beings. Because the believing citizen is a morally serious man, he believes that the greatest goods are the virtues. And because he believes that the gods want us to become altogether good human beings, he also believes that divine law promotes the complete virtue of a human being and that this brings happiness to both cities and individual citizens. Insofar as the devoted citizen recognizes that he believes this, he ceases to believe in the divinity of the laws of a city such as Crete and begins to accept the possibility that he can learn of a form of law that aims at the genuine goals of divine law. If the philosopher can show that he has a more complete account of virtue and of how it is related to happiness, he will have demonstrated to the serious citizen who believes in divine law that the philosopher has the authority to give rational guidance to politics and law. By paying attention to both the substance and the drama at the start of the *Laws,* we can recognize how the Platonic political philosopher makes every effort to avoid succumbing to the gravest dogmatism.

Chapter Three

THE EXAMINATION OF THE LAWS OF SPARTA

Part One—Spartan Virtue and Awe

After the Athenian Stranger describes the goals of correct law and the tasks of the legislator, he says that he wants to revisit the questions that he has just discussed with Kleinias. He says that he wants Kleinias and Megillus to say how the laws that Zeus gave to Minos and that Apollo gave to Lycurgus in fact aim at the goals of divine law that they have just described (*Laws* 632e). In addition, he wants them to reveal how they know that the laws of Minos and Apollo truly aim at these goals. He wants to know how those who have experience (*empeiro*) with the law have clarity about these laws while the divinity of the law remains unapparent to the rest of us. He wonders whether the divinity of the law is known through art (*techne*) or through habits while the rest of us remain unclear (*Laws* 632d4–7). In light of the care that he devoted to his opening examination of Kleinias, we might expect that he has sufficiently demonstrated that the laws of Crete and of Sparta do not aim at the highest goals and thus that they are not divine. We might think that he has already shown that the devoted citizen relies on reason to probe into his beliefs and to resolve the inconsistencies that appear within them.

In seeking to start from the beginning, the Athenian Stranger is not dismissing what he has shown through his opening conversation with Kleinias. What he is saying, however, is that his opening conversation is not decisive because he has yet to examine the beliefs of the Spartan Megillus. As the Athenian Stranger later points out, Megillus embodies the old-fashioned character of Sparta (*Laws* 696b, 699d). While Kleinias is talkative and evidently amenable to reason, Megillus is ever reticent and always respectful of the laws of Sparta, regardless of the arguments that he has heard from the Athenian Stranger (*Laws* 636e–37a, 638a, 646e–47c). If Megillus rather than Kleinias is the representative Dorian citizen, then the Athenian Stranger's success in speaking with Kleinias would not seem to have established that there is a tenable common ground between the devout citizen and the rationalistic philosopher. Perhaps Megillus has had some experience with the laws of Sparta that has eluded both Kleinias and the Athenian Stranger. If so, the Athenian Stranger wants to know what this experience is. Much like Socrates in the *Minos,* he wants to know if the citizen's belief in the law is based on some art or through some sort of habituation and if so what kind of art or habituation. Do we come to believe in divinity of the law through an art that is based in reason such as the art of arithmetic? Through an art such as medicine? Or do we recognize the law through the art of divination or soothsaying (cf. *Minos* 314b)? The Athenian Stranger has learned important things from his initial conversation with Kleinias. But having learned what he can from Kleinias, he now focuses his attention on what Megillus knows about the laws of Sparta and on how he knows it. For the remainder of the first three books, the Athenian Stranger continues to examine both Kleinias and Megillus. But the Athenian Stranger focuses his attention primarily on Megillus because he wants to learn whether the apparently more typically Dorian Megillus will confirm or contradict what he has learned from Kleinias about the origins and purposes of divine law.

When Kleinias asks what should be said at this point, the Athenian Stranger says that they should go back to the beginning and examine how the laws of Crete and Sparta teach the virtues. They should begin with examining how they teach courage and, using that as a model, continue to examine how the laws teach the other virtues (*Laws* 632e3). In the end, he says, we will show how the virtues that are taught by law are, in fact, virtue as a whole (*Laws* 632e5–6). It is notable that in starting over from the beginning, the Athenian Stranger does not call into question whether the principal goal of divine law is the cultivation of virtue. Having established this through his examination of Kleinias, he treats it as a hypothesis for the subsequent examination of Megillus.

Megillus, who has been listening to the discussion, seems to accept this hypothesis readily, for he suddenly speaks up to endorse the Athenian Stranger's proposal. At the same time, Megillus displays his Laconian character by suggesting that the Athenian Stranger begin his discussion with Kleinias, whom he calls this "one who praises Zeus" (*Laws* 632a1–2). The Athenian Stranger will not be put off, and says that he intends to begin his examination with Megillus. But, he adds, he will also continue to examine Kleinias since it is his intention to examine both of the Dorians and himself as well (*Laws* 632a3–5). The ensuing conversation constitutes the self-examination of the Socratic philosopher in that it tests whether divine law can be known through reason alone or whether it is known through some other, extra-rational experience. For the remainder of the first three books of the *Laws*, the Athenian Stranger must undertake an even more extensive, careful, and respectful examination of the laws of Sparta if he is to confirm that the philosopher is able to understand them and either challenge or verify their divinity.

The Athenian Stranger begins by reminding Megillus that it has been said that the laws of Crete provide common meals and gymnastic exercises in order to promote victory in war. What, he asks, do the Spartans do to teach the rest of virtue? In response, Megillus does not allude to how the Spartans teach virtues other than courage, but elaborates further measures that are intended to prepare young Spartans to endure pain. He says that he could name quite a few and mentions hunting, boxing, and theft. He says that the latter two involve suffering "many blows." He also alludes to the "secret service," a test which requires young men to endure cold conditions without adequate clothing or shelter. Similarly, they are required to participate in summer festivals, during which they must endure excessive heat (*Laws* 633b–c). By listing these practices and saying that he could do so indefinitely, Megillus does not seem to go beyond Kleinias's original claim that his city's lawgiver established laws that aim at victory in war. The Athenian Stranger effectively defines courage when he says that the Spartans acquire it by learning to combat and to endure pain (*Laws* 633c–d). The Athenian Stranger sums up how the Spartans teach courage by saying that they prevent the young from running away from pain and compel them to experience pain through force and through appeals to honor (*Laws* 634a–b).

Having granted that the Spartans teach courage through these means, the Athenian Stranger asks if they should define courage simply as the ability to combat pain or if it should be understood to include the ability to combat pleasure. The Athenian Stranger seems to be expanding the ordinary meaning of the word *courage* so that it includes what we might call "moderation" (Pangle 1988, 389; Strauss 1975, 11). But the Athenian Stranger suggests that some sort of moderation may be needed in order to preserve courage. He observes that there are desires, pleasures, and flatteries which can melt the spiritedness of those who think themselves most grave or solemn (*Laws* 633d). According to the Athenian Stranger's suggestion, true courage is endurance, the ability to stand firm while experiencing either pain or pleasure. The courageous individual remains serene and unaffected by passion.

When Megillus is hard pressed to say how the Spartans teach their young to combat their pleasures (*Laws* 634a–b), the Athenian Stranger anticipates that the discussion will lead them to criticize the laws of Sparta, and so he asks whether it is permissible for them to question the goodness or the truthfulness of those laws (*Laws* 634c). He argues that such criticisms are within the laws of Sparta and Crete on the grounds that many say that one of Crete's and Sparta's noblest laws is the one that proclaims to everyone that it is impious to question the laws but which permits an old man to make reasoned arguments regarding the law in private to the magistrates (*Laws* 634e). Upon hearing the Athenian Stranger describe this law, Kleinias says that the Athenian has divined the mind of the ancient lawgiver (*Laws* 635a1). By acknowledging that it is sometimes proper to question the laws, Kleinias grants that the lawgiver did not receive the laws from a god but must have claimed that he received them from a divine source in order to protect the laws from unwanted criticism (Strauss 1975, 10–11). In light of this, Kleinias associates the Athenian Stranger's incisive explanation of the purpose of the law with prophecy itself and agrees that it is permissible to criticize the laws in order to bring them into line with the laws that a god would legislate (*Laws* 635a–b).

Megillus does not object to examining how the laws of Sparta teach moderation. But instead of granting that they fail to do so, he says that the Spartans' common meals and gymnastics teach the young to master not only pain but also pleasure. The Athenian Stranger replies that these very institutions are not said to have made the Spartans more moderate but instead have helped to give Sparta a reputation for indulging in pederasty (*Laws* 636a–d). According to the Athenian Stranger, pederasty seems to be an ancient law that seems to be laid down in nature concerning the sexual pleasures not only of humans but also those of beasts (*Laws* 636b).[1] He says that it seems that sexual pleasure is according to nature only when males unite with females for the sake of procreation (*Laws* 636c). Furthermore, it seems that the mixing of males with males or of females with females is against nature and that those human beings who first broke with this law seem to have acted out of a daring that is rooted in a lack of self-restraint in regard to pleasure (*Laws* 636c). This reference to a "law in nature" is one of only two such references in all of Plato's writing.[2] Earlier in the dialogue, both Kleinias and the Athenian Stranger said that a prudent legislator devises laws in order to meet needs or to provide goods that are established by nature (*Laws* 625c–26a, 631d1–2). Yet it is not altogether clear what the Athenian Stranger could mean in speaking of a law in nature that would regulate the sexual pleasures of human beings along with all other animals. It is one thing to say that nature has instilled in living things an urge to procreate and that this urge tends to promote sexual activity in animals, and another thing to say that nature has established a morally binding rule that prohibits all animate beings from taking pleasure in any sexual activity that does not aim at procreation. Why, we wonder, should a principle that seems to govern what animals do or do not do apply to human beings? And since the Athenian Stranger has just prefaced this discussion by observing that it is almost impossible to find a rule that applies to every particular case (*Laws* 636a4–b1), we also wonder what it is about sexual activity between a man and a woman outside of a marriage that makes it, in particular, always illicit.

Immediately after speaking of the law, the Athenian Stranger adds some remarks about nature and pleasure that suggest one way that a principle or rule might be understood to apply to the sexual activity of human beings. He says that there are by nature two "springs," one of which brings forth pleasures and another which brings forth pains (*Laws* 636d). He says that those who draw from the correct spring at the correct time and in the correct amount are happy. But those who draw from one of the springs without knowledge (*anepistemonos*) and who draw from it at the wrong time live lives that are happy (*Laws* 636d–e). According to this image, nature provides everyone with pleasures and pains and leaves it to us to use knowledge to determine which particular pleasure should be taken and which particular pain should be endured in a given circumstance. In providing us with this image, the Athenian Stranger does not say whether the law is the standard of happiness that guides all our actions or the particular judgment that instructs us to pursue a particular pleasure or to endure a particular pain or both of these things. What is clear is that there is no universal rule that determines that a given pleasure is intrinsically bad or that a given pain is intrinsically good. Insofar as one relies on some rational faculty to deliberate about what is to be done in each particular case, this activity resembles the virtue *phronesis* or practical reason as it is described by Aristotle in the *Nichomachean Ethics* (Aristotle *Nichomachean Ethics* 1140a24–b30, 1141b28–42a32). If the rule that binds those who seek happiness is established in each case by practical reason or prudence, then this is not precisely the same law that guides other animals in regard to sexual pleasure. In order to show that sexual activity outside of heterosexual marriage is always against nature, the Athenian Stranger would have to show that it never leads to happiness but always leads to its opposite. He would have to explain the dangers that sexual or erotic desires always pose to the individual. At this time, at least, the Athenian Stranger does not provide such arguments. By repeatedly qualifying his remarks by saying that "it seems" that there is such a law and that "it seems" to prohibit certain sexual acts, the Athenian Stranger signals that he is not providing a conclusive demonstration of the proposition. What he is able to demonstrate, however, is that Megillus readily accepts this prohibition of all sexual pleasure outside of marriage or, more generally, that he believes that some pleasures are always bad regardless of the circumstances. We wonder whether some feature of the Spartan education has led him to conclude that some pleasures are always bad and why it does so. Accordingly, we also wonder what it is about Spartan education that leads him to this conclusion and whether this belief is shared by those who have been educated by the laws that the Athenian Stranger calls "correct" laws.

Megillus makes his views on pleasure more explicit in his response to the Athenian Stranger's criticism of Sparta's common meals and gymnastic exercise. Megillus does not defend the practice of pederasty but instead says that he believes that the Spartan lawgiver was correct in ordering the Spartans to "flee from pleasure" (*Laws* 636e). In his opinion, these laws are the noblest that can be found among human beings (*Laws* 636e8–37a2). Now, Megillus says explicitly that he does not accept the conclusions that the Athenian Stranger and Kleinias drew from the conversation at the opening of the dialogue. Megillus does not agree that the laws of Sparta aim only at victory in war and that laws that aim only at this good cannot be divine.

Megillus's primary evidence that the laws of Sparta regarding pleasure are the noblest laws is that the lawgiver has forbidden the drinking of wine, which leads people to succumb to the greatest pleasure and to indulge in the greatest insolence (*hubrisi*) and mindlessness (*Laws* 637a). The laws of Sparta ban all symposia and do not permit the Dionysian religious festivals, which offer an excuse for excessive drunkenness (*Laws* 637b). This strong criticism of wine-drinking and being drunk sheds new light on the Spartan virtue of moderation in regard to pleasure. The virtuous Spartan is moderate in regard to pleasure because he abstains from it altogether. Spartan moderation does not consist in keeping one's wits about one while enjoying certain pleasures but in denying pleasure to oneself.

The Athenian Stranger, for his part, denies that wine-drinking and Dionysia are intrinsically blameworthy and thus that simple abstinence is moderation. All such practices, he says, are praiseworthy where they are accompanied by endurance. But where this endurance is lacking, they become foolish (*Laws* 637b7–c2). Thus, one should be able to endure pleasures just as one is able to endure pains, taking them in or rejecting them in light of the guidance offered by practical reason. In this formulation, one needs not only practical reason but also endurance to enjoy certain pleasures in ways that are commendable and sensible. Practical reason is the leader of the virtues because it makes all other goods beneficial (*Laws* 631b–d). But one cannot always follow prudence unless one possesses a certain steadiness of soul.

Recognizing that evaluating the propriety of wine-drinking and drunkenness may seem trivial to men such as Kleinias and Megillus, the Athenian Stranger points out that what is at issue is the virtue and vice of the lawgivers

(*Laws* 637d). If he can demonstrate that drinking wine with prudence contributes some important good to human beings, he can argue that the laws
of Crete and Sparta do not provide what is best and thus are not correct.
Moreover, if he can get Megillus to acknowledge that this is a serious short-
coming of Spartan law, he will have taken an important step in confirming
that the Spartans' belief in their city's laws is rooted in the belief that those
laws aim at the greatest good and that they can be shown to do so.

In order to examine Megillus's beliefs about divine law, the Athenian
Stranger lists a number of nations whose laws permit the drinking of wine.
He says that in Scythia and Thrace women drink wine along with the men
and that they do so without any apparent limits. Persians, he says, also
drink a great deal of undiluted wine while remaining more orderly than
do other peoples (*Laws* 637e). When Megillus responds that the Spartans
are able to put all these peoples to flight in battle, Megillus signals that he
thinks that the laws of Sparta are best because they lead to victory in war,
as did Kleinias at the start of the dialogue.

The Athenian Stranger replies that victory in war cannot always be
traced to a single cause. Sometimes the size of one army enables it to overcome a smaller yet more virtuous opponent. Given the uncertain relation
between virtue and victory, the Athenian Stranger suggests that they focus
instead on reasoning about what is noble and what is advantageous (*Laws*
638b). The Athenian Stranger's observation that virtuous cities are susceptible to defeat at the hands of the large and strong qualifies his earlier
suggestion that those who have the virtues also have the external goods
and the goods of the body, and that those who have these goods have happiness itself (*Laws* 631b). By granting that a city can have virtue and still
lack happiness, the Athenian Stranger indicates that a legislator who seeks
to bring about the greatest goods will have to pay attention not only to
the whole of virtue but also to strength or size or to any other good that
is necessary to happiness. Some scholars have suggested that the need to
provide for the city's security might distract the legislator from promoting
the complete virtue of a human being (Pangle 1988, 432–34; Parens 1995,
65–75). To this point in the dialogue, the Athenian Stranger has not said
enough to clarify the relationship between virtue and happiness or about
how law would bring these things into being.

In response to the Athenian Stranger's claim that the powerful sometimes overcome the virtuous in war, Megillus seems to agree and thus to
accept that victory as such cannot be the goal of divine law (*Laws* 638e–
39a). This also seems to signal Megillus's agreement that the laws of Sparta,
which aim only at victory in war, do not aim at the highest goals and thus
cannot be truly divine. But Megillus might reply that the laws of Apollo

and Lycurgus sought to bring victory through courage rather than through mere size and strength. Moreover, he might say, the fact that the vicious sometimes prevail over the virtuous does not compromise the original Dorian claim that divine law aims at victory in war and at courage, for the serious citizen of Sparta might not expect dedication to the law to guarantee victory in every battle. The Spartans may not always exemplify the virtue that is taught them by the law. And even if they exemplify that virtue and still lose, it may be due to the gods' inscrutable will. After declaring that they will focus on what is advantageous for the city, the Athenian Stranger will make the defense of wine-drinking a principal theme of his discussion in Books I and II. If the Athenian Stranger can show that Megillus believes that wine-drinking provides some important good such as the virtue of the citizens, then he may be able to win Megillus's agreement that the laws of Sparta are defective in some serious respect. In light of the opposition between the way Crete and Sparta regard wine-drinking and the way that it is judged in Athens, the Athenian Stranger observes that many cities and nations have very different laws regarding such things. Rather than blame each other's city contentiously, they should consider how certain practices are done correctly and, in this case, the correct way to drink wine. Megillus agrees that if there is some better way of examining the matter, they should pursue it. Megillus is not concerned with winning the argument but with resolving it in a correct way. Upon hearing about the Athenian's claims, Kleinias rejoins the conversation and presses the Athenian Stranger to explain how they should recognize a correct kind of wine-drinking. The Athenian Stranger argues that every community needs a good ruler and that every good ruler must both know how to rule well and also have the endurance to use that knowledge in ruling (*Laws* 639c, 640a). Kleinias agrees that just as an army needs a courageous ruler, so must a drinking party need a ruler who has practical reason and who is sober (*Laws* 640c). The Athenian Stranger allows that he has not seen such a ruler himself. Since none of them have experience with such a ruler, he asks if it would be sufficient to show that such a ruler could oversee a drinking party (*Laws* 639e–40a). By granting that this would be an acceptable procedure for discovering a well-led drinking party, Kleinias and Megillus show that they are willing to recognize the authority of rulers of whom they have no experience. They seem willing to accept, provisionally, the authority of what is established by reasoned speech.

Urged by Kleinias to identify the good that comes from correctly run drinking parties, the Athenian Stranger says that it is good for education and that education produces good men and victories (*Laws* 641b–c). But immediately after saying that good education produces victories in war, the Athenian Stranger observes that such victories often lead to hubris, which undermines the education that led to martial success (*Laws* 641). But, he says, education never wins "Cadmean" (i.e. Pyrrhic) victories (*Laws* 641c4–5), thus suggesting that a genuine education would not allow victorious warriors to experience hubris but would prevent them from succumbing to that or other vices.

When challenged by Kleinias to explain how wine-drinking could contribute to education, the Athenian Stranger cautions that when so many disagree about such things, no one but a god could know about them with certainty (*Laws* 641d). He proposes that he will lay out an account of a correct education and about the use of wine-drinking in such an education and that they all will follow the argument until they "arrive at the god" (*Laws* 643a). The Athenian Stranger does not say which god will be at the end of the argument. England and Saunders suggest that the god is Dionysus (England 1921a, 249; Saunders 1970, 71). Strauss, on the other hand, suggests that the god is Zeus, whose cave is the interlocutors' destination (*Laws* 625a–b). According to Strauss, if they will be discussing education until they arrive at the cave of Zeus, then they will be discussing education throughout their whole conversation. If this is what is meant, then the entire dialogue will be devoted to the theme of education (Strauss 1975, 17).

The Athenian Stranger begins by offering his own account of education and by asking Kleinias to consider whether it is acceptable to him. Education, he says, consists in awakening a child's erotic love for that activity that will become his or her life's work (*Laws* 643b–d). Genuine education appeals to some inner, latent passion that will direct and sustain the child throughout his life. By calling this love "erotic," the Athenian Stranger suggests that the child will find his work alluring and beautiful. In love with his work, he will expect it to bring him fulfillment and will focus on it to the exclusion of other concerns. This erotic love of the art will enable the worker to draw upon all his resourcefulness, his powers and capacities, in his effort to carry it out. But an education that is truly worthy of the name does not arouse a love for any vulgar or illiberal activity (*Laws* 644a). Rather, a noble and liberal education consists in the awakening of an erotic love of citizenship. A truly educated citizen loves ruling and being ruled with justice (*Laws* 643e4–6). The Athenian Stranger's claim that the citizen harbors within him a latent passion for citizenship is the closest anyone in the Platonic dialogues comes to saying that man is by nature a political animal. The goal of divine law, it seems, is to awaken this love of citizenship.

To help explain what it means to be ruled with justice and how law would contribute to this, the Athenian Stranger offers an account of self-rule. He explains that everyone is moved by pleasure and pain, passions which he calls "imprudent counselors" (*Laws* 644c6–7). The person who rules himself is guided by "true reasoning" regarding what is best (*Laws* 645b4). Earlier in Book I, the Athenian Stranger said that nature is like a spring that brings forth pains and pleasures and that those with knowledge can consider the particular circumstances and can select among the pains and pleasures in order that they might be happy (*Laws* 636d–e). Now, he indicates that pains and pleasures are always accompanied by beliefs that claim to lead one to what is best. But those who have true reasoning are able to recognize that these passions do not counsel us prudently. Drawing on this true reasoning, the individual can weigh his particular circumstances and can prudently select which of his pains and pleasures he should follow in order to do or to acquire what is best for him. The Athenian Stranger says that when this sort of reasoning is applied to a whole city, it is called "law" (*Laws* 644d).

Kleinias and Megillus, however, do not understand this account of self-rule. In response, the Athenian Stranger offers a "myth" that says that we are divine puppets who are moved in various ways for reasons that we cannot apprehend. We do know, however, that what moves us in the most immediate respect are various passions that pull on us like strings pull on a puppet. We also know that we should be guided by reasoning, which comes to us in the form of law. Law, he says, is a golden, noble, and divine "cord" or "string" (*Laws* 644e). But this string is especially weak, and so it requires the help of something stronger to assist it. It is up to the individual to pull along with law and to struggle against the passions. The Athenian Stranger says that the contest between the passions and law brings to light the distinction between virtue and vice (*Laws* 644e4), suggesting that we first become aware of the distinction between virtue and vice when we find that our passions oppose what the law teaches. In light of this description of self-control, the purpose of education seems to be to cultivate certain passions that can help one pull along with the law and against the other passions. Kleinias and Megillus do not object to this second presentation of self-rule. The second version of self-rule seems more familiar to the two citizens. We still have to learn whether the second version fully accords with Megillus's understanding of virtue and whether or to what extent the two versions of self-rule are compatible with each other.

Having shed some light on genuine liberal education, the Athenian Stranger must explain how wine-drinking could contribute to it. The Athenian Stranger notes that those who are sick sometimes take medicines that make them feel worse but that eventually free them from sickness. He adds that athletes who train their bodies vigorously sometimes feel terrible immediately after vigorous exercise. By analogy, wine-drinking works like a medicine or a violent exercise in that it temporarily degrades the soul in order to bring about some good.

The degradation that wine-drinking brings about is well known: it intensifies the passions while weakening sensations, memories, beliefs, and practical reason (*Laws* 645d). In fact, wine-drinking strips away the effects of moral education (*Laws* 645e). One wonders how it could possibly contribute to education to undo all that moral education has achieved.

The Athenian Stranger begins to explain this by noting that the soul is subject to two kinds of fears. Primarily, there is a fear of the evils that we expect will afflict us. But in addition, he says, there is also the fear of the opinion that one has acted ignobly. This fear, which is called "shame," is so strong that it prevents us from indulging certain pleasures and compels us to endure certain pains (*Laws* 646e–47a). According to the Athenian Stranger, the lawgiver will revere (*sebei*) this second fear and will call it "awe" (*aidos*). The boldness (*tharros*) that is opposite to this fear is given the name "lack of awe" (*Laws* 647a). By associating this fear with reverence and awe, the lawgiver indicates that it goes beyond a fear of having a poor reputation among one's fellow citizens. The citizen who takes the law seriously also fears appearing shameless in the eyes of the gods. According to Rudolf Otto, awe is an emotional experience of dread, astonishment, and humility in regard to what is unspeakable or inexpressible about the divine (Otto 1958, 13–19, 39–41).[3] As such, it would be distinct from any rational knowledge about the intelligible attributes of the gods. Nor would it be reducible to any rational insight into the moral principles associated with a god. Rather, awe would be an encounter with something that is tremendous and terrible, something that overwhelms both the mind and the heart. In saying that the educator must always teach awe along with justice (*Laws* 647c, 670d), the Athenian Stranger confirms that one could experience a fear of shame that did not include a sense of moral responsibility or dread. At the same time, he indicates that the awe that is felt by the well-educated citizen must be accompanied by a strong concern with justice. The properly educated citizen will fear acting shamefully and unjustly in the eyes of his or her fellow citizens as well as in the eyes of the gods.

When the Athenian Stranger asks Kleinias whether the legislator will consider the lack of awe to be the greatest evil for the city and for the private individual, Kleinias agrees. The good Dorian citizen knows that shame and fear before the god is the core of virtue. The Athenian Stranger concludes that among the Dorians victory comes from boldness in the face of enemies and from a fear of vileness among friends (*Laws* 647b).

Having evidently confirmed that awe is the core of Dorian virtue and piety, the Athenian Stranger says that victory comes from boldness in the face of enemies and from a fear of vileness among friends. In light of these observations, it appears that the Spartans' fear of being thought shameful in the eyes of their fellow citizens and the gods compels them to stay in their ranks despite the dangers that might confront them. Insofar as courage is defined as the ability to overcome fear, neither the Cretans nor the Spartans would have courage in the strict sense but would instead be governed by an overpowering fear. In regard to pleasure, too, the Dorians seem to master that passion with fear rather than self-command. Most important, neither the devoted citizen of Crete nor the devoted citizen of Sparta would achieve the harmony of soul and happiness that Kleinias and the Athenian Stranger earlier agreed must be the goal of divine law.

These observations might seem to reveal crucial defects in Spartan virtue and thus in Spartan law. But when we reflect on the awe at the heart of Cretan and Spartan law, we must call into question the Athenian Stranger's entire criticism of the laws of Crete and Sparta. To this point, the Athenian Stranger's criticism of the most venerable codes of law has rested on the examination of Kleinias. While Kleinias's eagerness to discuss the goals of divine law and his readiness to use reason to think through the problems that emerge from the discussion brings to light his most strongly held beliefs about the gods and divine law, this eagerness and this readiness do not seem to be characteristic features of pious fear and awe in regard to the gods and their laws. Megillus, on the other hand, seems a more typical representative of the well-bred Dorian citizen. Megillus has joined the conversation to signal his agreement to a few points from time to time, but for the most part he has remained silent. Despite the criticisms of the laws of both Crete and Sparta, Megillus maintains a deep respect for the nobility of his city's laws (e.g., *Laws* 633a–b, 636a, 636e, 638a). His enduring respect for the laws of Sparta reflects his reverence for those laws. When contrasting Kleinias with Megillus, one cannot help but wonder if Kleinias has forgotten the awe that he felt as a young man or if he has always been somewhat oblivious to it (Strauss 1975, 20).[4] If Kleinias fails to feel that awe, it is possible that he also fails to recognize some sort of faith or wisdom that is given to those who feel the pious fear or awe that the law intends to teach. If the relatively free-speaking Kleinias does not experience the awe that is the very core of Dorian virtue, then his willingness to examine the origins and purposes of his city's laws and his responses to the Athenian Stranger's questions would tell us little about what a serious citizen believes regarding divine law. His agreement to the Athenian Stranger's argument would be of limited worth in the Athenian Stranger's endeavor to learn whether those who believe in divine law do so on the basis of reason or some other faculty. In order to confirm that the Platonic political philosopher understands divine law and has the authority to interpret it, the Athenian Stranger must examine the ostensibly reverent Megillus's beliefs about divine law to learn if they are the same as Kleinias's beliefs. The Athenian Stranger must find out whether Megillus is willing to hold contradictory views of divine law (e.g., *Euthyphro* 11c–d) or whether he will affirm, either explicitly or implicitly, that divine law must be grounded on a consistent and coherent account of what is best.

The Athenian Stranger does not, however, raise any direct questions about awe at this time. Instead, he returns to his thesis that wine-drinking contributes to education. Turning to how the Spartans teach courage, he recounts how they expose young people to numerous pains and fears in the expectation that the young will thereby learn to conquer these fears. As has been said, they triumph over their fear of the enemy through a stronger fear of their fellow citizens' and the gods' opinion of them. The Athenian Stranger says that just as the lawgiver teaches courage through exposing young people to various fears, so might he teach young people to feel the correct kind of shame by exposing young people to various pleasures (*Laws* 647c–d). He adds that the legislator should arrange for young people to drink wine in private until they become shameless. Alone, and in this condition, they should practice fighting off their shameless-ness (*Laws* 648d). The Athenian Stranger does not explain precisely how someone can learn to become more subject to shame while drinking wine. Perhaps the young will anticipate the shame that they could incur after the effects of the wine have worn off and through this anticipatory fear will conduct themselves in a solemn manner. The difficulty with this mode of education would be, of course, that drinking wine alleviates the concern with shame on which the young wine drinker is supposed to draw (Stalley 1983, 126). Rather than supply a satisfactory answer to this question at this time, the Athenian Stranger points out how useful wine-drinking would be for testing and revealing the natures and characters of those who are being educated in the virtues. He says that it is most useful for those who practice the art of caring for souls, an art that he characterizes as the political art (*Laws* 650b).

Part Two—A Model of Correct Education

Even though the Athenian Stranger has argued that wine-drinking reveals the character and nature of the wine drinkers, he has not yet demonstrated that wine-drinking makes a positive contribution to virtue. It is only at the start of Book II that the Athenian Stranger declares that drinking wine makes a substantial contribution to education. In order to show the greatest usefulness of wine-drinking, the Athenian Stranger needs to show its role in an education that is truly correct. Accordingly, he begins Book II by elaborating how one would educate a "perfect human being" (*Laws* 653b1–c4). If he can show that wine-drinking is the "safeguard" to such an education, then the Athenian Stranger can argue that the laws of Sparta or of any other city that fails to use it do not provide the noblest and best education.

According to the Athenian Stranger, the education of a perfect human being produces a harmony between the passions and reason (*Laws* 653b–c). This harmony is to be achieved by building good character. Those with such a character will be disposed to pursue the right kinds of passions and to resist the wrong kinds and as a result will be able to reason for themselves. While this education looks forward to this harmony, it does not begin by appealing to the child's reason. The Athenian Stranger explains that pains and pleasures move young children long before they develop the virtue prudence or before they hold "true opinions." In fact, he says, many never acquire this virtue even when they grow old (*Laws* 653a). In light of this, the goal of a correct education is to give young people the sort of character that will guide them prior to reasoning and will later enable them to reason for themselves should they develop the ability to do so. This account of a correct education sheds new light on the Athenian Stranger's earlier claim that education awakens an erotic love of "ruling and being ruled," which is further characterized as following "true reasoning" on one's own or in the form of law (*Laws* 643d–44a). It now appears that early education does not awaken a love of reasoning but instead arouses certain passions that can later assist reason if the young citizen eventually develops the ability to reason for him or herself.

The Athenian Stranger begins his account of how correct education takes place by noting that our primary experience takes place through pleasure and pain, and so it is through pleasure and pain that virtue and vice must be taught. The education begins by leading the young to experience the correct kind of pleasures and to avoid the incorrect kind of pleasures (*Laws* 653b–c). By repeatedly exposing them to the correct pleasures, the young should develop a habit of loving (*stergein*) the correct kind of pleasures (*Laws* 653c1–2). The result should be that harmony of passion and reason, which is said to be virtue itself (*Laws* 653b6).

While the goal of education is a harmony of passion and reason, the habituation that builds the citizen's character will not always be pleasant. Over time, the habits slacken or weaken and become "corrupt" or burdensome (*Laws* 653c). In the *Nichomachean Ethics*, Aristotle says that noble habits, those that contribute to our perfection, are intrinsically pleasant

(Aristotle *Nichomachean Ethics* 1099a10–20). But since correct habits are instilled long before the harmony between passion and reason takes place, it appears that they are not experienced by young people as aspects of their perfection. According to the Athenian Stranger, the gods recognized that even human beings with correct habits inevitably suffer, and took pity on human beings generally by introducing holidays and music to them. Through music, human beings are able to find enjoyment in the presence of the gods. But having said this, the Athenian Stranger remarks that "it is necessary to learn if the song that is now being sung is true according to nature." Looking to nature, reason (logos) says that every young thing is full of chaotic motion (*Laws* 653d7–8). But the gods have given us the ability to perceive and enjoy rhythm and harmony. By taking pleasure in certain rhythms and harmonies, we are able to bring a certain order to our passions (*Laws* 653d–54a). The Athenian Stranger also says that music has the power to imitate certain passions and dispositions, including the disposition to resist fear that we call "courage" (*Laws* 654e–55b). When young people are exposed to music that associates the virtues with beauty and pleasure and the vices with ugliness and pain, they come to enjoy and to assimilate themselves to the virtues (*Laws* 656b). In light of this, a correct education entails teaching young people to sing and dance in choruses. Even if one cannot fully articulate what is noble, one who takes pleasure in singing and dancing the noble things is the correctly educated human being. By helping young people to experience the orderliness and pleasure associated with noble virtue, the Muses and Apollo provide what the Athenian Stranger calls the "first education" (*Laws* 654a6).

According to the Athenian Stranger, some who receive the correct education will find that the music fits their character, and they will delight in the music and in the virtues that it portrays. But others will find that they take no pleasure in noble music or virtues (*Laws* 655e–56a). In fact, some will have natures or characters that allow them to enjoy music that portrays certain vices. In order to protect citizens from taking these illicit pleasures, it would be best to make sure that young people are never exposed to such music. Those who make good laws ought not to allow artists to present whatever music pleases them but should see to it that they sing only noble songs and dance only noble dances.

When poets present choruses to young people, it would be just to give them prizes and honors not for giving pleasure to the multitude but for giving correct pleasure that is sanctioned by prudent and courageous judges (*Laws* 659ab). The Athenian Stranger says that this was once the practice under the laws of ancient Greece and remains so under the laws of Egypt. For many years, he says, the law has established that noble music is regarded as divine and is not permitted to change. Should someone introduce new laws, he ought to follow the Egyptian example and mandate that only noble music should be played and that the noble music should never change. He ought to organize celebrations and contests in which those who sing and dance most nobly win honors and awards. The lawgiver should persuade the poets to make correct poems that celebrate those who are courageous, moderate, and completely good (*Laws* 660a).

In light of these reflections about the role that the arts can play in shaping the tastes of the citizens, the Athenian Stranger says that the argument has come around again to the theme of education. Offering a third definition of education, he says that it consists in "leading young people to accept the reasoning that is said to be correct by law and that is believed to be correct by those who are decent and oldest" (*Laws* 659d–60e). The Athenian Stranger points out that while the law intends to teach young people to have the correct kind of likes and dislikes, it is only decent, old men who readily take pleasure in these things (*Laws* 658d–e). But because children cannot be expected to be serious about these things without some further inducement, it is necessary to present what is correct through songs and games (*Laws* 659d). The Athenian Stranger explains that just as children can be led to enjoy healthy food by mixing it with pleasant-tasting things, so they can be led to enjoy what is correct by mixing it with pleasant music and games (*Laws* 659e–60a). According to the Athenian Stranger, the legislator must make sure that poets use correct rhythms and harmonies to depict the sounds and motions of moderate, courageous, and wholly good men (*Laws* 660a).

In saying that education consists in leading young people to "accept the reasoning that is said to be correct by law and that is believed to be correct by those who are decent and oldest," the Athenian Stranger appears to alter his initial account of education, according to which education consists in leading young people to rule themselves through reason (*Laws* 643d7–44b4, 644c1–d3, 645b4). By this earlier account, education would lead young people to regard reason as the standard of what is lawful (cf. *Minos* 315a). But here in Book II, in the third definition of education, the Athenian Stranger says that young people would be educated to respect the reasoning that has been established by law. Instead of reason being the measure for what is lawful, law is now the measure for what is rational. The third definition of education suggests that moral education does not appeal to reason but to the passions. But if education leads young people to feel passionate love for the arguments that they have been taught by the law, what might happen should they someday acquire the ability to reason for themselves? According to Bobonich, early education will help young people develop emotions that lead them to act rightly. Should they later develop a "reasoned appreciation of what is good and fine," they will acquire a "separate and additional sort of motivation for acting rightly" (Bobonich 2002, 115). But Bobonich does not explain precisely how we are to know that a passionate desire to do what the law requires will always coincide with what reason dictates about what is best. How do we know that our law-bred passions will always yield to the authority of reason? Why are these passions especially open to rational guidance?

Rather than pose such questions, Kleinias curses emphatically and questions the Athenian Stranger about which cities now use music correctly. In the name of Zeus, he says, do you know of anywhere except Crete and Sparta where music is used in this way (*Laws* 660b)? Kleinias's defense of the laws of Crete and Sparta helps us to recognize that law has the power to instill respect for certain beliefs even when those beliefs have been called into question by reasoned argument. For even though Kleinias has already accepted that the laws of Crete and Sparta do not aim at the whole of virtue and must have been corrupted (*Laws* 630a, 631b, 632e, 635a), his respect for those laws remains so strong that he asserts that they alone provide the correct education that the Athenian Stranger is describing.

In response to Kleinias's praise of Dorian law regarding music, the Athenian Stranger asks if the two cities do indeed regulate music as he has outlined. When Kleinias asks why they would not do so, the Athenian Stranger asks whether Crete and Spartan education says anything other than that the good man, who is moderate and just, is happy and blessed regardless of whether he is great or strong or small or weak (*Laws* 660d–e). At the start of the dialogue, the Athenian Stranger was able to examine Kleinias's beliefs about virtue by appealing to his admiration of the poets Tyrtaeus and Theognis. On that occasion, he contrasted Tyrtaeus's praise of battlefield courage with Theognis's praise of virtue as a whole. Now, in Book II, he attributes to Tyrtaeus the view that justice, along with piety, is the necessary condition for happiness and blessedness. The Athenian Stranger says that many seek fulfillment through health, beauty, and wealth. They believe that if they had these things, along with tyranny and immortality, they would be happy (*Laws* 661d–e). But, says the Athenian Stranger, they would not be happy unless they were also just and pious. For those who are not just or pious, these goods are in fact the greatest evil.

By ascribing this view to Tyrtaeus, the Athenian Stranger makes Tyrtaeus's poetry conform to the standards of correctness in music and in law. Kleinias, however, does not accept this reinterpretation of Tyrtaeus's teaching. In fact, Kleinias says that he cannot accept the claim that only the just and pious are happy and that the unjust and impious are always miserable

(*Laws* 661e). Injustice is surely shameful and justice is noble (*Laws* 662a) But he may have observed that the just individual must honor what is just whether it is done by him or by someone else (*Laws* 732a). Or he may have noticed that those who are just sometimes seem to suffer while those who are unjust sometimes seem to thrive (*Laws* 899e–900a). Thus, Kleinias's candor shows that even if reason were to counsel the citizen to do what is just, the passions might resist its guidance. According to Kleinias, justice seems to be noble and even choice-worthy, but often it does not produce happiness. Kleinias reminds us of the substantial obstacles that face the legislator who would teach that justice is the source of happiness. If the Athenian Stranger cannot persuade Kleinias that justice leads to happiness, then we wonder how successful a legislator will be in leading young citizens to believe that justice is the core of a happy life.

In order to allay Kleinias's doubts about justice, the Athenian Stranger describes a hypothetical conversation between Zeus and Apollo on the one hand and themselves on the other regarding the relation of justice to happiness. The Athenian Stranger would begin by identifying two ways of life that seem distinct. One would be guided by the pursuit of pleasure, while the other would be devoted to doing what is just. The Athenian Stranger expects that we will quickly recognize that the two ways of life are opposed. In fact, if there were never any conflict between doing what is pleasant and doing what is just, then pleasure would be a sufficient guide and we might never consider what is just. The Athenian Stranger says that if they were to ask the gods which of these two lives is happier, it would be strange for the gods to say that those who live the most pleasant lives are happier (*Laws* 662d). Before explaining why it would be strange, the Athenian Stranger says that it is not fitting to attribute such sayings to gods, and so he substitutes fathers and lawgivers for gods in his imagined conversation. More precisely, he now supposes that he is addressing someone who is both a father and a lawgiver. He says that it would be strange for a father who presumably wants his son to live as happily as possible and who never stopped urging his son to live as justly as possible to say that the life of pleasure is most blessed. Such a man, says the Athenian Stranger, could never speak in consonance with himself. The Athenian Stranger is able to substitute the fatherly lawgiver for the gods because devoted citizens like Kleinias believe that the gods are benevolent beings who establish laws and require that we follow them so that we may be happy (*Laws* 627e–28a, 628d–e, 631b).

Having brought this to light, the Athenian Stranger also points out that if the father were to say that the just life is the happiest, everyone would wonder what good and noble thing the just life provides that differs from pleasure but which leads to happiness (*Laws* 662e–63a). Because everyone recognizes that to act justly causes us to hold back from enjoying some pleasures, everyone must wonder what good comes from this holding back. The Athenian Stranger's primary response is that justice brings praise from human beings and from gods (*Laws* 663a3–5).[5]

As gratifying as this may be, one wonders whether this praise, by itself, is always an adequate compensation for the burdens that one must bear in being just. In addition to saying that a just life brings praise from men and from gods, the Athenian Stranger says that it is not unpleasant to refrain from doing injustice or to avoid suffering injustice (*Laws* 663a5–7). One might object that this last claim that justice is pleasant is incomplete because the Athenian Stranger does not explain how living a just life protects one from suffering injustice. But having just noted that the just are praised by their fellow citizens and by the gods, he may have in mind the possibility that the just will be protected by those fellow citizens and gods whom they have impressed with their justice. On the other hand, the fact that the Athenian Stranger does not elaborate why the just should expect protection leads one to wonder whether he thinks that either the just citizen's fellow citizens or the gods can always be counted on to provide protection to the just.

Rather than showing that the pleasures associated with a good name and a clean conscience compensate for the burdens of a just life, the Athenian Stranger points to what appears to be a further difficulty in proving that the just life is the happiest life: He observes that "no one willingly does what does not bring more joy than pain" (*Laws* 663b4–6). In showing why the just life is the happiest way of life, the Athenian Stranger says that he would have to show that the just life is the more enjoyable life. Having begun this discussion by distinguishing the just life from the pleasant life, he now says that the two ways of life must be brought together if we are to believe that the just life is also a happy life.

Implicitly admitting that he has not yet provided a conclusive proof that the just life is also the most pleasant, the Athenian Stranger begins the last part of this discussion by acknowledging that everyone who disputes which life is best perceives these things at a great distance and does not observe them clearly. But he assures Kleinias that the legislator will see these things clearly and will use habit, praise, and reason to persuade the disputants that the just things and the unjust things are mere shadows (*Laws* 66b6–c2; cf. *Republic* 514b–15a, 517d). Those who are unjust and wicked perceive the unjust things to be pleasant, but the just perceive the opposite (*Laws* 663c2–5). When the Athenian Stranger asks Kleinias if the better souls are the better judges of these things, Kleinias responds that according to what has been said it "appears" to be true (*Laws* 663c6). The weakness of his agreement may be due to his recognition that this last argument assumes what it is supposed to prove. Kleinias may also hesitate to agree that only those with defective souls think that one can be both unjust and happy because he has just expressed this view in his own name.

When Kleinias remains doubtful that the unjust are always miserable and that only the just are happy, the Athenian Stranger seems to recognize the weakness of this argument. Even if it is not true, he asks, is it not the most useful lie that a legislator could tell (*Laws* 663d–e)? He argues that it would be very effective in making everyone do the just things willingly. Kleinias says that truth is noble and lasting, but not everyone is easily persuaded by it. The Athenian Stranger responds that one can persuade the young of almost anything and says that the legislator should promote the conviction that is best for the city (*Laws* 663e–64a). Speaking in his own name, the Athenian Stranger says that the lawgiver should persuade the young to accept all the noble things that they are saying (*Laws* 664b). The lawgiver should tell them that when we claim that the gods say that the most pleasant life and the best life are the same, we are saying what is most true and persuading in the best way (*Laws* 644b–c).

In order to convey these teachings, the citizens should be organized into three choruses. The first is the chorus of the Muses, which is composed of young men. Next should be the chorus of Apollo, which is to be made up of men up to thirty years of age. The last chorus will include men who are thirty to sixty years of age. Unable to sing beautifully, its members will tell stories and dance in honor of Dionysus. The Athenian Stranger says that this Dionysian chorus will be the "savior of the city" and that it will be made up of the "best part of the city." Because it is the oldest and most prudent chorus, it will be the most persuasive and authoritative (*Laws* 665c). This chorus saves the city because it needs to supervise the music education as a whole. As we have noted, the Athenian Stranger argues that in order to teach young people to love the noble virtues, it is necessary to adorn those noble virtues with pleasant music. Moral education consists in presenting the young with pleasing "imitations" or "images" of the virtues (*Laws* 668b, 669c). The difficulty is that what brings pleasure is not necessarily beneficial or true (*Laws* 667c–4). In order to make sure that the music education is grounded in the virtues of what is beneficial or true, the Dionysian chorus must make sure that the poets and other artists who present the virtues to young people do not distort or mangle those virtues in their art. The chorus will not only need to know the virtues whose images are portrayed in art but also be able to judge whether the poets' rhythms, harmonies, lyrics, and dances are consistent with one another and with the images that they are attempting to present to the young (*Laws* 669b–70a). The Dionysian chorus must become good judges of both virtue and art and must use their judgment to supervise the musical education in virtue. This is especially important insofar as people often cease taking pleasure in music that has become overly familiar to them. Consequently, even the noble music that constitutes the core of moral education must change from time to time in order for it to bring pleasure to those who hear it (*Laws* 665c). The task of the Dionysian chorus is to use its knowledge of what is noble and its prudence to make sure that the new music conforms to what is correct.

In the course of presenting this account, the Athenian Stranger asks Kleinias which choruses should be sung (*Laws* 666d). When Kleinias replies that he and Megillus cannot sing anything other than the songs that they were taught, the Athenian Stranger takes this opportunity to level his most direct criticism of the laws of Crete and Sparta regarding education. He says that neither city has "attained the noblest song." Moreover, he says that each of these cities is like an armed camp rather than a city (*Laws* 666e1–3). He blames them for keeping their young in a flock, like colts grazing in a herd, and for failing to take each of them aside, to care for them individually and to educate them by calming them down. If the Cretans and Spartans did so, he says, the young man would become not only a good soldier but also capable of managing a city. He would be more of a warrior than the warriors who were praised by the poet Tyrtaeus (*Laws* 629b–e). The Spartans would honor courage as the fourth virtue and not the first for both individuals and the city (*Laws* 667a). At the start of his discussion of correct education, the Athenian Stranger described education as a preparation for virtue (*Laws* 653b). Now, he reveals that even a correct music education does not provide a complete education but is rather a part, and a somewhat crude part at that, of the preparation for virtue.

In response, Kleinias says that the Athenian Stranger is again belittling his lawgiver. This time, however, the Athenian Stranger does not say that they are not criticizing the lawgivers but those who corrupted the law. Instead, he says that if their lawgivers are criticized, it is not the Athenian Stranger who is doing it but the argument that they are following (*Laws* 667). Finally, the Athenian Stranger is willing to say openly that the laws of Crete and Sparta never originated from a god. But the Athenian Stranger still has not confirmed that the Spartan Megillus shares Kleinias's fundamental beliefs and expectations regarding divine law. So, at this point, the Athenian Stranger must continue to examine whether Megillus recognizes or believes in divine law through reasoning about its goals or whether his knowledge of divine law is rooted in inspiration or divination.

Finally, the Athenian Stranger is ready to explain how wine-drinking contributes to a correct education. As public censors, the Dionysian chorus needs to know whether and how the music fits the virtues that should be performed. The rhythms and harmonies might be associated with incorrect words or mixed in with incorrect images of virtue. In order to know precisely what the noble is and how it should be presented in music, the Dionysian chorus will need an education that is superior to that which comes through the choruses. It will be more precise than the education that is given to either the multitude or to the poets (*Laws* 670e). The wine-drinking is useful to those who need to learn more than one can learn from the correct music. Correct music leads young people to regard what the law teaches as what is reasonable and correct. But the censors will need to go beyond what the law teaches. They will need to reason about what is correct as such. This indicates why the Dionysian chorus is not a chorus in the literal sense. Its purpose is not to perform music in public but to engage in a critical examination of public morals and public art.

This is especially difficult for old men who feel shame more readily and more intensely as they become weaker and more diffident (*Laws* 666b–c). Becoming more and more fearful of their reputations, such men would become less and less willing to think and say critical things about what others regard as noble or shameful. But wine has a rejuvenating effect on the old. According to the Athenian Stranger, wine melts away feelings of despondency. Reviving hopes, it induces old men to speak freely (*Laws* 666b–c, 671b). In addition, it makes them unwilling to listen to authority (*Laws* 671c; Strauss 1975, 76). In short, wine-drinking seems to undo the work of the music education so that the most prudent element of the community can think and speak freely about the virtues that are taught and about the way that they are taught.

At the same time, wine-drinking poses a danger. Men who drink wine to excess can become overly bold and insolent. In order to curb such excesses, the Dionysian chorus must be led by an older, sober man who opposes shameless drinkers with the noblest fear that is accompanied by justice, namely, the divine fear called "awe" or "shame" (*Laws* 671c2–d2, 672d5–9). The Athenian Stranger does not explain precisely how the ruler of the symposium should do this. Perhaps he will remind the drunken individual of the shameful reputation among gods and human beings that he is incurring. Perhaps he will threaten him with some further punishment. Since the ruler must pay attention to each individual's actions, he may need to use prudence to determine what will lead each person to feel awe and to respect justice in each case.

Having argued for these uses of wine-drinking in education, the Athenian Stranger concludes by rejecting the traditional belief that wine-drinking is a curse directed toward human beings by vengeful gods (*Laws* 672b–c). Because we know that wine-drinking can greatly benefit moral education, it is not a curse. One could also dismiss the traditional belief that the gods imposed a curse on humanity on the grounds that the gods are benevolent beings.

The Athenian Stranger has argued that the laws of Sparta are defective because they fail to make use of wine-drinking. The Athenian Stranger argues that wine-drinking can help to free some members of the Dionysian chorus from the limits of old age as well as from some of the limits of their moral educations. In some cases, it can show the sober ruler of a symposium which wine drinkers have moderate natures and which have immoderate natures that are in need of further restraint. In the case of those who grow excessively bold and shameless when drinking wine, the sober rulers of the symposia can appeal to pious fear, awe, and shame to induce the drinkers to control themselves. In the end, the Athenian Stranger seems to have convinced Kleinias, at least, that drinking wine in the correct way is so useful for moral education that it not only is not a curse imposed on us by a hostile god but also that it must be a feature of a correct moral education (*Laws* 674c). If this is true, then the laws of Sparta and Crete manifestly fail to provide a suitable moral education for their young. Their laws do not aim at the goals at which divine law was said to aim. If this model of correct education can serve as a standard, the Dorian laws do not seem to be divine. However persuasive one may find these arguments, one must remember that the Athenian Stranger has not yet shown that Megillus shares Kleinias's beliefs or experiences regarding the origins and purposes of divine law. Megillus may know divine law through a divine fear or awe that is unknown to Kleinias. In light of such possibilities, the Athenian Stranger must continue to test whether Megillus will confirm that divine law has a goal that can be known to the philosopher through reason. He continues this examination in Book III.

Part Three—The Limits of Spartan Law

The Athenian Stranger's account of correct education suggests that the laws of Sparta do not aim at a correct education. But the examination of these laws is not complete. The Athenian Stranger began the dialogue by asking about the origins and purposes of the laws of Crete and Sparta. He has indicated why he believes these cities' laws do not aim at the highest goals. He has reasoned that this shows that they cannot have come from gods or from divine human beings. But he is not content to end the inquiry into the origins of the law. It would strengthen the Athenian Stranger's argument that the laws of Crete and Sparta are not divine if he can show that they can be traced to natural or human causes. More important, the Athenian Stranger must continue his examination because Megillus has not yet affirmed that divine law must aim at the complete virtue of a human being and at the civic and individual happiness that accompanies that virtue. Nor has Megillus said or done anything to indicate that it is through reason that he believes in the laws of Sparta. While he has occasionally participated in the conversation to this point, he continues to defend the nobility of Sparta's laws. He has listened to the Athenian Stranger's argument that correct education makes a place for wine-drinking but does not join Kleinias in saying that the Athenian Stranger has spoken beautifully (*Laws* 674c). The Athenian Stranger must continue to explore what Megillus knows about divine law and to learn whether he believes in it on the basis of reason or some other faculty.

At the beginning of Book III, the Athenian Stranger indicates that we can understand the coming into being of law by looking into how one regime becomes transformed into another. He will seek out "the cause of the transformation of one regime into another" (*Laws* 676c). According to the Athenian Stranger, the transformation from one regime to another is cyclical. There is a sequence of changes from one kind of regime into another that always recurs, subject to the unpredictable intercession of various cataclysms.

The Athenian Stranger begins the attempt to identify the cause of the transformation of regimes by alluding to certain ancient sayings that claim that the human race has always been subject to periodic great floods, plagues, and other catastrophes that have killed off most of its members. The few who survive these disasters live high in remote mountaintops and soon lose all but a few rudimentary arts (*Laws* 678a). According to the Athenian Stranger, the fact that only a few survive means that they are soon able to find adequate food and other necessities. And because they live neither in scarcity nor in abundance, they are neither jealous nor insolent toward one another, and thus they refrain from doing injustice. While these people are innocent of injustice, they also lack experience of many noble or beautiful things. These simple people believe everything that they are told about what is noble and what is base and accept without question what they hear about both human beings and gods.

According to the Athenian Stranger, these credulous people live in small families that are led by fathers who rule like monarchs. Within these small dynasties, people are guided by the habits and ancestral customs that develop within family life rather than by formal codes of law that are laid down purposely and carefully by lawgivers. The first patriarchs genuinely care about the good of their children, yet they do not reflect deeply about the fundamental purposes or principles of law. Despite the relative ignorance of the arts and of human and divine matters, these people nevertheless tend to acquire certain virtues of character. Remaining fearful of cataclysms and trusting in the rule of their fathers, these people lead modest lives. In fact, their great simplicity endowed them with a solid form of courage, moderation, and justice (*Laws* 679c–e).

The Athenian Stranger supports his account of the first regime by citing Homer's description of the Cyclopes. Homer says that these people dwell on mountaintops and are ruled by their fathers rather than by assemblies or by just rules (*Laws* 680b–c; Homer *Odyssey* IX. 112–15). It is only when the Athenian Stranger refers to Homer that Megillus breaks his extended silence. When Megillus says that the Athenian Stranger has brought forth a good witness for his argument, he indicates how deeply he trusts the authority of the divinely inspired poet *(Laws* 680c–d). By saying that Homer describes the Cyclopes as living a life of savagery, he suggests that he has some reservations about the Athenian Stranger's description of the primitive peoples' moral virtue (*Laws* 680d2–3).

The Athenian Stranger explains that this first regime gives way to a second when the population grows and people begin to forget about the dangers of living at low altitudes. Moving down into the foothills, several families join together to farm and to live under the protection of walls. Because each family has been accustomed to living according to its own ancestral customs, the first villages would be subject to numerous, conflicting customs and rules. In order to establish a common way of life and to provide a coherent account of the gods, someone must come forward to establish actual laws (*Laws* 681c). Lawgiving in the full meaning of the word begins not through a long series of trials and errors or from an emerging consensus but through a decisive choice among traditions.[6]

A third kind of regime comes about when human beings forget the dangers of life in the lowlands and boldly build great cities in the plains. At 681d–e, the Athenian Stranger once again quotes Homer to support his argument that the cities of the plains are a relatively late development. In the *Iliad,* Aeneas reports that Dardania was built in the foothills before Troy was built in the plain (*Laws* 681e; Homer *Iliad* XXII.16–18). In light of this, the Athenian Stranger says that his account of the third regime is supported by both nature and a god. He says that the poets are divine and that they are inspired by gods, and when the poets sing, they say many things that are true (*Laws* 682a). The implication is that one can discover the truth either through inspiration or through the study of nature.

In order to explain the coming into being of the fourth regime, the Athenian Stranger looks specifically at the war between Troy and the Greeks. After the Trojan War, the Greeks returned home to find that in their absence some young people had rebelled against their authority and committed grave injustices against them. As a result of the civil wars that raged in Greece, the Spartans founded a new kind of regime that would protect against such conflicts. In light of the discussion at the beginning of the dialogue, the Athenian Stranger now seems to be praising the Spartan regime. Its goal is not simply to win wars but to overcome the dangers of civil war (*Laws* 682d–e, 683d–e). The Athenian Stranger seems to recognize how these remarks relate to the beginning of the dialogue, for he says that it is as if they have been following a god and that they have now gone back to the beginning of their conversation about law or at least to the point from which they digressed to talk about music and wine-drinking (*Laws* 682e). While the Athenian Stranger's inquiry into wine-drinking and correct education may have impressed Kleinias, it did not persuade Megillus that the laws of Sparta are defective because they do not provide the education that is outlined in Book II. In order to learn whether Megillus shares Kleinias's fundamental beliefs about divine law, the Athenian Stranger must step back and restart the examination of divine law.

The Athenian Stranger says that if this inquiry into the cycle of regimes can reveal which laws are noble and which are base, which laws preserve things and which destroy them, and which make cities happy and which make them unhappy, then they ought to take up this argument again as if from the beginning (*Laws* 683b). Megillus agrees, saying that if a god were to promise them that a second attempt to discuss these things would be no worse than the first, then he would be willing to undertake that discussion. Megillus explains his interest by saying that this discussion would make the day pass quickly, even though it is the longest day of the year (*Laws* 683b–c).

Turning to the origins of the laws of Sparta, the Athenian Stranger says that the army that returned from Troy divided itself into three parts and founded the cities of Argo, Megeara, and Sparta. In each city, oaths were taken in accordance with the laws. Each of the kings swore that he would not rule harshly, and the people of each city swore that they would support the king if the king kept his oath. At the same time, each king and each people swore to come to the aid of the other cities' kings and peoples should they be treated unjustly (*Laws* 684b). The Athenian Stranger and Megillus agree that this powerful confederacy promised to be remarkably advantageous, noble, and strong (*Laws* 686a–b). It is a wonder, then, says the Athenian Stranger, that the settlement and the legislation turned out so badly. When Megillus asks what the Athenian Stranger blames in the confederacy, the latter points out that two of the three cities were quickly corrupted and only one maintained its laws. The Athenian Stranger says that they must focus on why the two cities became corrupted and why Sparta did not. Megillus agrees, saying that if they cannot learn why this confederacy failed, then they will not be able to identify the causes why any regimes and laws are able to preserve or destroy those things that are noble and great (*Laws* 686b–c).

After Megillus agrees that this investigation is important, the Athenian Stranger says that he has suddenly recognized that what they have just said about the desirability of Sparta being a partner in a greater confederacy may be in error. He says that we often see noble things and imagine that we might do wonderful things with them if only we knew how to use them. But, he says, this may turn out to be a mistake and not according to nature. We admire military power that could bring freedom and empire, great wealth, and an illustrious family name because we believe that these things can satisfy all of our desires and bring us happiness. These hopes reflect how everyone wants all things to come to pass in accordance with their soul's desires (*Laws* 686d–87a).

When the Athenian Stranger notes that we pray that everything will happen according to our heart's desires, Megillus agrees (*Laws* 487b3). After the Athenian Stranger and Megillus reflect on the great power that Sparta would have possessed had she remained a partner in a confederacy with two other cities that sadly fell into corruption, the Athenian Stranger says that he has suddenly recognized that what they have just said about the desirability of Sparta being a partner in a greater confederacy may be in error. He says that we often see noble things and imagine that we might do wonderful things with them if only we knew how to use them. But, he says, this may turn out to be a mistake and not according to nature (*Laws* 686c–d). We admire military power that could bring freedom and empire, great wealth, and an illustrious family name because we believe that these things can satisfy all of our desires and bring us happiness. These hopes reflect how everyone wants all things to come to pass in accordance with our heart's desires (*Laws* 686d–87a). When the Athenian Stranger asks Megillus whether we pray to have everything that we want, Megillus agrees. The Athenian Stranger notes, at this point, that a father is a friend to his son, and his son is a friend to his father (*Laws* 687d). But, he asks Megillus, does a father always pray that all his son's prayers will be answered? In response, Megillus says that a father will not join his son in prayer if his son lacks intellect (*nous*). Having begun by accepting that fathers are friends to their sons, Megillus agrees that fathers owe it to their sons to watch over their prayers and to ask whether their prayers are mindless, apparently on the grounds that friends are obliged to save their friends from doing things that are harmful or unjust. Furthermore, the Athenian Stranger reminds Megillus that fathers sometimes make ignoble and unjust prayers regarding their sons, such as the prayers that Theseus made while cursing his son Hippolytus (*Laws* 687e). Because sons are also friends to their fathers, as friends, they owe it to their fathers not to join them in praying for what is unjust or base. When the Athenian Stranger asks whether a son should join in the fervent prayers of a father who does not know what is noble and just, Megillus replies that one should not pray for whatever one desires but should instead pray that one's desires are guided by practical reason (*Laws* 687e).

Megillus's responses to the Athenian Stranger in this passage mark a crucial point in the dialogue. For this line of reasoning indicates not only what fathers and sons owe one another as friends but also what fathers and sons must do in regard to prayer and more generally what they must do in order to act piously. In a strong, patriarchal tradition, one might expect that a father's authority over his sons would be absolute. But Megillus's reasoning shows that because he believes that the gods expect both fathers and sons to act as friends to one another, the gods also expect them to look to what is best for one another and to prevent them from doing things that are harmful or base or unjust. It follows that in order to do what the gods demand of fathers and of sons when they pray, fathers must not guide their sons with absolute authority and sons must not simply obey their fathers. In order for each to do what is pious, each must be guided not only by justice but also by intellect or practical reason. Precisely because the gods expect fathers and sons to love each other and care for each other, the gods expect them to reason well. Moreover, this argument indicates more generally that while the gods want us to worship and obey them, they are not satisfied if we worship and obey them with unthinking, speechless awe. The gods want us to act in ways that benefit those for whom we are responsible and those to whom we are responsible. Moreover, the gods hold us responsible for what we do, and so they require that we understand what we do when we act. Genuine piety consists in a reverence for the gods that is combined with practical reason or intellect regarding the welfare of those for whom and to whom we are responsible. The problem of Spartan piety is that it emphasizes only the fearsomeness of the gods and understates the gods' concern for the good of the city.

Megillus recognizes that his insight into the correct way to pray has implications for politics as well as for every individual: "The city, and every one of us," he says, "ought to pray and seek to have intellect" (*Laws*

687e). Likewise, the Athenian Stranger understands that if the city and its inhabitants must be guided by prudence or intellect, then the virtues of the mind must be a principal concern of the lawgiver. The "statesman-lawgiver," he says, "will look to this in ordering the laws" (*Laws* 688a–b). By connecting Megillus's remarks on how we should pray for prudent wishes to the law, the Athenian Stranger brings to sight a standard for measuring the correctness of the law. If a code of law promotes practical reason or intellect, then that code may be correct. If, however, a code fails to promote those virtues, then that code is defective and cannot have originated from a divine source.

The Athenian Stranger says here that he is reminded of the opening of the dialogue, when Kleinias and Megillus said that divine law aims at victory in war and at courage and when he argued that it aims at the whole of virtue, which is led by an erotic desire of intellect, practical reason, and opinion (*Laws* 688a–c). The Athenian Stranger now summarizes his discussion with Megillus and claims that it is dangerous to pray without intellect (*Laws* 688c). Furthermore, the Athenian Stranger says that this is the very same argument that he himself made at the outset of the dialogue (*Laws* 688a; cf. 631a ff.). By identifying Megillus's arguments here in Book III with his own arguments from early in Book I, the Athenian Stranger points out that Megillus has now confirmed some of the important conclusions that he and Kleinias reached regarding the purpose of divine law in the opening conversation. Specifically, Megillus has confirmed that the gods and their laws want us to have and to use certain virtues and that these include justice and especially the virtues of the mind. And if one bears in mind the questions regarding law that were raised in the *Minos,* one will see that Megillus has confirmed that the serious citizen relies on reason to draw conclusions about what the gods and their laws demand of us.

Megillus's comments on prayer obviate the objection that the Athenian Stranger has based his account of law on the beliefs of Kleinias, whose general lack of awe shows that he is not a good example of someone who is seriously devoted to the divine law of his city. For even if Kleinias lacks the depth of awe that is manifest in a man like Megillus, Megillus's reflections on how we should pray show that the serious citizen's awe of the gods and of divine law is always accompanied by the belief that the gods want what is best for us and by the further belief that the gods want us to recognize with our own minds the great good at which they aim. The serious citizen of Sparta who has been raised to revere the gods and feel awe is able to recognize what is lawful by asking himself what the gods want of us and by deducing that they must want us to use practical reason or intellect so that we might do what is noble and just. Thus, contrary to many contemporary scholars, it is not Plato who assumes that the gods are rational. Rather, Plato shows through the dialogue that when devoted citizens like Kleinias and Megillus are questioned about the purposes of their cities' laws, it is they who affirm that the gods' purposes are both knowable through reason and also prudent and rational.

Megillus's reasoning about the gods has important implications for the question of whether the laws of Sparta are divine. Megillus has agreed that divine law must aim at something higher than awe. It must aim at the whole of virtue led by the virtues of the mind. This means, in principle, that the laws of Sparta cannot be divine. But Megillus has not drawn this conclusion or spoken of it explicitly. The Athenian Stranger's goal is to find out whether Megillus will draw this conclusion or will accept arguments that imply it strongly.

The Athenian Stranger follows Megillus's remarks saying that Argos and Messina became corrupt, not merely because their rulers and peoples lacked courage or knowledge of military affairs but because they lacked the whole of virtue and especially knowledge of human affairs. He identifies the lack of virtue as a whole as the greatest sort of ignorance and says that its absence is what has destroyed cities in the past and will destroy them in the future (*Laws* 688e).

Before explaining in more detail how this ignorance led to the downfall of Argos and Messina, the Athenian Stranger pauses to give a more elaborate account of ignorance and wisdom. According to the Athenian Stranger, those who lack practical reason suffer the greatest ignorance. This ignorance is accompanied by a dissonance between the passions and reason. We are ignorant when we hate what we believe to be noble or good and when we love what we believe to be wicked and unjust. The Athenian Stranger says that this ignorance belongs to the greatest part of the soul, which is the part that feels pain and pleasure. When these passions obey their natural ruler, which is knowledge or opinion or reason, then there is agreement or consonance. But when they do not, they achieve nothing (*Laws* 689a–b). The Athenian Stranger compares this disorder in the soul with the disorder that one finds in those cities whose majority population refuses to follow the guidance of their rulers and the law. He says that in cities there may be a majority who can calculate and who are quick-witted, but they might nonetheless still lack practical reason. But one may also find select individuals who lack rudimentary knowledge of the most basic things but who are nonetheless prudent and wise. While making this argument, the Athenian Stranger suggests that one has the virtue practical reason whether one follows genuine knowledge or mere opinion. Insofar as the greatest wisdom is reducible to self-control, it does not seem to matter whether one controls oneself through rational knowledge or through some other means.

Sparta and the Best Regime

The Athenian Stranger says that Argos and Messina lacked the consonance that marks practical reason (*Laws* 690e–91a). He says that the problem was not any disobedient populace but imprudent kings. Given to luxury, the rulers took more than a measured amount and did not make good use of what they took (*Laws* 690e). Sparta's rulers, however, never took more than their due measure and avoided the greatest ignorance (*Laws* 691d). According to the Athenian Stranger, Sparta avoided this great ignorance not because of the moral education that it provides each citizen but because of the arrangement of its political offices. Sparta has proved itself to be superior to the monarchies in Argos and Messina because its regime is "mixed" (*Laws* 691e–92a). The Spartan monarchs were unable to overstep their limits in part because the monarchy was divided into two separate lines.

Recognizing that this division of the monarchy was not incorporated into any of the confederates' monarchies at the start, the Athenian Stranger attributes it to divine providence. A god, he says, must have recognized that a single monarch would grasp for more than is measured and arranged for the queen to give birth to twin sons (*Laws* 691d–e). After this, he says, a human being who had some divine power must have recognized that the monarchy was still too feverish and thus must have established the moderate council of elders and must have given it a power equal to that of the kings (*Laws* 691e). Finally, some third savior must have seen that the ruling officers were still swollen and irritated and decided to harness them by establishing the democratically selected *ephors* (*Laws* 691e–92a).

The Athenian Stranger seems to have found a standard for distinguishing regimes that were established with a divine mind from those that were not. He says that it is now easy to recognize that the arrangement of Sparta's offices keeps the city in due measure. He adds that it is also clear that the founders of Sparta did not understand how to arrange a regime correctly, for if they had they would not have thought that mere oaths would suffice to establish a stable order (*Laws* 692b). The Athenian Stranger goes on to explain how Argos and Messina fell into corruption and shows that this corruption prevented them from joining Sparta and Athens in defending Greece's freedom against the invading Persians. He says that any lawgiver who establishes powerful, unchecked ruling offices is worthy of blame. A lawgiver should instead legislate with an eye to making the city free, prudent, and a friend to itself (*Laws* 693b).

It sounds like Sparta is a model regime because it remains within "due measure" (*Laws* 693d). But we must wonder whether keeping within this measure is truly the same as pursuing or practicing virtue as a whole, led by intellect. The Athenian Stranger's response to this question is to remark in passing that they have been using different names to refer to the same things. Moderation, he says, is the same as friendship and practical reason (*Laws* 693c). But is moderation the same thing as reasoning about our passions and deciding which ones lead to happiness or which is best (*Laws* 636d, 644c–d)? Is it impossible to be moderate without exercising this virtue of the mind? After all, there seem to be some who are moderate because their passions are relatively weak or because they master their passions through a profound fear of shame or awe (*Laws* 647a).

When Kleinias asks what the Athenian Stranger means when he says that the lawgiver should seek freedom, practical reason, and friendship, the Athenian Stranger says that monarchy and democracy are the two kinds of regimes from which all other regimes are woven. Some combination of the two is needed for friendship, freedom, and practical reason. In order to understand what each of these regimes is, it is useful to consider how monarchy and democracy appear in their pure forms. He says that Persia under Cyrus exemplified monarchy at its best and Athens under its ancient laws did likewise for democracy (*Laws* 693d–e). Before describing these regimes, he says that even though both were once well measured, they did not remain in this condition. The enduring regimes of Crete and Sparta, however, are more measured (*Laws* 693d).

He says that Persia under Cyrus allowed those with practical reason to speak freely. This resulted in freedom, friendship, and a common sharing in intellect (*Laws* 694b). It seems that the extreme form of monarchy brought forth a greater virtue than one finds in well-measured cities like Sparta. But the defect in the Persian model is that it did not endure. In order to show why it failed, the Athenian Stranger turns to divination (*Laws* 694c). This divination follows from the reasoning that he has already laid out in his conversation with Kleinias and Megillus. He says that the Persian monarchy must have failed because Cyrus did not provide a proper education to his successors. Giving all his attention to his conquests, Cyrus must have allowed his heirs to be educated by their mothers and by slaves, who were unaccustomed to having great wealth and mistakenly allowed their children to live in luxury and to do as they wished (*Laws* 694e–95b).

Consequently, Cambyses murdered his brother and eventually lost his rule. Later, after Darius restored the monarchy, his son, Xerxes, received a similar education and came to a similar end (*Laws* 695d–96a).

The Athenian Stranger contrasts these regimes with Sparta, which, he says, does not honor great wealth but instead honors virtue. The Athenian Stranger does, however, note that the Spartans do honor their hereditary kings on the basis of their birth. The Athenian Stranger says that the Spartans do not honor virtue unless it includes moderation (*Laws* 696b). When Megillus asks what he means, the Athenian Stranger responds by asking Megillus if he would accept someone to live in his home or neighborhood who had courage but not moderation. In response, Megillus says that he would not and that he would not welcome someone who had justice or wisdom in some art but who nonetheless lacked moderation (*Laws* 696c). While agreeing that virtue without moderation is not good, Megillus nonetheless goes on to confirm that in his view moderation by itself does not deserve honor (*Laws* 696d). Moderation is necessary but insufficient to win honor or to constitute the best way of life. Moreover, moderation is not simply equivalent to a virtue of the mind such as practical reason or intellect (cf. *Laws* 693c). If moderation is not the same as practical reason and virtue as a whole, then one suspects that Sparta's well-measured, orderly, and moderate way of life is not truly equivalent to a life led by practical reason or intellect.

Having indirectly raised these questions about the ranking of the Spartan regime, the Athenian Stranger turns to how one should measure the piety and the wisdom of a lawgiver. He says that if a lawgiver honors the greatest goods first and lesser goods later, according to their rank, then the lawgiver is correct. He should honor the goods of the soul above those of the body, and those of the body above external goods like wealth (*Laws* 696e–97b). But if he honors lesser goods above greater goods, then he will do something that is neither pious nor statesmanlike (*Laws* 697c3). In response, Megillus agrees emphatically (*Laws* 697c4). But he does not say anything to clarify what this agreement implies about the divinity of Sparta's laws. For if intellect is a greater good than being well measured or moderate without intellect, then the lawgiver who provides only the latter virtue would not be of the highest rank.

The Athenian Stranger describes how in ancient Athens the people were voluntarily enslaved to the laws and that their master was awe (*Laws* 698b). While they were deeply afraid of the law, they were also greatly afraid of the Persians and this secondary fear led them to develop an especially strong friendship under the law (*Laws* 698b–c). During the Persian invasion, the Athenians took refuge in their own community and in the gods.

They banded together to defend their temples, graves, fatherland, relatives, and friends. Their awe comes to sight as a powerful fear that gave them a common purpose (*Laws* 699c–d). In this light, awe seems to be a kind of fear in which the Athenians placed their trust and hopes.

The Athenian Stranger finishes his examination of Megillus by discussing democracy in ancient Athens. He says that the ancient Athenians placed great emphasis on music and music education. Moreover, those who had knowledge regulated the sacred music very carefully and forbad innovations and misuse. When the music was performed, the people listened reverently, in solemn silence, and lived in an orderly way (*Laws* 700a–d). But later, after the Persian crisis had passed, the poets sought popular acclaim and began to change and mix the music to please the people. The poets introduced music that stirred and pleased the people, and the people came to regard themselves as authorities in music and in all other things. Free from their traditional restraints, the people of Athens became shameless and brazen and failed to respect the authority of parents, laws, and oaths (*Laws* 700d–1b).

The Athenian Stranger concludes by saying that they must look back over the argument and must "pull it up" like one pulls on the reins of a horse so that the horse does not carry one away by force (*Laws* 701c–d). According to this simile, arguments have a force of their own, and the best way to guide them is to draw them up or to pause to consider the questions that generated them and how the argument responds to those questions. According to the Athenian Stranger, they have agreed that a lawgiver must aim at freedom, civic friendship, and intellect (*Laws* 701d). Looking at the most despotic and the freest cities, they have discerned that when either the most despotic or the freest city was well measured, it did well, but when either went to its extreme, no good came from it (*Laws* 701e). It is to learn these things that they began the discussion of the cycle of regimes and the founding of Sparta. In addition, this is also the purpose of the discussion of music and drunkenness and even of the things that were said before that (*Laws* 702a–b). Revealing his purpose in raising the conversation, the Athenian Stranger says that from the beginning they have been investigating these matters to learn the best way to establish a city and the best way for a private individual to lead his life (*Laws* 702a–b).

In saying that he has been examining the best way to establish a city and how one ought to live as an individual, he does not explicitly say how these two questions are related. If we recall Socrates's concerns in the *Minos,* we will remember that he wanted to know how we come to recognize or believe in the law and specifically whether we do so through a rational art or science or through some extra-rational faculty such as divination.

The Socratic philosopher wishes to know these things because he is alert to claims made by defenders of divine law who say that law is rooted in a profound wisdom that transcends the limits of human reason. By examining how the best city comes into being, by learning whether those who are devoted to divine law believe that the best city comes into being according to rational principles and for the sake of rational ends or if they believe instead that it comes into being through miraculous means for the sake of unknowable ends, the Socratic philosopher is able to shed important light on whether the life of reason is just and good.

Since early in Book I, the Athenian Stranger has been examining in particular the origins and purposes of the laws of Sparta. In the course of the conversation, he and Megillus have agreed that if a lawgiver establishes a regime that is not well measured, then that lawgiver is neither pious nor statesmanlike (*Laws* 697c1–2). The Athenian Stranger says that in order to do what is pious and statesmanlike, a lawgiver must apportion honors correctly. He must give the greatest honors to the greatest things, secondary honors to secondary things, and other appropriate honors to lesser things. When Megillus agrees emphatically at (*Laws* 697c4), he indicates that they have found an intelligible standard for recognizing which laws are well measured and which are not. Looking back to what they have said about the laws of Sparta, Megillus and the Athenian Stranger have agreed that the Spartan law seem divine because of the prudence that guides the arrangement of its offices. According to this argument, it is not the mark of a divine legislator to require that kings take oaths before the gods to uphold justice. A divine legislator would recognize that kings will not keep their oaths and that just gods should not be counted upon always to save the city. Instead, a divine lawgiver would arrange the regime in such a way that the powerful are unable to abuse their offices. But the prudence in the arrangement of offices is preventative. It does not extend to the other laws and innovations. Under Cyrus, Persia honored and was guided by intellect. Under divine law, old Athens was led by knowledgeable men who guided the authoritative, sacred music. Sparta, however, is said to be "well measured" and to honor moderation rather than virtues of the mind such as intellect or practical reason. By expressing admiration for Persia's concern with intellect under Cyrus and for Athens's reverence for knowledge under divine law (*Laws* 696d, 701b, 702a1), Megillus implicitly acknowledges that the laws of Sparta do not aim at the highest ends.

Looking back to the opening question about the origins and purposes of the laws of Sparta, it is now apparent that Megillus has come to recognize certain deficiencies of those laws. He has agreed that a monarchy under Cyrus was led by intellect. And he has agreed that a democracy in ancient Athens was led by music guided by knowledge. The Spartan regime, however, is merely well measured and moderate. And Megillus has agreed that Spartan moderation, one of its defining characteristics, is not the highest virtue. Without saying it openly, he has accepted the argument that the Spartan lawgiver did not establish the best possible virtue or the best possible city. If a divine lawgiver would have established better laws, then the laws of Sparta are not divine. Beyond this, he has accepted the argument that none of the regimes that have been known to exist has established lasting laws that aim at the highest virtues. It is because he does not yet know what sort of laws would be established by a god that Megillus agrees with the Athenian Stranger that they "are somehow desirous of law" (*Laws* 697a7).

At the end of Book III, the Athenian Stranger asks Kleinias how they might test whether their conversation has been useful (*Laws* 702b). Kleinias reveals that he has been asked to help establish the laws for a new colony of Crete's. He asks the Athenian Stranger and Megillus if they are willing to select from among the things that they have said so that they might establish a "city in speech" that could serve as a model for those laws (*Laws* 702c–d). The Athenian Stranger says that Kleinias is "not declaring war," a proverbial expression which, in this context, means that he will not be legislating with an eye to victory in war but to virtue as a whole and civic and individual happiness. Megillus, too, agrees to join in the conversation. He does not assert that the laws of Crete or Sparta ought to be applied or adapted to the new colony whose laws are to be the best.

It will be up to the Athenian Stranger to try to elaborate the best code of law, drawing on his own reasoning and knowledge of the political art (*Laws* 650b). He will try to show that human reason can both comprehend and accomplish the goals of divine law. He will play close attention to discover whether this code of law can meet Kleinias's and Megillus's expectations of divine law (*Laws* 649d–50b, 657a–b, 839b–c). Much like the natural theology that attempts to use human reason alone to demonstrate the existence of a god, the Athenian Stranger's procedure in the *Laws* is an attempt to show that human reason can establish a code of divine law.

Chapter Four

DIVINE LAW AND MORAL EDUCATION

In the *Minos*, Socrates asks his Athenian companion what law is and how we come to know or recognize that it is authoritative. In the course of their conversation, Socrates points to the inherent limits of law, showing that even though law presents itself as just and therefore good for everyone, law's breadth and rigidity prevent it from supplying the needs of each individual who is subject to it. This deficiency would seem to make it impossible to recognize that any particular political command is truly lawful and authoritative. Yet Socrates also indicates that the examination of law cannot be complete until he takes up the examination of divine law. It is only by examining how divine law is understood by those who live under and believe in it that the Socratic philosopher can learn what divine law is, how it is known, and whether it can overcome the apparent limitations of law. In the first three books of the *Laws,* the Athenian Stranger has examined how Kleinias and Megillus understand the origins and purposes of divine law. In the subsequent books of the *Laws,* the Athenian Stranger will try to lay out a correct and complete code of law. This code will show us whether or to what extent divine law can provide the soul with the goods that it needs and that divine law is expected to provide.

In Book IV of the *Laws,* the Athenian Stranger prefaces his elaboration of the laws by discussing some of the preconditions of legislation for the new colony of Crete. It is while he is discussing these preconditions that he sheds light on what his conversation with Kleinias and Megillus has taught or confirmed for him about what divine law is. The first of these preconditions is the location of the new colony. We might have thought that it is very important to select a site that provides the colony with the greatest safety and military prowess. But the Athenian Stranger insists that it is more important to select a location that will promote virtue; bearing this in mind, he says that founders should always choose a site that is far from the sea, so that the city will not succumb to the political and moral vices associated with commerce and the possession of a powerful navy (*Laws* 705d–e, 706a–c, 707d). In calling for an inland site that will be defended by a hoplite army, the Athenian Stranger and Kleinias implicitly agree that neither the laws of Minos nor those of Athens are suitable for a city that is under divine law (Pangle 1988, 438–39).

The Athenian Stranger's remarks about the preconditions of legislation include a discussion of the best kind of population and the best kind of political founder for a new colony. Yet, as the Athenian knows, the location, population, and founders of the new Cretan colony have already been selected. The disparity between the best possible setting for a colony and that of the actual, new colony leads the Athenian Stranger to reflect on the role that chance plays in legislation. He claims that no human being ever truly legislates, for chance usually determines whether regimes and laws succeed or fail (*Laws* 708). Yet he qualifies this statement by saying that both god and art, which is gentler than either god or chance, also play a role in determining how regimes and laws fare (*Laws* 709a–c). The precise roles that divine providence and human art play in bringing about divine law remain to be clarified.

As the three interlocutors turn to their task of legislating for the new colony, the Athenian Stranger calls upon a god to join them in setting up the city and its laws (*Laws* 712b). By making this invocation, the Athenian Stranger signals that he aims to elaborate a code of divine law. But what sort of assistance does he hope to gain from the god whom he invokes? The fact that he invokes the god at the start of Book IV underscores how he has relied on his own reasoning to this point in the dialogue. And since what was said in the first three books is to be the basis on which the laws are established (*Laws* 702a–b), the invocation indirectly reminds us that the Athenian Stranger has not needed divine assistance to this point in order to elaborate the ends of divine law. Moreover, the Athenian Stranger's willingness to ask the god for help indicates that he believes that he possesses the practical reason or intellect that we need if we are going to pray correctly and safely (*Laws* 687e–88a, 709d). Now, if he has these intellectual capacities, we wonder what sort of assistance he is seeking from the god. Is he saying that his own reasoning must be complemented with some extra-rational insight or faith? Or does he make this invocation while remaining confident in his own ability to understand divine law?

When the Athenian Stranger takes up the subject of the kind of regime (*politeia*) that is fitting for the colony, he says that the only regime that is truly a regime and that is not a despotism is the rule of a god (*Laws* 712e–13a). In order to clarify his meaning, the Athenian Stranger offers what he calls a myth and an oracle about how Kronos ruled human beings. According to the Athenian Stranger, Kronos long ago recognized that by nature human beings succumb to hubris and injustice when they seek to rule themselves (*Laws* 713c). As a result, he established daimonic spirits to rule over the different cities in the manner that shepherds look over their flocks. These daimonic spirits established peace, awe, good laws, and justice for those cities and brought concord and happiness to human beings (*Laws* 713d–e). The Athenian Stranger declares that there will be no rest from evils for cities that are ruled by human beings rather than by gods (*Laws* 713a; cf. *Republic* 473c–d). Even though Kronos no longer rules human beings and the daimonic spirits no longer stand over the cities like shepherds, this does not mean that divine rule over human beings is now impossible. The god can still rule over human beings through law. The Athenian Stranger characterizes the rule of law as the distribution of intellect (*Laws* 714a1–2). The Athenian Stranger does not say here why divine rule should be identified with the rule of intellect. But we have learned from the discussion with Kleinias and Megillus in the first three books that the gods establish laws so that we may develop not only each of the particular virtues but also the complete virtue of a human being. And when the gods promote those virtues they also intend to establish civic harmony and individual happiness. Insofar as we are able to discern the gods' purposes through our own reasoning, through intellect, it would appear that intellect is something that we share with the gods. Intellect would be a divine element in human beings.

Now, if divine law is the distribution of intellect, then when the Athenian Stranger invokes a god to join them in making the regime and the laws, he is praying that they will be guided by intellect rather than by some extra-rational faculty or art. Inasmuch as he already seems to possess intellect, by nature and by divine dispensation (*Laws* 642c–d, 875c), his invocation of a god who will guide the three of them in laying out the laws seems to be a prayer that intellect will also guide Kleinias and Megillus as they go on to discuss the laws.

After the Athenian Stranger claims that intellect is the source of divine law, he addresses those who challenge the claim that law ought to rule. These challengers say that there is no such thing as the rule of law, for law is always made by some part of the city as it rules over the other parts. Moreover, they say, the ruling part always makes laws that will preserve its rule over the city (*Laws* 714b–d). The Athenian Stranger responds that law should rule because it is the only form of rule that can aim at the preservation and good of the whole city (*Laws* 715b). He has already claimed that no human being can resist the temptation to use political power to gratify his own desires at the expense of the needs of others (*Laws* 713c, 875b–c; but see 875c3–d3).

Bearing in mind the thought that the rule of law alone looks to the good of the whole city, the Athenian Stranger says that the highest offices in the city should go to the most obedient servants of the laws (*Laws* 715c). When the city's rulers are "slaves" to the laws, he says, the city will be safe and will enjoy all good things (*Laws* 715d). By characterizing those who administer the laws as "servants" and "slaves" of the law, the Athenian Stranger suggests that the office holders are not free to do as their own intellects determine but must follow the law to the letter.

At 715e, the Athenian Stranger presents a speech whose purpose is to introduce them to the theocratic rule of law. He begins by alluding to an ancient saying that claims that "the god holding the beginning, middle, and end of all beings together completes his straight course while revolving according to nature" (*Laws* 715e–16a). By describing "the god" as a deity that never changes, the Athenian Stranger leads us to wonder whether he believes that the highest god intercedes in human affairs (cf. *Republic* 380d–81c, 382d–83a). But after causing us to wonder whether the supreme god ever engages in particular providence to support divine law, he adds that this god is accompanied by Justice, a god who avenges those who defy divine law (*Laws* 716a–b). In order to escape the punishment that befalls those who forsake the law, the colonists should be humble and orderly (*Laws* 716a). If they are measured and moderate, that is, if they follow the law, then they will be loved by the god and will find happiness (*Laws* 716c–d). Underscoring the importance of piety in the new colony, the Athenian Stranger says that the good man is happy if he always communes with the gods through prayers, sacrifices, and every kind of service to the gods (*Laws* 716e).

After honoring the Olympian gods and the gods of the underworld, colonists must honor the daimonic spirits and heroes. After these, they must honor ancestors and living parents. If we do all these things, he would tell the colonists, we will get what we deserve from the gods and from those who are greater than we are. And we will live in good hopes (*Laws* 718a). Regarding how we should honor children, family, friends, and fellow citizens, the law will provide the necessary guidance.

The Athenian Stranger concludes by indicating that some will be persuaded by the law while others will be persuaded only through punitive violence and justice (*Laws* 718b). In order to explain how law can persuade those who are subject to the law, the Athenian Stranger takes up a criticism of law that could be made by a poet. Speaking on behalf of the poet, the Athenian Stranger says that the lawgiver should not forbid poets from presenting things that contradict the law, since the poet who would persuasively depict different kinds of people necessarily portrays them saying things that contradict what others say (*Laws* 719c). Some of their persuasive albeit conflicting statements are bound to contradict what the law says. But law, says the poet, is unable to make different speeches in regard to the same thing (*Laws* 719d). Because law always says the same things to all people, it fails to give what is fitting to different kinds of individuals. For example, says the poet, if the law could direct different kinds of people to do what is fitting, it would direct wealthy people to provide lavish funerals, people with moderate wealth to provide moderate ones, and poor people to provide simple ones. But the breadth and rigidity of the law prevents it from giving what is fitting in particular cases (*Laws* 719d–e; cf. *Minos* 317d and *Statesman* 294b–c). The poet says that the lawgiver must find a way to overcome this limitation in law if he wishes to say that reason (*logon*) has become law (*Laws* 719e5).

In response to this criticism of the law, the Athenian Stranger agrees that the law must speak with more than one voice if it is to be genuinely persuasive. In all other cities, he concedes, the laws speak bluntly and harshly, like tyrants (*Laws* 722e–23a). He compares these laws to commands given by enslaved doctors who minister to other slaves. For these doctors do not know the nature of the body and its diseases, so they rely on a set of written rules and do not attempt to consult with or instruct their patients (*Laws* 720c). But the divine laws that will be established in the new colony will speak with more than one voice. These laws will be prefaced by "preludes" that will persuade many, if not all, of those who are subject to the law to follow the law on the grounds that it is good for them. These preludes will speak to the citizens in the way that citizen-doctors speak to patients who are free citizens: They will explain the reasons for the laws, looking to nature and consulting with and explaining the best treatments with their patients (*Laws* 720d–e). Yet the Athenian Stranger's description of the preludes and the laws makes clear that the preludes are distinct from the laws (*Laws* 722e1, 723a5). The laws themselves are blunt commands that coerce rather than persuade. In characterizing law as a blunt command, the Athenian Stranger does not mean that all laws are arbitrary or that all laws are equally beneficial or harmful. When the Athenian Stranger discusses the doctor who is himself a slave, he says that this doctor follows rules that are laid out by the free doctor who is an expert in the medical art. If law resembles the medical treatment administered by the slave doctor, then it, too, can be guided by someone with intellect who knows the political art (Strauss 1974, 64–65). But the blunt commands are not persuasive in themselves. Even though divine law may wish to be the discovery of what is or the dispensation of intellect, it appears that it cannot make itself known to us as law without the help of some supplementary reasoning. Exactly what this supplementary reasoning should be and precisely how it supplements the law remains to be clarified.

Following the analogy of the doctors, the preludes and the laws would be recognizable as divine law if they bring health to the soul. But do the preludes and laws, like medical doctors, merely alleviate or cure diseases of the soul rather than instill positive strength, beauty, and health? According to the account of correct law that emerged at the start of the dialogue, divine law must aim at virtue or excellence, at the positive, glowing health of the soul. It may be that divine law both cures diseases of the soul and promotes its positive health. But if we are to recognize divine law by the good that it brings to the soul, we need to know more precisely what those goods are. What virtue or virtues would the divine preludes and divine laws bring forth?

The speech to the colonists in Book IV indicates that the principal virtue of a citizen consists in piety and in devotion to the law. The sequel to that speech that begins Book V enjoins the citizens to honor the soul by caring about what is noble and about the better things (*Laws* 727d–28a; 728c). But the Athenian Stranger does not present a full, clear account of what those things are. Nor does he delineate all the virtues that we would develop through dedication to divine law. He praises the "real man" in the city who dedicates himself to punitive justice (*Laws* 729d, 731b, 731d) and the trustworthy man who honors justice more than himself (*Laws* 731e–32a). But he does not lay out a full account of all the virtues that divine law would bring forth in those who live under them. He does not explain which forms or versions of the virtues would be taught in a city under divine law. Nor does he explain how these virtues would come together or be recognizable as the complete virtue of a human being. In the rest of Books V and VI, Kleinias, Megillus, and the Athenian Stranger consider how property should be distributed, how the ruling offices should be filled, and how marriages should be regulated in a city under divine law. The arrangement of each of these institutions will have some effect on the citizens' virtues and vices. But it is difficult to determine what this effect could be without some further knowledge of the virtues that are taught through divine law. In order to get a clearer picture of the virtue that is to be taught by divine law, we need to look at the Athenian Stranger's account of the laws regulating education in Book VII. The laws regarding education provide us with the clearest vision of the virtues that the law aims to teach its subjects.

Education Based on Divine Law

The Athenian Stranger's account of what the lawgiver should do to produce the best education comes in Book VII. At first, this discussion of education may appear to be a mere supplement to the discussion of correct education in Book II (e.g., Stalley 1983, 132). But Book VII does more than add gymnastic exercise to the musical curriculum. It would promote different forms of the virtues that are discussed in the account of correct education in Book II. The looming question is why the Athenian Stranger believes it is necessary to present two different accounts of moral education and two different accounts of the virtues that can be taught by law.

The Athenian Stranger begins his account of the best education under law by observing that law does not seem to be fully suited for establishing fixed, binding rules for education. He points out that education must begin at a very early age and thus that it must be carried out in private homes. He acknowledges that it may seem petty and intrusive for the legislator to make rules regarding how parents and nurses interact with very young children. Nonetheless, he says, the unwritten laws or customs that govern education are the bonds of the whole regime. If these unwritten laws are established in a noble way, they will save the written laws. But, he says, if educators deviate from what is noble, young people will develop disparate kinds of characters and will become accustomed to acting contrary to the law. Such dispositions will undermine not only the law but also the city itself (*Laws* 793b). Consequently, the legislator needs to make unwritten rules regarding early childhood education not only to help build good character but also to supply the law with crucial strength and authority.

The Gymnastic Education

Near the start of Book VII, the Athenian Stranger says that education should begin not with musical training as he had in Book II but with gymnastic education. According to the Athenian Stranger, the education of the body cannot begin too soon. In fact, the legislator should encourage expectant mothers to exercise for the sake of the offspring whom they are carrying. Soon after they are born, infants should be carried and moved about constantly by their mothers and nurses to help with their digestion and nutrition. This constant motion is good not only for the very young but also for people of all ages. The Athenian Stranger says everyone should accept as an axiom that the best thing for everyone's body and soul is to be in constant motion all day and all night. Everyone, he says, should spend his life in motion as if he were on a ship at sea (*Laws* 790c–d). This continuous movement benefits the soul because of a very important but previously undisclosed inborn passion. In Book II, the Athenian Stranger said that every young animal is born with an innate "jumping motion" (*Laws* 653e) and that education consists in calming that motion by introducing regular habits and by exposing it to noble music (*Laws* 654a). But in Book VII we learn that human beings are born not with an otherwise nondescript "jumping" motion but with an inner motion that inclines them to feel terror (*Laws* 790e–91b). This terror, which is readily visible in infants, has no discernable cause or object (*Laws* 790c5–90e2, 791a1–5). Although this nameless and elemental terror may seem to wane as children grow older, it never fully departs. We see it reemerging, for example, in adults who suffer from insanity and who can be calmed only by rocking motions and music (*Laws* 790d–e). If most adults do not fall back into this overwhelming terror, they remain prone to excessive fearfulness. Accompanying this terror is a proneness to fear every pain beyond reason. If allowed to remain unchecked, this fearfulness can give one a character that is cowardly, gloomy, and irritable (*Laws* 791b7–8, 792a–b).

In light of the spontaneous terror that afflicts the very young, the first task of education is to combat this passion so that young citizens do not develop a cowardly disposition. Courage is more important than Kleinias and Megillus recognized in Book I. They neither knew how important courage is to establishing a good order in the soul nor how to bring courage into being. In order to counter the dangerous fearfulness to which human beings are prone, the legislator should see to it that each citizen becomes accustomed to being in motion throughout his or her life. The Athenian Stranger recommends this regimen because he has observed that terrified infants are relieved of their fear when someone rocks them and sings to them gently. Similarly, he has noticed that those who are caught up in the frenzy of Bacchic celebrations are also filled with terror and that these people, too, are calmed by music (*Laws* 790d). The lesson that the Athenian Stranger draws from these examples is that music is an external bodily motion whose regular movements have the power to distract or occupy those who would otherwise be overwhelmed by internal passions or "motions" such as fear (*Laws* 791a). By leading everyone to adopt a lifelong regimen of bodily exercise, the legislator would provide them with an even steadier and more effective counter-motion to fear. These exercises cannot eradicate the inborn terror, but a constant gymnastic regimen can keep the inborn terror at bay. By establishing a steady counter-motion in the soul, this regimen builds a kind of flooring on which a more positive form of courage may be built.

In order to protect the young from becoming too fearful and to help them develop some inner strength or toughness, educators should make sure that even very young children should never suffer any extremes of pain or pleasure (*Laws* 792b). In Sparta, young people develop the ability to fight pain and fear by being exposed to pain from an early age. But, in order not to become overly sensitive to pain, young people should not experience any intense pains or anxieties during their early years. Nor should they be allowed to experience great pleasures, for these, too, can soften one's character and make it more difficult to master one's passions as one grows older.

This new advice about avoiding the extremes of pain and pleasure leads to a new account of how young people should understand the relation between pleasure and virtue. Back in Book II, the Athenian Stranger acknowledges that the virtues themselves are not intrinsically pleasant (*Laws* 653c). But he indicates that citizens can learn to take pleasure in seeing and practicing the virtues if the virtues are properly adorned with beautiful music. If public art is guided by those who know what is noble and what is not, it can establish images of noble virtue that appeal to young citizens. For those who have developed the correct kind of likes and dislikes, there is, in principle, no limit to the pleasure that one might find in observing and in practicing virtue. In Book VII, however, the Athenian Stranger does not provide the very young with a standard that would inform them which pleasures are correct and can be pursued without limit. Instead, they are taught to hold back from every great pleasure just as they are taught to avoid great pains. By exercising this restraint, they will learn to pursue a "middle way" between pleasure and pain. This temperate, middle way of life is endowed with a certain grace (*Laws* 792c). But what makes this way of life graceful is not that it leads one to pursue noble pleasures or to endure any particular pains because it is useful to do so but instead that it helps one to resist pleasure and to endure pain, as such. Those who successfully hold themselves back from intense pleasure and pain would achieve a kind of serene independence from the passions rather than gratify some deep or pressing desire.

After saying that young people ought to adopt this posture toward the passions, the Athenian Stranger says that an oracle ascribes this gracious middle way to the god (*Laws* 792d). On the one hand, this appeal to "the god" is an appeal to the citizen's piety. Wishing to be godly, the citizen should prove himself to be a divine human being by enduring pain and resisting pleasure in the manner of the god. While the Athenian Stranger is appealing to the citizen's desire to be worshipful or pious, he is also presenting a new aspect of what a god is. According to this account, the gods do not live in blissful happiness. The gods are not joyous but imperturbable, for they accept some pains as necessary and endure them quietly. The Athenian Stranger says that the gods are tough, serene beings who do not yield to their passions, and pious men and women who follow them adopt this way of life. Moreover, according to this presentation, the gods are not omnipotent. They calmly endure pains and resist pleasures because they accept that they are subject to certain necessities (*Laws* 792d). Their own need to endure hardships suggests that they cannot perform any miracle that they might wish to bring about. By presenting "the god" in this manner, the Athenian Stranger suggests that when human beings are threatened by great pains or when they seek great pleasures, they should not expect divine assistance. Rather, the god expects human beings to be courageous and moderate in the face of both adversity and temptation.

These claims about "the god" may seem like assertions on the part of the philosopher. How could the Athenian Stranger know that every god is subject to necessities? In one respect, the Athenian Stranger has already established one necessity to which the gods must submit. At the opening of the dialogue, he has shown that the serious citizen recognizes the divinity of the law only insofar as it aims at human virtue as a whole along with civic harmony and individual happiness. To this extent, at least, the gods are under the necessity of making laws that promote virtue as a whole and happiness for the cities to which they give laws. Gods who give such laws are necessarily benevolent and just. And these gods are also necessarily rational insofar as their laws must carefully promote forms of the particular virtues that will culminate in virtue as a whole and happiness. But the Athenian Stranger has not yet indicated precisely why these gods must endure pain and pleasure in the manner of a continent human being, unless he means that gods who are altogether rational and just would not give way to great pains or pleasures in their efforts to do what is just and what is best.

Kleinias responds to the Athenian Stranger's statement about the importance of a middle way regarding pain and pleasure by giving his and Megillus's full assent. He affirms that one should avoid both the life of unrestrained pain and the life of unrestrained pleasure and that one should "cut it somewhere in the middle" (*Laws* 793a). By seeking the mean somewhere between the extremes, Kleinias suggests that one does not find the mean by looking to some positive standard of what is correct but by looking to and avoiding the two extremes of pain and pleasure. Knowing precisely how to act courageously or how to act moderately in a particular situation is not crucial to acting nobly because what is important to know is that one must not respond to great pain or great pleasure, for endurance itself is what is noble.

Having argued that young children should learn to endure pain and pleasure, the Athenian Stranger says that at the age of six both boys and girls should undertake an extensive program of physical education. This education consists in leading young people to play carefully supervised games and competitions. Beginning at this early age, children will learn to compete in an orderly, restrained, and just way (*Laws* 794a–b). These games and contests help children to combat their fears and to develop courage in two ways. Primarily, when the body gains in health and strength, the soul takes confidence in that newfound vigor. In addition, the competitive nature of the games and contests encourages young people to indulge their spiritedness or love of victory. This spirited desire to overcome an adversary and to win honors is extremely helpful in combating both pain and pleasure. As Socrates says in the *Republic,* spiritedness is "irresistible and fearless" (*Republic* 375a–b). Under its influence, one seeks to win a victory over one's adversaries regardless of the threat of pain or injury.[1] It is for this reason that he says a founder of a city should recruit spirited young boys to serve as guardians for the "city in speech." In the *Laws,* all young citizens are encouraged to exhibit this passion in order to help them overcome their own passions and to help others do likewise (*Laws* 807c).[2]

By learning to play games justly (*Laws* 794b6), the young will begin to absorb some lessons in justice. But the justice that they learn is a specific form of justice: they learn that justice consists in playing by the rules in a competitive game. Left at this, they would learn that justice entails limiting how one competes as one tries to win a victory for oneself. They would not learn that justice is caring for the good of others (*Laws* 627b–e; *Republic* 332d).

The contests in which the children will participate must take on a decidedly military character. Since boys and girls should play only those games that contribute to their prowess in war, at the age of six boys and girls should learn to ride horses, throw javelins, and develop other military skills (*Laws* 794c–d; Morrow 1960, 333). Some argue that the militarism at the core of the citizen's education shows that divine law cannot be concerned solely with the promotion of virtue but must give some attention to matters of public safety, thus diluting or limiting the virtue that it would teach its citizens (Pangle 1988, 438–39; Parens 1995, 69–75). Yet the need to provide the city with a strong defense would not explain why every exercise and game must have a military use. The key reason for the militarism in gymnastic education is that when young boys and girls learn to combat enemies in war, they learn to confront and, as far as possible, to accept the possibility that they will suffer violent injury and death. They learn to combat their fears of violent injuries and death not by countering them with a deeper fear of shame or with a deep fear of the gods but by putting them aside in the course of a spirited desire for victory over their enemies and over their own fears.

Reverence and Courage

After the Athenian Stranger, Kleinias, and Megillus have sketched the lessons that will breed spirited courage among the young citizens, the Athenian Stranger says that they have omitted many important things, including the very first things that should be said to everyone (*Laws* 796e). He says that he must first say something frightening about gymnastic education and about moral education as a whole. After some hesitation, he says that it is crucial that generation after generation of young people should always play the same games. If the "serious customs" (*Laws* 797b) surrounding games always remain the same, then the laws will, too. But wherever the games change, he says, young people never love the same things and never call the same things "good" or "bad." Wherever such changes are found, the young fail to honor what is ancient and to dishonor what is new. But if someone is fortunate enough to live where no one has heard of things being any different than they are, then this person's entire soul feels pious reverence (*sebetai*) for whatever is established and fears changing it (*Laws* 798b). According to the Athenian Stranger, human beings begin to revere laws and customs that are both familial and old. Citizens associate old laws with divine laws because of their respect for their cities' laws. Believing that their city's laws are the best, they also believe that the laws and customs that established their way of life must have come from a source that is supremely wise and good. Consequently, they readily accept that old laws and customs originated with gods or with divine human beings. In order to make the citizen revere the games and contests, the lawgiver should follow the model established in Egypt, where songs and dances have not changed for thousands of years (*Laws* 799a). This discussion of piety affirms that reverence does not arise solely from fear of the gods, as it may have seemed to when the Athenian Stranger was discussing the laws of Crete and Sparta (*Laws* 646e–47c), but also on a profound trust that the gods are benign and powerful beings.

The Athenian Stranger justifies this new conservatism on the grounds that things that are in the best condition are not subject to change, while those that are ever changing are defective (*Laws* 797d–98b). If the games and contests are the best, then there should be no need for innovation and any change is a change for the worse. The observation made in Book 2 that people tend to take pleasure in what is new is not repeated here. In the earlier account of correct education, the Athenian Stranger argues that young people should be instilled with a taste for the pleasure of seeing and doing what is correct. In Book VII, however, the goal is to induce citizens to feel reverence and awe for what is traditional or ancestral. By establishing a strong tradition in respect to the games and contests, the lawgiver can establish reverence for the citizens' whole way of life and for the law itself.

The Athenian Stranger says that they have forgotten to mention the need for this conservatism and that it should have been said at first. He omitted to mention this first because the initial goal of education is not to instill reverence but to learn to combat the primal terror and proneness to fear that afflicts human beings. The Athenian Stranger turns to the importance of teaching reverence in the context of what he has said about the need to combat cowardice by promoting a kind of courage based on steady habits, confidence in physical strength, and a spirited love of victory. In this context, reverence is important because it adds something crucial to this sort of moral education. But what precisely does it add to education and especially to the education in courage? The Athenian Stranger provides us with an answer to this question by now turning his attention to the laws regarding music and music education.

Sacred Music and Civic Virtue

The Athenian Stranger says that this new conservatism in gymnastic education should be accompanied by a similar conservatism in music. Like the ancient Egyptians, the music in the city should never change any more than do the games. By recommending this extreme conservatism in music as well as in gymnastics, the Athenian Stranger underscores how greatly the education that is described in Book VII differs from the education that is described in Book II. In that earlier account of correct education, the Athenian Stranger said that music should be used to teach young people to take pleasure in the noble things. Because the music had to remain pleasing in order for it to lend charm to the virtues, it was necessary for the music to change from time to time. And thus it was necessary for the Dionysian chorus to oversee the production of new music to make sure that it conformed to the unchanging standards of the noble virtues. Now, instead of leading young people to take pleasure in those things that please the oldest and best citizens, the goal of music is to lead them to experience reverence and awe in regard to what is sacred. Therefore, innovation in music, and in all things, should be kept to a minimum, and the role of the Dionysian chorus is barely discussed. The Athenian Stranger mentions the chorus and recalls

ng the music, the Athenian Stranger calls for three specific
which shed new light on the problem of moral education.
erns music's power to convey and intensify grief at the death
e. The Athenian Stranger says that every time someone is
orm a sacrifice, a great number of choruses appear and utter
phemies. These blasphemies consist in the words, rhythms,
I harmonies that move the listeners and cause them to weep.
these choruses as those that are produced by the great tragic
e says that these are the choruses that win the prizes (*Laws*
)–c). Crying and wailing express feelings of great loss. They
pirited hope that someone or something might help to bring
sorrows to an end. The Athenian Stranger links tragedy
cause tragedians often present great suffering as something
transfiguring. By portraying the people's pains and fears, the
able the people to express their sorrow and win fame and
s for themselves in the process. But by enabling the citizens
ir suffering as something beautiful and even admirable, the
dermine the stern habits and disposition to endure pain that
lation of the courage that is taught by law (*Laws* 700d–1a).

ian Stranger does not ask young men and women to take
obly combating pain, as he had in Book II. Nor does he ask
egard the loss of a loved one, as Socrates does in the *Repub-
he Athenian Stranger recommends that citizens keep their
of grief within limits. The grieving citizen remains composed
he period of mourning and does not seek music to help him
the pain that he may feel within. If the occasion calls for
presses great sorrow, then the musicians, singers, and dancers
rformed by foreigners rather than by the citizens themselves
e, 960a–b).

citizens how they should mourn, the Athenian Stranger sheds
on the correct kind of piety that he would instill in the citi-
start of the dialogue, the Athenian Stranger linked piety with
e and fear of the gods. But in Book VII, he says that it is not
moved by great pains or fears. On the contrary, the gods want
xhibit the virtues, including the virtue courage. Therefore the
each citizen to bear up under terrible adversity and to remain
face of pain. Wishing to do what the gods require, the pious
s great pains along with great pleasures. But how, one might
is differ from the Spartan teaching that one should not fear
ath at the hands of the enemy lest one suffer an even more
sgrace before the city and its gods?

how its job is to know whether the m
of virtue (*Laws* 812b–c). But there is
wine-drinking or of the knowledge of
Instead, he says that a supervisor must
rus teachers and will make sure that th
do not change the way the sacred musi

The goal of these innovations in
emphasis in education from seeking
an erotic love of citizenship and to pla
virtue. In the law-based education outl
not led to find deep pleasure in the be
moderate and orderly and to take prid
stood to consist in being able to rise ab
longer are children taught to seek a cor
in principle, good without limit. There
correct. No one will be permitted to ap
zens to new music and other customs (
well-educated young people will take
music. As the Athenian Stranger says, e
kind of pleasure (*Laws* 812). But he als
time from childhood until the age of adu
ing a moderate and orderly Muse, then
he will hate Her and will proclaim Her t
is brought up with the common and sw
opposes this Muse is cold and unpleasan
education that is outlined in Book VII p
is unfamiliar rather than to enjoy what i
Moreover, the pleasure that the young
have become accustomed is likely to pa
others take in hearing music that is new

This new conservatism in games and m
games and music that will be selected an
the oldest games and music. The conserva
music will be new to the city. One wond
the new sanctification of customs, some o
as the extension of gymnastic education t
thought that the new, correct laws are n
are based on what is natural, which is ete
be (Strauss 1975, 25). But it must be note
to respect what is natural because it is nat
respect it because it is old and therefore sa

In reform
innovations
The first co
of a loved
about to pe
complete b
and mourn
He identifi
poets when
800d, cf. 75
also reflect
the chorus
with grief
beautiful a
tragedians
other rewa
to regard t
tragedians
are the fou

The Ath
pleasure in
them to di
lic. Instead
expression
throughou
give voice
music that
should be
(*Laws* 800

By telli
further lig
zens. At th
fear of sha
pious to b
citizens to
gods expe
steady in
citizen re
ask, does
injury or
fearsome

The second innovation concerns the music that accompanies prayers. As the Athenian Stranger argued back in Book III, one should not pray without intelligence. Prayers are requests that are made of the gods, and one must not risk praying for something that turns out to be evil. No prayer should be uttered unless it conforms to the city's lawful and just version of what is noble and good (*Laws* 801a–d). As a result, no poet will be permitted to present a prayer until that prayer has been scrutinized and approved by judges and by the guardians of the law.

Following this, the third innovation forbids poets from composing encomia for living people and from praising them for anything other than what is both noble and sanctioned by the law (*Laws* 801e). Presently, poets praise some for actions taken outside or beyond the scope of law. The Athenian Stranger's innovation suggests that encomia for such people weakens the law, insofar as much of the law's strength lies in its ability to provide individual citizens with a lasting fame that will help them overcome the limits of their mortality. By restricting the composition of encomia to those who have scrupulously followed the law and by prohibiting them from honoring anyone prior to his death, the lawgiver would ensure that those who seek lasting glory will seek it within the limits of the law all their lives.

Here we see one important way that piety in the new colony will differ from the kind of piety that characterizes a city such as Sparta. In Book I, the Athenian Stranger associates Spartan piety with fear of disgrace before the gods. If piety were grounded entirely in fear, then laws that teach citizens to have courage would undermine piety. But the opening of the dialogue has shown that serious citizens recognize divine law insofar as they aim at providing citizens with the whole of human virtue along with civic and individual happiness. The citizen believes that the gods expect him to have courage. In a city under divine law, citizens will exhibit courage not only because they fear the gods' disfavor but also because they hope that the gods will allow them to win lasting fame and honor for having followed the laws. This new piety is needed to support the new, more spirited courage that the Athenian Stranger says is crucial to virtue. At the same time, one could say that the new sort of spirited courage that the Athenian Stranger promotes is needed to bring about a kind of piety that is more conducive to the whole of human virtue.

The Problem of Divine Lawgiving

The Athenian Stranger says that the three of them must distinguish by some outline which songs are suitable to women and which are suitable to men. Alluding to a natural difference between men and women, the

Athenian Stranger says that each is inclined toward a different kind of virtue. He says that what tends toward the virtues magnificence (*megaloprepes*) and courage should be called "manly" and that what tends toward orderliness and moderation should be called "womanly" (*Laws* 802e). If men and women tend to have different virtues, then it seems that neither would be naturally inclined to the whole of virtue. In order to lead either a man or a woman in the direction of the whole of virtue, different educations would be needed for each.

Instead of elaborating how law must be applied to different kinds of human beings, the Athenian Stranger says that he is providing only an outline of how the laws ought to be laid out. He says that "As the shipwright first lays down the lines of the keel, and thus, as it were, draws the ship in outline, so do I seek to distinguish the patterns of life, and lay down their keels according to the nature of different men's souls; seeking truly to consider how we may go through the voyage of life best" (*Laws* 803a–b). Having said that this is only an outline of the best laws, the Athenian Stranger says that he is having difficulty taking these matters seriously. He says that one should be serious only about serious matters and that by nature the god is worthy of the most complete and blessed seriousness. A human being, however, is but a plaything (*paignion*) of the god, and this is the best thing about one. While human beings are not serious in themselves, every man and every woman should be serious and should play the noblest games (*Laws* 803c). At present, he says, people mistakenly think that what is serious is for the sake of play, in that they take war seriously and think that it is waged for the sake of peace (*Laws* 803d). They are mistaken in that they do not recognize that peace is more serious than war. For in peace human beings can partake of education and of the serious "play" that consists in sacrificing, singing, and dancing (*Laws* 803e). In this pious statement, the Athenian Stranger indicates that the goal of life ought to be the worshiping of the god. As he has just indicated, even lawgiving is nothing great when one compares human things to the divine (*Laws* 803b). But the Athenian Stranger quickly adds that the result of the sacrificing, singing, and dancing that one does for the gods is to make the gods propitious to oneself and to defeat enemies in battle (*Laws* 803e). The difficulty that arises from this remark is that it causes one to wonder whether the gods should be worshiped for their sake or for ours. Is the goal to worship the gods or to win the gods' favor in order to win a victory in war (Pangle 1988, 486; Strauss 1975, 106)? If someone were to say that it is both, the citizen would still be confronted with the problem that when we reflect on the greatness of the gods and on their overwhelming superiority to humanity, we inevitably wonder why the gods would take human things seriously enough to give us laws and to come to our assistance when we are in need.

The Athenian Stranger says that he will not take the trouble to discuss the sort of songs and dances that are needed, since this has already been indicated in the outline. Quoting a passage from Homer, he says that it should be left to the legislator and to oracles to provide a more detailed account of those songs and dances (*Laws* 804a–b). Human beings should live out their lives singing and dancing, for we are puppets of the gods, sharing in only a small portion of truth (*Laws* 804b3–4).

As the Athenian Stranger declines to discuss the songs and dances that should be sung, the long-silent Megillus breaks in and objects to the Athenian Stranger's claim that human things are puppets and not worthy of any seriousness. He says that the Athenian Stranger is deprecating the human race in every respect (*Laws* 804b5–6). The Athenian Stranger apologizes and explains that when he said these things he was "looking to the god" rather than to human beings and went too far (*Laws* 804b7). Megillus seems to accept the Athenian Stranger's acknowledgment that he has turned his eyes beyond the horizon of the citizen and failed to take citizenship seriously enough. But precisely why does the Athenian Stranger at first deny and later grant that human affairs are weighty enough to merit the serious attention of a god?

One can begin to account for this by saying that the Athenian Stranger has an especially lofty notion of what a god is. But what provokes him to express such a low view of human beings at this point in the dialogue? Does not the philosopher's attention to divine law begin from the premise that the gods take human beings most seriously? The Athenian Stranger has come to doubt the seriousness of human things in general and in lawgiving in particular because of what has come to light regarding law and moral education. In Book II, the Athenian Stranger described the education of the perfect human being. This person would take pleasure in the correct passions and would develop virtues of character that eventually harmonize with the virtues of the mind. But in Book VII, we learn that in an actual city the education must address a profound and innate terror and fearfulness. Education cannot expunge these passions but it can distract the citizen from them through vigorous activity, physical confidence, and spiritedness. Unable to master every pain or fear, young people must not be exposed to them. At the same time, neither are young people able to master every pleasure and hope. Temperance or endurance is the model of moral virtue. In order to follow the gracious middle way between extremes of pain and pleasure, the well-educated citizen is guided by reverence for the law rather than by a passionate love of or taste for the pleasure of acting virtuously. As we piece together the disposition of the citizen who is educated by law, we find that he is falling short of the virtue of the perfect human being. The god wants the citizen to take pleasure in the virtues of character to be guided by prudence and (or) intellect. But the primary goal of the law-based education is to enable young boys and girls to resist the fearfulness that ordinarily leads most human beings to cowardice and irritability. In light of this, the Athenian Stranger wonders how the gods could take lawgiving seriously, insofar as it seems to produce such limited virtues.

Yet the Athenian Stranger acknowledges that human things are worthy of some serious consideration. What he may find serious in human things is reflected in the Athenian Stranger's reference to the two alternative goals of worship. On the one hand, he says that human beings should take up the "serious play" that consists in education and in the artful celebration of the god. The problem or defect with war is that it makes no place for these sorts of activities. What is serious in education and in the artful celebra-tion of the god is the use of intellect or mind. In order to worship the god, we must know what the god is. Consequently, worshipful human beings make some use of the mind, which has been associated with the divine part of the soul (*Laws* 714a). On the other hand, the Athenian Stranger's further statement that the gods are worshiped to win their favor and to win victories over enemies suggests that one looks to the gods as means to achieve human ends. If the goal of worship is winning the gods' favor and achieving victory in war, this seems like a less serious end. The citizens seem to care for the gods in order to secure worldly goods that are beneath the concern of the gods.

In defense of citizens such as Megillus, we should note that from the start the serious citizen's piety and knowledge of the gods are based on the conviction that the gods care about human beings, make laws for them, and expect them to obey their laws. When asked to determine which of more than one code of law are divine, the citizen knows that the gods make codes of law that aim at what is best and that this is the whole of virtue, led by intellect or prudence. As Megillus understands it, a crucial aspect of divinity is a deep concern for human beings and for cities (cf. Maimonides *Guide for the Perplexed* 1. 54). Moreover, Megillus might also point out that human beings may find greater dignity in war than the Athenian Stranger has allowed. After all, it is in war that the citizen must draw on and display the whole range of virtues of action or of character. Under the duress of combat, the good citizen shows that he can put aside his concerns about his own pains and pleasures and remain courageous, moderate, just, and prudent. War, especially in its harshest forms, proves that one is a trustworthy friend (*Laws* 630a–d). Under the duress of battle, the citizen can manifest a courage in the face of death that is not experi-enced by immortal gods. Insofar as the full range of moral virtues should be taken seriously, both human beings and legislation would seem to be worthy of great attention. If it is agreed that human beings are worthy of some seriousness, then the question remains whether we are serious because of the virtues of the intellect, which enable one to know what is divine, or because of the virtues of character, the moral virtues, which enable one to do noble things.

The Family and Moral Education

Having accepted that legislation is worth our serious attention, the Athenian Stranger turns his attention to reforms that alter the role of the private family in daily life. According to the Athenian Stranger, moral education should be both public and mandatory. Children, he says, belong more to the city than to the private family (*Laws* 804d). Furthermore, a similar public education should be provided to both boys and girls. Even if males and females are disposed by nature to develop different kinds of character (*Laws* 802e), the educator must strive to teach courage to both.

According to the Athenian Stranger, traditional education neglects to teach women to fight in combat, with the result that Greek women fail to join in the city's defense. He adds that when danger approaches, women run into temples instead of joining in the fighting. By failing to fight for their children and their cities, these women act shamefully and fall short of the example set by female animals who vigorously fight to defend their offspring (*Laws* 814b). In order to join in the fighting if needed, girls must undertake military training and must also take part in martial games and exercises.

While these measures should make women better able to combat their fears and to contribute to the common defense, other measures are needed. Like the men, adult women should not dine at home with the children but must take common meals along with the other women (*Laws* 806e–7b). Furthermore, both women and men must be engaged in political activity not only during the day but long into the night. Sleep should be kept to a minimum so that each citizen can participate day and night in civic activities (*Laws* 807c–8c). By keeping in constant motion, the Athenian Stranger says, citizens will develop courage (*Laws* 808d1). But why would constant motion have this effect? If we consider this reform in the context of the other reforms in this section, we note that the all-day and all-night civic activity shares with public education and common meals the consequence that it intrudes on the private family. Thus far, the danger associated with strong familial bonds is that the grief that is felt by family members can be so overwhelming that it undermines one's ability or disposition to endure pain and fear. The Athenian Stranger warns that family members who have lost a loved one should not hear excessively mournful music lest they give way to grief (*Laws* 800b–e). In the *Republic,* Socrates says that in order to teach courage to young guardians, they should never encounter poetry that depicts heroes feeling grief at the death of a son or a brother. They should believe that the loss of such a relation is nothing terrible and should not cry or wail (*Republic* 387d–88e). Later, Socrates acknowledges that it is impossible for actual human beings to detach themselves from the grief associated with the death of a close family member and says that citizens should grieve privately (*Republic* 603e–4d).[3]

In the *Laws,* on the other hand, the Athenian Stranger does not ask men or women to display such toughness in regard to the death of their loved ones. But by limiting the time that children and adults will spend together in the intimacy of the private home, the Athenian Stranger's proposals would place limits on familial bonds. Armed with a vigorous martial education and engaged in various civic activities, both men and women are less likely to give way to the grief that can undermine a courageous disposition. But in addition to making the citizens bolder, these reforms would make an important contribution to the citizens' piety and understanding of the gods. As has been noted, the Athenian Stranger says that Greek women run into temples during times of danger for the same reason as female animals fight: they, too, want to protect their children (*Laws* 814d). The difference is due to the way that women, and men, turn to providential gods for help when they fear for their loved ones and despair that they cannot protect them or save them by themselves. The problem with this appeal to the gods is that the Athenian Stranger has already argued that the gods endure both pain and pleasure. According to his argument, the gods do not always come to our assistance, but they expect us to learn to endure without giving way to our passions. After agreeing that the human things should be taken seriously, the Athenian Stranger has proposed reforms that tend to draw young boys and girls away from the circle of the private family so that they may better maintain both the spirited courage that combats fear as well as the refined, tempered piety that goes along with that courage.

The Laws as the Standard for Public Art and Literature

If there is some peaceful activity that is higher than war, the guardian of the law will have to provide an education to support it (*Laws* 809a–c). The last part of the best education under law must give instruction for these peaceful activities, which the Athenian Stranger has already associated with education and the singing and sacrificing associated with worshiping the god. This education concerns what is written without meter (*Laws* 809c).

From the ages of ten to thirteen, all the students will study mathematics for practical use in war, household management, and the management of the city. In addition, they will study astronomy for similar purposes, so that they can know the seasons and establish sacrifices and festivals according to nature. From the ages of thirteen to sixteen, these students will learn to play the lyre (*Laws* 809e–10a). If nature urges them to do so, they shall proceed further with the higher education (*Laws* 810b). The higher education will begin with a focus on poetry. In a traditional education, boys learn different poems by heart. According to the Athenian Stranger, some of this poetry is serious, while the rest is comic. He adds that some of the poetry is noble, while the other part is not (*Laws* 811b). He says that it is the task of the guardian of the laws to determine which poems are to be taught. He adds that the guardian will need a standard for measuring which poetry is appropriate and that the speeches of the three interlocutors are the best model for judging which poetry is best. He suggests that the speeches they have made should be recorded and studied. He also suggests that their conversation could serve as a model for selecting other poetic works. Their speeches can serve as the standard for all literature in the city because they are "well measured" and "divinely inspired" (*epipnoias; Laws* 811c8). We might conclude that in saying that these speeches have been inspired by something divine, the Athenian Stranger is saying that they are not fully intelligible to those who rely solely on their own reason. Yet one must not move to this conclusion too quickly. The Athenian Stranger refers to what he has just said as a myth, so one must consider whether it has the same status as most of his other remarks (*Laws* 812a). More important, the Athenian Stranger has said that the gods rely on intellect (*nous*) to establish the laws (*Laws* 714a), indicating that inspired laws would reflect a wisdom that is discernable by human intellect.

At 812a, Kleinias is not sure that this is correct as a whole. Kleinias does not say what his reservations are, but it is evident that he does not yet accept that the Athenian Stranger's laws are divine. The Athenian Stranger replies that the validity of the argument may not be evident until the entire discussion has reached its end. We must pay close attention to what it is that finally persuades or dissuades Kleinias of the legitimacy of the laws.

Gymnastics Revisited

Next, the Athenian Stranger returns to the topic of gymnastic education by taking up the choral dancing that will be taught in the city. There are, he says, two kinds of dances. The first consists in presenting beautiful bodies making solemn movements; the second, in presenting ugly bodies making shameful or ridiculous movements. The first kind, the serious kind, is further divided into dances that are either warlike or peaceful. The warlike reflect courage, while the peaceful manifest the virtue moderation (*Laws* 814e). The moderate dances are further separated into some dances that imitate human beings who are escaping evils and other dances that imitate them becoming better and gentler. These latter dances present the virtues that the citizens have been learning since the beginning of life. But these are not the only dances that are needed. In addition, there are dances that are not serious. These consist of Bacchic dances in which drunken celebrants imitate nymphs, pans, *sileni,* and satyrs (*Laws* 815c–d). At the start of Book VII, the Athenian Stranger associates those who are moved by the Bacchic music with people who suffer from a great terror, apparently regarding the gods. This music and the drinking seem to alleviate the fear. This indicates that despite all the training, many citizens will never experience the consonance between passion and reason that is the object of divine law.

But there are also some unserious plays that are political and comical. The Athenian Stranger indicates that while comedies are needed to teach practical reason, tragedies are suspect in the city under divine law. The tragedies are not to be admitted to the city unless they prove to say the same things as or to say better things than the lawgivers say (*Laws* 817d). The Athenian Stranger once again points to the conversation that the interlocutors are now having as a model for tragedy. The city that they are now describing, he says, is the imitation of the noblest and best way of life (*Laws* 817b). The different kinds of tragedies present the noblest and best way of life very differently. Traditional tragedies present the noblest human beings undergoing great conflict and suffering. According to Aristotle, tragedy moves the audience to pity and fear (Aristotle *Poetics* II, 13–14). But the city described by the Athenian Stranger claims that the best life is one of harmony and happiness. Accordingly, this city would discourage poetry that ennobles conflicts, suffering, lamenting, and tears, for such poetry would make people softer and more susceptible to excessive fears and hopes.

The banning of conventional tragedies seems consistent with Socrates's guidance in the *Republic.* But unlike Socrates in the *Republic,* the Athenian Stranger says that comedies should be performed in the city. He says that comedies should be accepted in the city because they promote practical reason (*Laws* 816c–d). In order to understand how comedy might contribute more to *phronesis* than tragedy can contribute, we must recall that comedy presupposes tragedy insofar as comedy is the debunking of what tragedy presents as serious. Comedy succeeds by showing that what we ordinarily fear or respect is not as fearsome or as respectable as we have believed. It presents the objects of comedy as boasters, as people who claim to be more than they really are. The Athenian Stranger admits comic poetry into the best city because some of the things that the citizens will fear and respect will not be worthy of their seriousness. This is a further sign that their education is not altogether successful in cultivating the correct passions and diminishing the incorrect ones.

Mathematics and the Study of Necessity

After discussing the education in the choral art, the Athenian Stranger says that there are three subjects which are appropriate for free men: arithmetic, geometry, and astronomy. He says that the purpose of teaching "numerical necessities" and other aspects of mathematics is to make young people familiar with necessity (*Laws* 817e–18a, 818c; 809c–d). Necessity is so comprehensive that the person who first uttered the proverb "even a god never fights against necessity" must have been considering the "divine necessities" (*Laws* 818a–b). This education is needed for those who would be "divine" or who would be able to "exercise serious supervision over human beings" (*Laws* 818c).

In order to learn how the study of mathematics and other, related disciplines helps to teach rulers how to rule, one must consider what the Athenian Stranger has said about the study of numbers back in Book V. In that book, he says that the study of numbers "awakens him who is sleepy and unlearned by nature, giving him ease of listening, memory, and sharpness, and thus making him surpass his own nature by a divine art" (*Laws* 747b3–6). In the *Republic,* Socrates says that the study of mathematics can "awaken" the intellect (*Republic* 526a–b). In the *Laws,* the Athenian Stranger says that as a result of studying numbers and geometry, the student will be able to learn about "the greatest god" and the whole cosmos (*Laws* 821a).

The Athenian Stranger points out that most Greeks are terribly ignorant about great gods such as the Sun and the Moon. These and other stars are called "wanderers" (*planeta*) on the grounds that they do not keep regular motions in the heavens (*Laws* 821b). But through the study of mathematics, astronomers have learned that these gods always move in regular, circular motions (*Laws* 822a–c). Some Greeks, he says, blame those who study these motions. But, he reasons, this blame is not pious, for the gods surely want to be worshiped, and therefore they surely want to be recognized accurately (*Laws* 822b–c).

These studies seem important for learning about nature and for properly worshiping the heavenly gods. But precisely how would these studies help rulers to govern cities? According to the Eleatic Stranger in the *Statesman,* kingly rulers need practical reason (*phronesis*) in order to make discerning and discriminate decisions about particular individuals in varying circumstances (*Statesman* 294a–b). By teaching young people that the whole cosmos is subject to necessity, these lessons may help to persuade potential statesmen that they cannot rely on the gods to solve each and every problem for the city. But what about the gods who are not heavenly? How do we know that they are not subject to human necessities? How do we know that they are subject only to the kind of necessities that move the heavenly beings? We know from the opening of the dialogue that the serious citizen recognizes or "believes in" *(nomizo)* the divinity of a code of law because he understands that it aims at the greatest good. This sort of citizen believes that the gods are necessarily benevolent and prudent in making laws for cities. But it is not yet clear how the study of numbers, geometry, harmony, and astronomy would seem to supply any further insights into the purposes or concerns of lawmaking gods such as the Olympians. We must therefore continue to ask how this aspect of the higher education under the law contributes to ruling over human beings.

The last part of the education consists in learning to hunt wild game. This teaches physical and intellectual skills. In this passage, the Athenian Stranger says that one cannot learn to hunt by following rules or laws (*Laws* 823c). By forcing young people to go beyond the letter of the law, this education draws on a certain prudence in learning to hunt. Still, this culmination differs markedly from that of the philosophic education in Book VII of the *Republic*. There, Socrates says that the peak of education is "dialectics," a form of argument through which the young citizen learns to raise questions about what the law teaches regarding what is good and noble and just (*Republic* 534e). In the *Laws,* the need for this is less pressing or less obvious. The need for it has yet to be seen. The Athenian Stranger concludes by saying that the laws concerning education are at an end.

Conclusion

In order to understand the kind of virtues that divine law can bring forth among those who live under it, we look to the laws regarding education and virtue. We note that the Athenian Stranger elaborates these laws in a second and markedly different discussion of the best possible form of civic education. Having reached the end of Book VII, we are able to draw some conclusions about why the Athenian Stranger believes that it is necessary to supplement his earlier account of the best education with a second account in Book VII. The education that is outlined in Book II uses the power of music to promote a passion for the correct kinds of pleasure.

The well-educated citizen takes great pleasure in the beauty of the noble virtues, and he exercises these virtues as much as possible. The moral education that is outlined in Book VII, however, does not begin by focusing on cultivating the correct kind of pleasures. The educator cannot rely on the correct pleasures to lead the young to virtue because of the presence of a deep, innate fearful passion. Initially, this ineradicable fear does not seem to have a natural object. But we tend to develop many fears, most especially the fear of death. While this inborn fearfulness may remain with us, the young can be distracted from it through the introduction of new, orderly "counter-motions" in the soul. Gymnastic exercises, games, and contests establish these new motions, which are strengthened and supplemented by the appropriate music.

In addition to gaining confidence from their physical strength, young people are spurred to a spirited love of victory that enables them to resist both great pleasures and great pains. In addition, all the exercises, games, and music will remain unchanged so that the young develop great reverence for them and for all things ancient. This produces a stable and spirited courage which would sustain the individual citizen when faced with grave dangers. But it is not yet clear how this courage is to be harmonized with the other dispositions of character such as moderation and justice and with the practical reason that is supposed to be the most important of the particular virtues. In order to learn more precisely how the law-based virtues manifest themselves in action and how they affect one another, we need to look to a fuller account of how those who have absorbed the education in Book VII would act in civic life.

Chapter Five

THE PROBLEM OF EROTIC LOVE AND

PRACTICAL REASON UNDER DIVINE LAW

In Book VII, the Athenian Stranger describes the best education that could be established under the rule of divine law. While we can anticipate some of the results of that education on the citizen, it remains to be seen how well-educated citizens will spend their days and how the virtues will emerge and work together in their lives. Knowing this, we will be better able to understand the kind of virtues that divine law can promote. To shed light on the character of the law-based virtues, it is useful to look at Book VIII, which takes up how the citizens will occupy themselves as they grow up and act from day to day as citizens. In Book VII, the Athenian Stranger says that the citizens should spend their days and nights in political activity. Some will assist the foreign teachers in the program of education, but that accounts for the activity of only a few. In Book VIII, the Athenian Stranger reveals that much of their time will be spent in the many religious festivals and celebrations that take place in the city. Even though they involve a great amount of choral singing and dancing, these activities also include military contests that so closely re-enact what takes place in actual battles that some participants are bound to be killed (*Laws* 830d–31b). Thanks to their constant activity in the city, the citizens are not affected by the primal terror that was said earlier to lurk in the soul (*Laws* 709e–10b). Their spirited love of victory, which was carefully cultivated in their early education, enables them to overcome their fear of violent injury or death without flinching. While facing up to such great evils, they do not pray to the gods to protect or rescue them. Their implacable character enables them to worship the gods in the way that the gods want to be worshiped (*Laws* 830e; cf. 792d).

After describing how these festivities will fill the citizens' time and after pointing to the success of their early education in building confidence or courage, the Athenian Stranger observes that the very success of the moral education that he has described in Book VII will threaten the young citizens' virtue. The threat arises because well-educated young men and women will be freed from the drudgery that usually weighs upon and breaks the spirits of young people. Physically healthy, strong, and beautiful, these courageous, young men and women will spend their days dancing, singing, and engaging in challenging martial contests. And as they display their own beauty, and grace in worshiping the gods, they also are bound to feel erotic love for one another (*Laws* 835d). The danger is that their erotic passion will weaken their virtue and will undermine the law itself. How the well-educated citizen will respond to erotic passion reveals the kind of virtue that he has acquired through the law.

Earlier in the *Laws,* erotic love was presented as a passion that supports civic virtue and law. In Book I, the Athenian Stranger says that erotic love can move a person to take up an art and to pursue it as his life's work (*Laws* 643d–e). He says that the goal of a genuinely liberal education is to arouse and to deepen an erotic love of citizenship or of ruling and being ruled with justice. Thus, erotic love first comes to sight as the very spirit that animates the highest form of citizenship (*Laws* 688b). Later, in Book VI, the Athenian Stranger speaks of erotic love in a new way. He says that it has only three objects: food, drink, and the procreation of offspring. Rather than speak of a positive, erotic love of justice or civic virtue, he says that erotic love is an indeterminate passion in that it can lead to either virtue or vice, depending on one's upbringing (*Laws* 782d–83cc). But in Book VIII, the Athenian Stranger describes erotic love chiefly as a passion that leads even well-educated men and women into degradation and as a "sickness" that threatens law itself (*Laws* 836b2–4).

In Book VIII, the lovers seem to be moved not simply by bodily pleasure or procreation by the beauty of their beloveds' bodies and souls. The desire to be together with one's beloved is overwhelming, and unless it can be checked by fear or law or reason, lovers will pursue their beloveds without limit or restraint (*Laws* 836a–b). Erotic desire is so powerful that it can move a lover to undergo terrible deprivations and to suffer the greatest hardships in pursuit of the one whom he or she loves (e.g., *Symposium* 182e–83b). Yet from the point of view of the law, lovers who stop at nothing in order to gratify their passion are in no way admirable or impressive. They are, instead, utterly shameless and indifferent to good sense and virtue. According to the law, young people should learn to find beauty in correct images of courage and moderation or should revere the gracefulness of those who can endure pain and resist pleasure. But the lover's intense desire to be together with a beautiful beloved eclipses any affection or respect that he or she may have felt for the beauty of the virtues that are taught by law. Moreover, the lover's guiding passion undermines the character that law has sought to build. Moved by strong desires for the beauty of the body and soul, lovers abandon the steady habits that are the foundation of courage and self-command. The lover abandons the "gracious middle way" that consists in enduring both pain and pleasure in the manner of a god (*Laws* 792). In its place, the lover is overcome with a great desire for a pleasure that seems altogether beautiful and gratifying, a means to immortality and happiness (*Laws* 721c, 782e–83b; see *Symposium* 206a–7a, 207c–d, 208e). As lovers find themselves being moved by great pains and pleasures, they lose the steadiness of character and inner toughness that helps to give them their courage and self-command. And by flattering and importuning their beloveds, they often undermine their beloveds' good character as well (*Laws* 836d–e). Unmoored from the moral virtues that were instilled by the law, the lover scoffs at any limitations that law would place on his erotic passions (*Laws* 839b). Moreover, those who feel erotic love are no longer restrained regarding any other passion that should arise. The Athenian Stranger notes that erotic passion affects different people in different ways. Recalling a fundamental distinction between moderate and courageous human beings, the Athenian Stranger says that those lovers who are moderate by nature will seek riches and will turn into merchants. But, he says, those who are courageous by nature will pursue not only wealth but also rule: they will turn into thieves, warriors, and tyrants (*Laws* 831e–32a; cf. *Symposium* 209a, d). Thus, it seems that the education that produces courage in the young citizens inevitably gives rise to a form of immoderation that threatens the rule of law.

These criticisms of erotic love are not departures from Socrates's treatment of erotic love in the *Republic*. While describing the relations between the male and female guardians in the city in speech, Socrates suggests that these guardians will be moved by "erotic necessities" to join together (*Republic* 458d). Rather than allow the guardians' erotic desires to guide them, Socrates says that the rulers of the city will have to arrange brief "sacred marriages" for selected male and female guardians (*Republic* 458e). Yet it is not enough to prevent lovers from marrying and establishing private families. The wise ruler must suppress the erotic desire to procreate offspring who would provide them with a form of immortality. According to Socrates, when any of the female guardians are pregnant, neither they nor their husbands are to know who their children are. Familial love is blamed not only because it is the source of an unjust favoritism in civic life (*Republic* 330c, 415a–b), but also because family members feel an extremely powerful love for their own. The most important consequence of this sort of love is that when a family member, especially an offspring, dies, the grief is overwhelming. When moved by great sorrow, or even by great fear for the safety of their loved ones, family members will call on the gods to assist them or their family members (*Laws* 814b). But this distorts the grieving person's understanding of the gods, for the philosopher argues that the gods are perfect, unchanging, and disinclined to assist all who call upon them (*Republic* 379b ff.). At the same time, Socrates's argument that citizens must not grieve over the death of loved ones is qualified. As Socrates himself acknowledges, it is not possible for a human being to be indifferent to the death of a brother or a son (*Republic* 603e). Consequently, he says, the guardians must be allowed to grieve but should do so discreetly and in private (*Republic* 604b–c). In the *Laws,* the Athenian Stranger does not attempt to suppress familial bonds. While saying more than once that it would be best to eliminate the private family, he says that it is not possible to do away with it (*Laws* 739c, 807b). But he does recommend several measures that are intended to weaken familial bonds. Education will take place in public rather than in the private home. Parents will not share their meals with their children, but dine in common. These measures, as well as the constant political activity during both day and night, are intended to limit familial bonds. In addition, the Athenian Stranger emphasizes that family members must not be permitted to grieve excessively for the loss of their loved ones. Funeral music and other signs of grief should be temperate in order to limit as much as possible the anguish that loved ones feel for those whom they have lost (*Laws* 800b–e, 960a).[1]

In order to understand how to protect the citizens against this loss of virtue and disregard for the law, the legislator must learn to distinguish among three different forms or "ideas" (*Laws* 836d7, 837a3) of erotic love. The first kind is the love of what is similar to oneself. Being a love of like for like, it is gentle, mutual, and lasting (*Laws* 837b). This could be the sort of friendship that develops between people who share similar interests or who are kindred spirits. But the love of what is opposite to oneself is a needy kind of love. As we see in the love of those who need and lack wealth, it is terrible and savage and tends not to be mutual. This would be the yearning, desirous love that old lovers feel for young beloveds or that passionate lovers might feel for beloveds who seem unusually striking and exotic. According to the Athenian Stranger, when either of these two forms of erotic love becomes intense, it is called "erotic love" (*Laws* 837a). Yet there is a third form, which seems to be some combination of the first two. The person who has this form of erotic love is uncertain what he wants because he is torn in two directions. The Athenian Stranger praises the sort of lover who looks at the beauty of the body but regards gratifying the desire for the body as wanton (*Laws* 837c). Instead, he desires the beloved's soul and feels awe and reverence for moderation, courage, magnificence, and practical reason. Because the lover loves the young beloved for these qualities and does what he can to help him become as virtuous as possible, the lover wishes that he and his beloved will remain chaste (*Laws* 837d).

After discussing these worse and better forms of erotic love, the Athenian Stranger says that he has a "certain art" and that through this art he will propose laws that will help avoid the dangers of erotic love (*Laws* 838a). The Athenian Stranger acknowledges that many will find it implausible that any effective restrictions could be placed on erotic love. But the Athenian Stranger also says that many are able to resist sexual or erotic longings for members of their own family because everyone says that such a thing is altogether impious and hateful to the gods (*Laws* 838a4–e1, 839c2–d5). In order to discourage this form of erotic desire, the Athenian Stranger points out that poets present those who engage in incest as choosing to die as a penalty (*Laws* 838c). He argues that if everyone were to join in saying that the gods hate those who engage in sexual acts that are not aimed at procreation within marriage, then erotic passion could be mastered by the citizens (*Laws* 838d–e). This sort of piety resembles the awe or pious fear that the Dorians feel in regard to the gods and their laws. In addition, it also reminds one of how people were said to hold their beliefs about what is noble and what is divine in the primitive regime that was described near the start of Book III. According to the Athenian Stranger, these people believe whatever they are told because they never heard anyone or anything contradict it. Now, he suggests that everyone still fears and reviles incest because everyone agrees that it is hated by the gods.

Having argued that a universal agreement about extra-marital sexual and erotic love would be effective, the Athenian Stranger concedes that nowadays lawgivers might not be able to achieve such a consensus among contemporary, sophisticated Greeks. In order to persuade such a people to restrain themselves, the legislator would have to appeal not to fearful piety but to a love of victory. The Athenian Stranger points out that those who compete to win victories in wrestling deny themselves erotic pleasure, which the many say is happiness (*Laws* 840b). But the citizens who are challenged to win a victory over erotic love are challenged to win an even greater and nobler victory than do athletes in the Olympic Games (*Laws* 839e–40c). This appeal to the love of victory over passion is an appeal to pride or to the love of honor. In order to underscore that the contest is a great one, the Athenian Stranger says that the adversary is not simply erotic pleasure but pleasure itself (*Laws* 840c1–2). Earlier in the dialogue, the Athenian Stranger said that passions such as pain and pleasure are so fundamental to our experience as living beings that early education must

consist in training them correctly (*Laws* 653a–b). Now, he presents pleasure as an opponent who can and must be conquered in order to demonstrate one's worthiness. In order to underscore the challenge to overcome
pleasure, the Athenian Stranger points out that there are numerous kinds
of birds and animals who are able to reproduce without becoming base,
unjust, and impious. He says that these animals are celibate, pure, and
chaste until they mate, after which they pair off and live lives of piety and
justice (*Laws* 840d). To fail to exercise self-control over erotic desire is to
sink to a level that is lower than that of these beasts. And to rise above
pleasure is to display a pure and pious virtue of the soul. In some respects,
this recalls the Athenian Stranger's earlier claim that pederasty and other
extra-marital forms of sexual activity should be outlawed because they are
against a law in nature (*Laws* 636b). But here, the Athenian Stranger does
not refer to such a law. Nature is not the standard for law because not
all animals are orderly or chaste in regard to their mating. The animals
that are to be admired and emulated are selected because of the virtues
that they seem to display. Virtue, not nature, is the standard to which the
Athenian Stranger looks in making law.

In his earlier conversation with Megillus, the Athenian Stranger noted
that moderation in itself does not seem to be as noble as the other virtues
(*Laws* 696d). It may, after all, reflect the weakness of one's passions or a
steadiness that does not seem moving to those who witness it. But now the
Athenian Stranger describes the moderation of those who defy pleasure as a
courageous kind of moderation (*Laws* 840a). One needs courage to resist the
demands of pleasure. By presenting the exercise of self-control over pleasure
as a great conquest that manifests manly virtue and that wins honor, the
Athenian Stranger indicates that the source of the strength with which one
will overcome desire is spiritedness or the love of victory. The lover relies
on his own spiritedness or love of victory to overpower his erotic passion
and pleasure. His moderation is a form of self-overcoming: he is "superior
to himself" or to passions that are always present to him (cf. *Laws* 626d–e,
645b). The citizen does not need a new education to triumph over pleasure.
The wise lawgiver will have sought to promote this tough, proud asceticism
from the start of the education. The Athenian Stranger brings up the challenge that erotic love poses to law because it engages or tests the virtues that
have been learned through the public, law-based education. According to the
Athenian Stranger, the test will show that the regimens and lessons instilled
by the legislator can foster a spirited courage and moderation.

Summarizing what he has said about controlling erotic love, the Athenian Stranger says that there are three ways to master it. The first of these
measures is reverence for the gods, which he has said could be used to

promote chastity and faithfulness in marriage. The second is the love of honor, which is evidently at the core of the love of victory (*Republic* 581c–d, 586c). The third is the erotic love of the soul, for this passion enables the lover to resist the erotic love of the body so that he or she may enjoy the greater gratification found in loving the beauty of the soul (*Laws* 841c). In formulating a law to enable well-educated citizens to control their erotic passion, the Athenian Stranger has suggested that the second kind be used. As he has said, contemporary Greeks may be too corrupt to believe or to fear the gods would punish them for licentiousness. The third form is apparently too rare or too weak to be counted upon as an effective check on the lower form of erotic love.[2]

The Athenian Stranger indicates that even though the better citizens will be able to master their erotic passions, many others will be corrupted by the dissolute examples set by other Greeks and barbarians and will most likely succumb to their desires for bodily gratification. As a result, the "guardians of the law" will need to establish a second law (*Laws* 840e). The second law attenuates the pleasures by subjecting citizens to vigorous exercises (*Laws* 841a). In addition, the law would permit citizens to engage in sexual relations only when they are filled with awe, on the grounds that this would make such relations less frequent (*Laws* 841a–b). According to the Athenian Stranger, those who fail to master "the pleasures" should be blamed and punished (*Laws* 829d–31a). He proposes two laws to deal with such people. The first would proscribe sexual activity with anyone other than one's own wife but would not outlaw the non-sexual, erotic love of the soul between one male and another. The second would not blame those who manage to keep their extra-marital affairs secret but would punish anyone who is caught having extra-marital sexual relations with a woman and would forbid all forms of erotic love between men, including the chaste love of the beauty of the soul (*Laws* 841c–e). The first of these two seems to follow from what has been said about the evils of the low form of erotic love and the nobility of the high form. The second makes an allowance for those men who will not be faithful to their wives. Rather than make a law that will not be kept by many in the city, the Athenian Stranger proposes a law that many will find easier to avoid breaking. But while the second law seems to make an allowance for the strength of heterosexual desire for the body, it gives no scope to any form of erotic love, including the higher, non-bodily form, of one man for another. Despite his earlier praise of this nobler love, the Athenian Stranger now disallows it, as if the strength of the love of the body were so great that the lawgiver cannot expect citizens to counteract it on the basis of their erotic love of the soul. Having described both laws, the Athenian Stranger does not say which of the two is best. In fact, he presents the two incompatible laws as one (*Laws* 841e–42a). This confusion in the law is rooted in the inherent limitations of law. Speaking universally, it cannot give each kind of citizen the law that is fitting. Consequently, he seems to propose a first law that would be fitting for the most virtuous citizens and a second law that would be more fitting for citizens with less virtue. In order for law to give what is fitting to both kinds of citizens, it would have to say different things to different kinds of people. But because law must speak universally, it cannot do this. The difficulty surrounding the elaboration of two laws shows why the Athenian Stranger said earlier in Book VII that reason is "attempting" (*epixeiron*) to become law (*Laws* 835e4–5). It merely strives to formulate laws because what reason would declare in erotic matters cannot be translated fully into law.

Self-Rule and Practical Reason

Returning to the question of whether the law-based education fosters virtue as a whole, the discussion of how the well-educated citizen responds to erotic love suggests that the lawgiver can foster a kind of moderation or self-control that is compatible with the citizen's courage. The citizen is able to endure great pains and to resist great pleasures. But it remains to be seen whether or to what extent this citizen also possesses practical reason, the virtue that is said to be the leader of the virtues and the hallmark of divine law (*Laws* 631c).[3] In order to shed light on this question, it is useful to consider more precisely what is meant by practical reason. According to what is nearly a definition of practical reason in Book III, it is that state of soul in which the passions obey the better part of the soul, which is knowledge or opinion or reason (*Laws* 688e–89b). If the citizen is willing and able to follow rational guidance, then he would seem to have practical reason in regard to his own soul. But how or why do the citizen's passions lead him to follow the better part of his soul? Does it make a difference whether the passions submit on the basis of knowledge or of opinion?

In order to clarify what it means for the better part of the soul to lead the worse part, it is useful to examine how the Athenian Stranger first describes self-rule in Book I. In this early passage, he says that in each of us there are two "imprudent" (*aphrone*) counselors (*Laws* 644c7) called pain and pleasure. He says that pain is attended by the expectations we call "fear" and pleasure by the expectation we call "daring." The individual who can rule himself is able to calculate about which of the pleasures and pains (or fears or hopes) is better and which is worse (*Laws* 644c–d). By calling pain and pleasure "counselors," the Athenian indicates that they are more than mere urges. Each of our pains and pleasures is accompanied by some sort of counsel or opinion about what is good and what is bad. The individual described in this image uses reason to think through what each pain and pleasure claims is good and to weigh this in light of what is truly best. In this first image of self-control, when calculation *(logismos)* shows that the belief that accompanies a given passion does not lead to what is best, the mistaken belief will give way, and the passion will yield to reason, because the imprudent counselors will have been shown to be mistaken. As the Athenian Stranger puts it, the individual uses "true reason" on the passions and also uses it to guide his own life (*Laws* 645b4–5). By correcting the "imprudent" counselors through reason, this individual is able to rank the passions in light of the genuine goods or evils that accompany them. When thought through and ranked in light of what is best, each pain and each pleasure will find a place in the soul, and the passions will achieve a kind of harmony or consonance through "correct reason" (*Laws* 696c; *Republic* 443d2–44a1). To rule oneself by reasoning about one's passions would bring about the harmony between passion and reason that is called "virtue" at the opening of Book II (*Laws* 653b–c). If we consider how this account of self-rule compares to the description of practical reason in Book III, we find that it corresponds to the form of practical reason that consists in the passions willingly obeying knowledge or reason (*Laws* 688e–89b).[4]

The prudent individual may need to calculate about his or her passions on many occasions and in varying circumstances. According to an image in Book I that appears just before the Athenian Stranger begins describing what it means to exercise self-control, nature gives us many pains and pleasures. It is up to us to select which of these should be gratified at the correct time and in the correct amount so that we may be happy (*Laws* 636d–e). The prudent individual does not brand each passion as good or evil or as noble or base, but considers whether or to what extent each one contributes to his or her happiness in a given circumstance. We may add that those who are able to rule themselves in this manner would be better able to make prudent judgments about things other than their own passions (*Laws* 689d5–e1). The Athenian Stranger concludes his description of self-rule by saying that when this individual's reasoning is adopted by the whole city it is called "law" (*Laws* 644d3). By this account, law is not the source of this prudence. On the contrary, legislation consists in taking someone's prudence in regard to his own passions and applying that prudence to every other person in the city. The Athenian Stranger does not explain here how this prudent self-rule could come into being. Nor does he comment at this time about the difficulties that would arise from law's inability to take into account changes in circumstance or the various needs and abilities of many different individuals within the city. He has, however, provided us with an image of self-rule and practical reason in the most complete respect.

When Kleinias and Megillus each complain that they do not understand this image of self-rule, the Athenian offers them a second description of self-rule. It is important to note that the Athenian Stranger explicitly distinguishes the first account of self-rule at 644, which he calls an "image" (*Laws* 644c2), from the second, which he calls the "myth of virtue" and the "myth about us being puppets" (*Laws* 645b1–2).[5] In the myth of virtue, the individual is pulled in different directions by many passions, which tug on one like strings pulling a puppet. In the myth, reason appears in the form of law, which is described as a sacred, golden, and noble string which pulls us along with the passions, except that it is weaker than those passions. In order to help the law prevail against the passions, one must summon one's own strength and pull along with it in order that the "race of the gold" (*to krusoun genos*) might prevail (*Laws* 644e1–45a7). While the Athenian Stranger does not identify this "race" or family explicitly, he suggests that it includes the gods and all those higher beings who are liberated from the passions and able to follow the laws that the gods establish. As one compares the initial image with the subsequent myth, one may expect that the person in the myth recognizes reason in the law which is given to the city as a whole and follows it as one might follow calculation or reason in the original image. After all, the Athenian Stranger says that reason declares that one should always follow law because law is the sacred and golden "pull" of calculation (*Laws* 644d4–45a1). But even if law is said to be a sacred and golden form of reasoning, it does not seem to act in the same way that reason acts in the first example of self-control. As we know from the *Minos* and the *Statesman*, the great variety of human types means that what is best for a given individual is not necessarily best for each person in the city (*Minos* 317d; also *Statesman* 294c1–4). And when one looks closely at the two descriptions of self-control, one finds important differences in how and why one controls oneself. While the individual in the first image hears imprudent counsels from his passions and reasons about which of them is truly best for him, the person in the myth does not hear the passions counseling anything at all. Instead, the passions are inarticulate strings or cords, brute forces that pull on him as if he were a puppet. This person is not concerned with reasoning about these passions or even with discovering what is best for him or herself. Instead, he strives to assist the law because it is sacred, golden, and noble. But since it was said at the start of the myth that we human beings are puppets who do not know what ends the gods have in store for us, he cannot know with certainty the final result of his coming to the assistance of the law (*Laws* 644d7–9). He wants to add his own force to the law because the law is sacred, golden, and noble, and he wants to honor that which is sacred, golden, and noble (*Laws* 645a).

The reference to a struggle between the passions and the law reflects a further important difference between the two descriptions of self-rule. In the first image, the reasoning concerning what is best is not said to be weak, and there is no mention of any struggle that takes place when it is followed. The calculations are strong because they show the individual that they must either follow or resist a given passion if he or she is going to do what is best. In the myth, however, the person struggles against the passions in order to assist a law that is always weak. The Athenian Stranger says that the law is weak because it is golden (*Laws* 645a3). But weakness is a relative term. The law is weak in relation to the passions because the passions are strong or "made of iron" (*Laws* 645a2). In relation to law, the passions seem to be strong and tough because they do not listen or yield to reason. Moreover, the person in the myth endures a struggle against the passions that appears to be unending. There is no suggestion that the citizen somehow transforms his passions when he triumphs over them so that they come to support the law. The lower yet stronger passions are defeated through strength rather than through reason or persuasion. Yet the thought that the second figure struggles against the passions does not seem to diminish his accomplishment. On the contrary, the struggle is at the core of what makes his self-rule seem impressive. The Athenian Stranger says that for this person it is always necessary (*dein*) to assist the noble pull of law because noble calculation is weak (*Laws* 645a4–b1). This necessity differs from the necessity that seems to guide the individual in the first image at 644. For that first individual is compelled by a necessity that follows from calculation; if he or she is to do what is best, he must either gratify or resist a particular passion, and as long as he or she is reasoning he or she cannot choose otherwise (*Laws* 645b5). But when speaking about the figure in the myth, the Athenian Stranger says at 645a4–7 that one must follow the guidance of the law "if the race of the gold is to be victorious over other races." If this person does not come to the assistance of noble calculation, then it is possible that the lesser "races," which is to say, the passions, will prevail. Thus, in the myth, one is in a position to choose between submitting to the passions or doing what is sacred, golden, and noble. Through this struggle and this choosing, one seems to come into one's own. As this person summons the strength to oppose the passions, he becomes aware of himself as something other than a puppet, as a willing being who chooses to act or not to act in accordance with the law.[6] Yet his thoughts do not linger on his newfound selfhood. In striving to overcome his passions, he tries to win a victory for the sake of something beyond himself. By fighting his own passions for the sake of what is golden, noble, and divine, he not only demonstrates his own freedom from what is base or expedient or mortal but also shows that he cares for and is akin to a higher race of beings (*Laws* 645a7). Those who are able to support the sacred, golden, and noble law are thereby transfigured and made sacred, golden, and noble.

It is in the myth rather than in the initial image that virtue and vice are said to dwell and where virtue and vice are said to become more distinct from one another (*Laws* 644e, 645b–c). This is because it is only in "the myth of virtue" that one seems to be choosing to act either nobly or basely. The virtue that one possesses is not practical reason in the sense that the passions willingly obey reason or the "better part" of the soul. Instead, this virtue is like that of the Cretan citizen who was said at the beginning of the dialogue to be "better than himself" when he was overpowered by his own passions (*Laws* 645b; cf. 626d–e). The individual who applies "true reason" to the passions and who lives according to what true reason says is not said to be "better than himself" because he is not like a Cretan or Spartan who gets the better of his own passions, but rather like the individual who finds out how to gratify those passions that are compatible with what is best (*Laws* 783a). He achieves the inner consonance that Kleinias and the Athenian Stranger had earlier agreed is a higher and more important goal of divine law (*Laws* 628c–e).

Self-Rule under Divine Law

As we consider how each of these models of self-control compares with the self-control of the citizen who has been educated by divine law, it helps to ask how that citizen would control his own erotic longings. The Athenian Stranger says that the legislator should appeal to the citizens' love of victory and should urge them to triumph over erotic desire in a contest that is greater and more honorable than the Olympic Games. Like the figure in the myth of virtue, the well-educated citizen is not invited to reason about whether his erotic passions lead to what is best. He does not abstain from sexual relations because abstinence will fulfill his love of the beauty of the soul. Rather, he rejects such relations because erotic desire, and even pleasure itself, is an enemy that is trying to defeat him in life's greatest contest. His goal is to overcome his passions just as the figure in the myth of virtue seeks to overpower the cords that pull on him. And, like that figure, he also wants to follow law so that he might overcome the disgraceful passions and live like a higher order of being. In competing against indefatigable adversaries like erotic love and pleasure, the erotic citizen does not reach an agreement with them. Insofar as they continue to compete against him throughout his life, he cannot claim that these passions obey the better part of him or that he fully possesses the virtue of practical reason as it is described in Book III. Like Megillus, he will regard certain pleasures as evil regardless of the circumstances (*Laws* 637a–b). If, however, an erotic citizen were able to use true reason to calculate about which erotic passions will lead to what is best, the erotic love of body would become subordinate to the erotic love of the soul. The lover could gratify the highest form of erotic love and might thereby achieve the consonance of the passions and reason that characterizes practical reason in its truest form. But the Athenian Stranger does not ask the well-educated citizen to rely on true reason to curb or guide erotic passion. The same citizen who harbors great fears beneath his or her courage (*Laws* 791b) is also threatened by great erotic hopes. The best moral education under law does not enable the citizen to exercise practical reason in the most complete sense. Lacking practical reason in this way, the well-educated citizen would achieve neither the virtue as a whole nor the happiness that is supposed to accompany it.

One might grant that the well-educated citizen does not manifest practical reason in regard to erotic love but still wonder if he could possesses this virtue in regard to other passions. But can the citizens' erotic love be set aside? One should recall that erotic longings for immortality and happiness will be very strong and influence many aspects of the citizens' lives. Yet if one were to set aside how the citizen rules him or herself in regard to erotic love and considers how he or she responds to passions such as pain or fear, one will still find that the citizen bears a stronger resemblance to the figure in the myth of virtue than to the one in the first account of self-rule. As a result of the education that is described in Book VII, the citizen learns always to remain firm when faced with pain and fear. The citizen will regard these passions as weaknesses or adversaries. Courage consists in having the ability and the will to overcome these passions in accordance with the law (*Laws* 633c–d). Those who are able to withstand both pains and pleasures thereby prove themselves to belong to a higher order of being: one becomes a divine or godlike human being (*Laws* 792c–d).

Equipped with such an understanding of courage, the devoted citizen will remain at his post regardless of the risk to his own safety and, in this respect, will seem a noble citizen. But it is not clear that this sort of courage is always prudent either for the city or for the individual citizen. The citizen who fights with law-based courage may prefer to stand his ground and fight even if it is better for the city for him to withdraw to fight another day. As for the individual, he may act nobly, yet he will not reason about his strong pains and/or about his strong fears as does the individual who exercises true reason in regard to his passions. And because he does not reason about his passions, he will not establish a consonance in his soul and will not possess either genuine practical reason or virtue as a whole.

One might respond that those who exercise the sort of self-rule that is described in the myth of virtue might eventually come to acquire the sort that is described in the earlier image of true reasoning. After all, the moral education that is outlined in Book VII is said to be a preparation for the arrival of practical reason. Perhaps it teaches citizens images of virtue (*Laws* 669a) that provide them with a disposition to act virtuously, and when reason arrives, the citizens are able to welcome its guidance. Christopher Bobonich suggests that those who are educated with the correct emotions will find that their "reasoned appreciation of what is good and fine" will give them a "separate and additional sort of motivation for acting rightly" (Bobonich 2002, 115). One difficulty with this proposal is that the Athenian Stranger says that the first image describes a form of self-rule that occurs in an individual who rules him or herself prior to and independently of the rule of law (*Laws* 644d, 645b). More important, the citizen who associates virtue with self-overcoming and devotion to law will not recognize that those who reason about which of their passions is best have the virtue practical reason. Like the figure in the myth of virtue, the citizen who is educated by law considers virtue to consist in having the desire and strength to overcome the base passions and to follow the sacred, golden, and noble law. From the point of view of this citizen, the individual who calculates about which passions will lead to what is best does not always face great, inner challenges and does not rise above his or her own low passions in order to live like a higher sort of being. Nor is the calculating individual concerned with a law that has been established and favored by a god. Moreover, the citizen who is educated by divine law knows that it is always noble, pious, and good to combat pain and fear and to resist pleasure and bold hope. It will not occur to the citizen to ask whether under some circumstances it is better to yield to certain pains or fears or to permit oneself certain pleasures or hopes. In particular, such a citizen will never ask whether it is always best to remain in his place courageously or whether it is sometimes better to withdraw or take flight. The prudent individual, on the other hand, would weigh every passion under different circumstances and would determine whether or not it leads to what is best or to happiness. The serious, law-bred citizen will regard this openness to the passions as a sign that the prudent individual does not aspire to live like a better, transfigured being. In light of these considerations, it seems that when divine law teaches its version of courage and of "courageous" moderation to the citizens, it inadvertently places obstacles before them that stand in the way of their development of practical reason. And if moral education under divine law does not promote practical reason, then can it promote the whole of virtue?

The laws' limitations are not accidental: they will be found in any code of law that teaches moral virtues. According to the Athenian Stranger, terror and erotic love are powerful passions that always threaten many individuals and that always undermine the rule of law. The Athenian Stranger has shown that some forms of law control these passions by instilling an even greater fearfulness. The laws of Crete and Sparta, for example, master those passions by appealing to the fear of shame and fear of the gods. But the law-bred fear that underlies Cretan and Spartan virtue undermines practical reason and virtue as a whole. The Athenian Stranger explains how the best laws would use habituation and a love of victory or of honor to instill a kind of courage and a kind of courageous moderation. These virtues would enable the citizen to keep terror and erotic love at bay. But these nobler virtues still stand in the way of practical reason and virtue as a whole.

The Athenian Stranger himself does not draw this conclusion explicitly in either Book VII or VIII. But he does confirm it at the end of the dialogue. Near the end of Book XII, as he is completing his account of the best laws (*Laws* 960b), the Athenian Stranger says that the laws are in danger of "wandering" and of failing to hit their target (*Laws* 962b–c, 962d–e, 963b). Kleinias is surprised, for, as he says, they have been designing the laws all along to teach virtue (*Laws* 963a). But the Athenian Stranger explains that while the laws have been teaching the different particular virtues such as courage and practical reason, they have not been teaching them in such a way that they bring about virtue itself or virtue as a whole. The laws do not provide a moral education that enables the citizen to lead a complete and coherent life of virtue (*Laws* 963a–e). Moreover, it is not simply that the virtues do not fit or work together. As we see from a reading of Books VII and VIII, the virtues can undermine one another. The laws teach a sort of confusion about what virtue is, and as a result of this confusion the laws may come undone. For example, as we have just seen in Books VII and VIII, law can teach a kind of courage. By cultivating physical health and strength, the law enables young citizens to put aside their fears and instills a steady confidence. Along with this confidence, the law promotes a spirited love of victory and a love of honor that enables each citizen to stand firm against pain and fear. But this very courage also emboldens the citizens' erotic hopes and longings. In a city teeming with healthy, strong, and daring young men and women, they are bound to feel erotic passions that overwhelm what the law teaches about the need to resist strong pleasures and hopes.

The Athenian Stranger also shows that the law can promote a kind of courageous moderation that enables lovers to triumph over their own passions, but neither the law-based courage nor the law-based moderation promote practical reason in the fullest sense. Neither enables or even invites the citizen to think through what makes each passion, each desire or aversion, good or bad. Thus, the end of the dialogue alludes to a problem in moral education that was not explicitly acknowledged in Books VII and VIII but is displayed there and later confirmed at the end of the legislation.

Some will argue that the laws will promote practical reason by attaching preludes to all the laws. In Book IV, the Athenian Stranger wins Kleinias's agreement that law ought to speak to citizens in the manner of a doctor who cares for free citizens rather than as a doctor who looks after slaves. The former sort of doctor, he says, persuades his patients to follow his guidance by explaining to them the nature of bodies and how the remedies will treat the patients' diseases (*Laws* 720, 857). Applying this reasoning to their own cases, the free patients willingly follow their doctor's orders. By contrast, the doctor who looks after slaves does not know the nature of bodies. Following written rules, he gives commands to his patients and expects them to obey without understanding or accepting his orders. In order to arrange it so that the laws speak to the citizens in the manner of a free doctor, the Athenian Stranger suggests providing preludes to each law that will explain the reasoning of each law to each citizen. But however much the Athenian Stranger might wish that the citizens could use their own practical reason to understand the purposes of the laws, he knows that the citizens have been raised by a moral education that prevents them from exercising practical reason in regard to their own passions and conduct. As some have noted, the preludes do not appeal simply and directly to reason. They speak very broadly and frequently persuade through praise and blame, in the manner of rhetoric, rather than that of straightforward rational discourse (Laks 1990, 224–25; 1991, 427–28; 2001, 114; also Stalley 1994). Bobonich responds to this by acknowledging that both the preludes and laws speak generally and by claiming that individuals will be compelled to think about particular applications of the preludes and laws in their own lives (Bobonich 2002, 113). But the problem with this suggestion is that many citizens who have learned courage, moderation, and other virtues from the law will not be able or willing to consult and apply practical reason in their own lives. The well-educated citizen strives to follow the law in the manner described in the myth of virtue and will strive to support the divine, noble, and golden law rather than to reason about what is best in their own, particular case.

Speaking up on behalf of the rule of law, one might respond that law must have authority and that law cannot be authoritative if individuals are to be free to consult their own practical reason before deciding whether or how to comply with the law. According to Joseph Raz, this does not require that law exercise authority without reason or without offering us reasons (Raz 1986, 47–48). Rather, law offers "exclusionary" reasons that explain why we should not consult our own judgment regarding certain matters and on certain occasions. In fact, John Finnis openly acknowledges that law tries to "absorb and take over, the 'good citizen's' schema of practical reasoning, and to give it an unquestioned or dogmatic status." He speaks of a moral principle that law should "provide directly applicable and authoritative guidance for the reasonable man and eliminate the need for him to weigh up (as the legislature had to weigh up) the pros and cons of many possible courses of action . . ." (Finnis 1980, 318).

In response to this objection, we could grant that laws are needed and that legal authority necessarily supersedes an individual's own practical reason. But this does not undercut the criticisms of law that emerge from the Platonic account of civic education under law. Considered from the viewpoint of practical reason, obedience to the law requires that one cease deliberating about our many desires and aversions and thus that one sacrifice the very foundation and core of practical reasoning. For if we are not able to weigh for ourselves the "pros and cons" of our passions, we would never acquire either the knowledge or the inner harmony that comes from practical reason.

If this were the Athenian Stranger's last word on moral education under divine law, it would seem that divine law would never be able to produce the complete human virtue and civic and individual happiness that is believed to be the true goal of divine law. Divine law would always fall short of its end. In the *Minos,* Socrates said that law wishes to be the discovery of what is (*Minos* 315a), thus suggesting that law strives to disclose what is without ever fully accomplishing its goal. In Book IV of the *Laws,* the Athenian Stranger says that law is the distribution of intellect (*Laws* 714a). But as we think through divine law's efforts to promote the whole of virtue, it appears that it does not present citizens with a complete account of what that virtue is. Perhaps Plato means to teach in these passages that while the divine lawgiver is perfect, divine law is necessarily imperfect. But this would present us with a great difficulty, for, as we saw in Book I, the serious citizen is able to recognize and identify which code of law is divine only by looking at each code and by considering its goal. The serious citizen believes that the divine code is the one code that aims at the whole of virtue and happiness. If no code aims at such a goal, then it is unclear how any code could be identified and recognized as divine. But this cannot be the Athenian Stranger's last word on the divine law and moral virtue. After all, if neither the laws of Crete and Sparta nor the Athenian Stranger's laws promote practical reason and the whole of virtue, why would the Athenian Stranger regard the latter laws as superior to the former (*Laws* 702a–b)? Why would he later suggest that the lawgiver and the guardians of the law should try to save the laws by learning what the whole of virtue is (*Laws* 964b–65a)?

In order to look into this matter more deeply, we need to consider two arguments that the Athenian Stranger makes during the dialogue. The first is his initial characterization of "virtue as a whole." Early in the dialogue, he claimed that there is such a virtue and that it is "perfect justice" (*Laws* 630a–c). Even though the moral education in Book VII does not include extensive training in justice in its curriculum, this virtue would seem to play a decisive role in the complete virtue of the human being and citizen. And so we must examine what perfect justice is, how citizens come to acquire it, and whether or to what extent it resolves the problem of wandering that the Athenian Stranger identifies at the end of the dialogue. In addition to this, we must also consider the Athenian Stranger's further statements in Book XII indicating that the laws not only need but also might find an "anchor" and a "savior" (*Laws* 961c, 961d). In order to discern what Plato is suggesting about divine law and its ability to achieve its aims, we need to consider what it would mean to save the laws and what would have to be known and done to save them.

Chapter Six

PERFECT JUSTICE AND DIVINE PROVIDENCE

At the start of the dialogue, the Athenian Stranger and Kleinias agree that divine law is the law that aims at the highest end. They say that correct law must aim at the whole of virtue and at the human goods that together with virtue bring happiness to individual citizens and harmony to the city as a whole. But at the end of the dialogue, the Athenian Stranger says that the laws that they have just outlined, the best possible laws, fail to aim at the highest end. Instead of achieving their goal, the laws "wander" (*Laws* 962c–d). The laws, he says, are unstable because they aim at a multitude of virtues rather than at virtue as a whole (*Laws* 962c–d). This is not surprising to those who reflect on the discussion of courage and moderation that is described in Books VII and VIII. In Book VII, we find that young citizens must follow an inflexible regimen in order to resist fear and to develop the disposition that is called "courage." And in Book VIII we find that this courage is bound to awaken an erotic love that threatens the rule of law and the steady virtues that it promotes. In order to curb the dangerous erotic passions, the legislator must persuade young citizens to regard pleasure itself as a great adversary that must always be conquered in order to do what is just and pious and in order to win honor. It seems that law can promote forms of both courage and moderation, but each of these law-bred virtues requires an inflexibility in regard to the passions that is incompatible with a practical reason that consists in calculating which of our pains and pleasures is best.

Yet Kleinias is surprised to hear the Athenian Stranger say in Book XII that the laws fail to aim at a single, coherent goal (*Laws* 963a). From the beginning of the dialogue, he has believed that he knows what virtue as a whole is. And from the beginning of Book IV, he has believed that the laws that they are outlining will aim at that virtue. Kleinias and the Athenian Stranger say from the start of the dialogue that the whole of virtue includes the four virtues courage, justice, moderation, and practical reason. But they also agree that some say this virtue is the "greatest virtue" and that this virtue is "perfect justice" (*Laws* 630c, 643e–44a).

But precisely what do they mean when they speak about perfect justice? Why is one virtue, justice, associated with the whole of virtue? And why say that justice rather than some other virtue, such as moderation or practical reason, is the whole of virtue? Moreover, we need to consider what the Athenian Stranger's remarks near the end of the dialogue about the instability of the laws imply about the law's attempt to promote perfect justice. Does he mean that the laws try but fail to promote perfect justice? Or is it that when the laws promote perfect justice, they nonetheless fail to promote virtue as a whole or at what is supposed to accompany that virtue? In order to clarify what he means when he speaks of perfect justice and whether or to what extent the law aims at it, we need to take a closer look at what perfect justice is and at how it is taught.

When speaking about justice in Book I, the Athenian Stranger refers to justice in two distinct ways. In one respect, it is said to be the whole of virtue, a virtue that includes within it the other three virtues (*Laws* 630c). But he also speaks about it as one of the particular virtues, as a virtue that is distinct and separate from courage, moderation, and practical reason. As one of these particular virtues, justice is the disposition to be equitable in regard to property: a person is just if he or she gives and takes what is owed (*Laws* 632b). But when the Athenian Stranger speaks of "perfect justice," he is referring to a different disposition of the character. Near the start of the dialogue, the Athenian Stranger and Kleinias agree that law should aim at a kind of virtue that is superior to the martial courage that wins victories in foreign wars and also superior to the self-command that allows one to triumph over our base passions. The Athenian Stranger says that the citizen who possesses the virtues courage, moderation, justice, and practical reason deserves more praise than does the citizen who is merely a courageous fighter in battling foreign enemies. The worthiest man is the man who is trusted by his fellow citizens in the course of civil war (*Laws* 630a–b). During civil wars, parties and factions form, alliances shift, and loyalties are tested. As the city breaks down, laws and customs lose their force and many citizens are swept up by fear, anger, and vengeance. In this turmoil, those few who remain unaffected by faction, lawlessness, and the intense passions that engulf the city seem to stand out. These few never exhibit the cowardice, immoderation, injustice, and imprudence that seem commonplace during civil war (*Laws* 630b). Keeping their eyes on what the law established as correct, they rise above partisanship, and they, alone, seem to be especially concerned with the good of the whole community. They are just not only in the sense that they give and take only what is owed according to the law but also because they care about the city as a whole (*Laws* 627c–28a). To have perfect justice, one needs both to care about the common good and to have the courage, moderation, and practical reason that will be needed to care for the city during times of crisis.

To have perfect justice in a city under divine law, one not only must care about the good of the whole city but also must devote oneself to the city's laws. In Book V, the Athenian Stranger describes the best person in the city as the one who best serves the laws throughout his life (*Laws* 729d–e). The "great man in the city" is the one who helps to carry out the laws, even when it requires him to inflict punishments on those who defy the law (*Laws* 730d). He is generous with his possessions and never envies his fellow citizens (*Laws* 730d–31a). The Athenian Stranger says that the great man should not trust his own judgment regarding what is noble and good and just but should honor what is just, whether justice is done by him or by someone else (*Laws* 732a–b). In addition to following the law closely, the just citizen must discern what the lawgiver praises and blames when the lawgiver is making laws. The "more perfect" praise belongs to the citizen who lives in constant obedience to what the lawgiver praises and blames (*Laws* 822e–23a).

Perfect justice seems especially difficult to teach because it is the virtue that requires that we be concerned with the good of others (*Republic* 347d). The law calls on each citizen to endure all of the hardships, fears, pains, and sufferings that are praised (*Laws* 727c). Because this virtue places great demands on the citizen, it is little wonder that many regard it as something that is noble yet difficult and burdensome (*Laws* 718d–19a). In light of the demands that justice places on the citizen, it would seem that the moral education in the *Laws* would make the greatest effort to teach justice to young citizens. In Book I, the Athenian Stranger's first definition of education is that it consists in awakening an erotic desire for citizenship or for ruling and being ruled with justice (*Laws* 643e–44a). If we look to the moral education outlined in Book VII, we find that the legislator would use gymnastic and musical training to promote the other virtues. But if we look carefully at the education that is laid out in Book VII, we find that the Athenian Stranger says nothing about how the virtue justice should be taught. He says that poets must not produce any works that contradict the lawful and just teachings about what is noble or good (*Laws* 801d). But there do not appear to be any teachings or exercises that are intended to instill a distinct passion for justice or a dedication to the common good.

One possibility is that the legislator can lead the citizen to care for the city and its laws through the preludes that precede each of the laws. The Athenian Stranger says that the law should speak to each citizen in the way that a free doctor speaks to citizens when giving them medical advice. The free doctor persuades his patients to obey him by explaining to them the course of diseases and the nature of bodies and by showing them how his orders will lead to their health. But the slaves who give medical attention to other slaves merely take medical advice from written books and simply command slaves who are sick to obey without explaining to their patients why their orders are fitting (*Laws* 720a–e). According to the Athenian Stranger, the legislator should place prefaces or "preludes" before each law that explain the purposes of the law so that the citizens can come to understand and support the laws on their own (*Laws* 722a–23b). In reasoning with the citizens about the purposes of the laws, the preludes may help citizens to discover that the laws benefit them as well as the city as a whole.

In order to provide an example of the sort of prelude he has in mind, he describes a prelude that could precede a law requiring every citizen to marry. The hypothetical prelude would explain to the citizens that every citizen should marry since everyone is moved by an erotic desire for immortality that can be satisfied through having offspring. After pointing to the benefit that accrues to the individual citizen, the prelude adds that it is impious for someone willingly to refrain from marrying and raising children (*Laws* 721b–c). By appealing to each citizen's concern with his own good, this prelude seems to show the prudence inherent in the law. But will every law appeal to every citizen's self-interest? Does every citizen benefit from seeking immortality by procreating offspring? When the Athenian Stranger later describes the actual prelude for the laws regarding marriage, he changes it significantly. The actual prelude declares that it is best for the city that everyone marries a spouse with an opposite background and temperament. It claims that those who are wealthy should marry those who are poor. Those who are impatient and who do things hastily should marry those who are patient and orderly (*Laws* 773b). By nature, says the prelude, we are attracted to what is similar to ourselves (*Laws* 773b6–7). This is reasonable, if each of us wants a share of immortality and if we can pursue this immortality by leaving behind an offspring who is like us. But, the prelude says, if each citizen is permitted to marry whomever he or she desires, then the city will become "uneven" or divided (*Laws* 773b). In order to forestall this unevenness, each citizen should select a spouse in light of what is good for the city rather than in light of what gratifies the individual citizen (*Laws* 773a). Reflecting on the actual prelude, it seems that it appeals to those who are already convinced that what seems good to the individual should be subordinated to what is good for the city. But preludes such as these would not necessarily persuade every individual, especially those who feel a strong erotic love for a beloved, to marry those who differ from themselves for the sake of the city. Yet something must persuade these citizens that they should honor what is just and put aside their "excessive" self-love. Far from teaching perfect justice, the preludes tend to presume some pre-existing desire to subordinate one's own good to that of the city.

If the legislator does not attempt directly to instill public-spiritedness or dedication to the common good through education, then he may promote these things indirectly, through the laws as a whole. The laws place many burdens on the citizens. Because of the character of law itself, all laws are broad and inflexible rules that do not seem to fit every individual in every circumstance. Moreover, civic virtue under divine law places great demands on the citizen. When first discussing the model of a correct education in Book II, the Athenian Stranger says that the educator should try to teach young people to take pleasure in the correct kinds of things (*Laws* 653b–c). But when he outlines the actual laws regarding education in Book VII, he indicates that the citizens should learn to resist both great pains and great pleasures. Virtue will consist in learning to endure the desire for pleasures without gratifying it rather than in learning to enjoy the correct ones (*Laws* 792c–d; also 716c–d). Given our natural desire for pleasure and aversion to pain, citizens are bound to regard these laws as burdens. But some will not regard these burdens as evils but will embrace them in the belief that they are somehow good for them. Precisely because the laws are demanding, they will awaken a desire to serve an end that is difficult yet noble and just. In the *Minos,* Socrates indicates that some codes of law can have such an effect when he compares divine laws to the divine music that was composed by Marsyas and Olympus. In that dialogue, Socrates says that the flute music that was composed by Marsyas and Olympus is widely recognized as divine (*Minos* 318b–c). The musical art differs from many other arts in which the artist carefully gives what is fitting to each object under his or her care. Even though the musical artist will broadcast the same music to all his or her listeners, good music will make a special appeal to those listeners who have good natures. Divine music will move these select listeners deeply, and it will awaken in them a need for the gods (*Minos* 318b). In light of the comparison that Socrates draws between divine music and divine law, he suggests that divine law makes a similar appeal to those citizens who have suitable natures. Just as some people who have good natures are able to recognize good music, some citizens with the appropriate natures will embrace the demands associated with divine law, thinking that they benefit them in some important way (Bruell 1999, 14–15). To such people, divine law would speak with the power of great music; it would awaken in them a longing for the divine. It may be in this respect that education can be said to arouse an erotic love of citizenship or of ruling and being ruled with justice (*Laws* 643e–44a). Insofar as divine law is like divine music, it would not teach perfect justice to the citizens through habituation or instruction, but it would arouse a dedication to perfect justice in the souls of those whose natures are disposed to it.

This possibility may help to overcome a problem regarding law that came to sight in the *Minos*. As Socrates suggests in the *Minos,* a "true" law can be distinguished from a false one insofar as the former is just. But if justice consists in giving everyone what is fitting, then law cannot be just in this respect, for it cannot distribute what is fitting to every individual in every circumstance. What Socrates is suggesting in the *Minos* through his comparison of divine law to divine music is that we might be able to distinguish divine codes of law from less legitimate codes of law by noting how divine codes seem to give what is fitting to citizens with the correct kind of natures. Even if divine codes of law cannot provide each and every citizen with the goods that each needs, their ability to select out those who can be moved by their appeal may set them apart from codes that rarely if ever give what is fitting to any of their citizens.

Justice and Happiness

Even though some citizens may seem to welcome spontaneously the opportunity to serve the city and its laws, the Athenian Stranger notes that it is important for the lawgiver to encourage citizens to believe that the just lead happy lives and that the unjust lead lives of misery. The Athenian Stranger discusses the relation between justice and happiness thematically in two passages of the opening books. In Book I, when the Athenian Stranger describes the goods at which "correct law" aims, he refers to each of the particular virtues as "divine goods." He does not claim that the virtues by themselves bring happiness. Instead, he says that when one has all of the divine goods, one also will acquire the human goods, which are said to be wealth with practical reason, strength, beauty, and health. Those who have both the divine and human goods will be happy (*Laws* 631b–c). In Book II, the Athenian Stranger again discusses the relation between justice and happiness (*Laws* 660e ff.). Here he says that if someone has great goods such as health, wealth, and even immortality but lacks justice and the whole of virtue, he will nevertheless live in misery (*Laws* 661b–c, 662a). But if he has these goods and justice too, then, and only then, will he be happy. In this second formulation, the Athenian Stranger does not declare that having all the divine goods will necessarily supply the citizen with all the human goods and happiness. Rather, he leaves open the possibility that justice is a necessary but not sufficient condition for happiness.

When presented with this ringing praise of justice and correspondingly strong criticism of injustice, Kleinias hesitates to agree that the unjust are always unhappy (*Laws* 661e). Perhaps because he has observed that the just sometimes seem to suffer while the unjust sometimes seem to thrive (*Laws* 899e–900a), he suspects that those who have great wealth, health, courage, tyrannical power, and immortality would be very gratified without needing to concern themselves with justice. To be sure, Kleinias believes that injustice is base and disgraceful. He would not be unjust. But his suspicions about the goods that the unjust appear to enjoy underscore the difficulty of proving that justice is indispensable for happiness. Despite Kleinias's conviction that the unjust can be happy, the Athenian Stranger insists that the just must be persuaded not only that the just are happy but also that only the just are happy. In fact, they must be assured that the unjust are utterly miserable. In saying that the just need this assurance, the Athenian Stranger concedes that he has not yet offered a very strong argument to support it (*Laws* 663d).

Before considering what that argument might be, we should first examine why the Athenian Stranger thinks that it is necessary to assure young citizens that only the just are happy and that all of the unjust are miserable. What prevents the Athenian Stranger from saying that justice is very noble but that it requires great risks and sacrifices, including, at times, the loss of one's happiness and pleasure? One might think that those who are truly just will remain devoted to justice even if it makes them miserable and even if the unjust seem to thrive. But by saying that citizens must be assured that the just are happy and that the unjust are always miserable, the Athenian Stranger suggests not only that citizens need to believe this in order to lead a just life but also that justice itself requires that the just be rewarded and that the unjust be punished.

In order to explain why the Athenian Stranger thinks that the just need to be assured that the just alone are happy, we need to consider more carefully how the morally serious citizen understands the relation between justice and happiness. At the outset of the dialogue, Kleinias agrees that those who have perfect justice or the whole of virtue not only will bring happiness to their city but also will find happiness as individuals (*Laws* 631b–d). In Book III, Megillus agrees that the goal of both the virtuous citizen and the virtuous city is happiness (*Laws* 687a1, 697b). But why should citizens who take justice seriously expect that a thoroughly just life will bring them happiness? How do they know that a just life will not require them to sacrifice their own happiness for something more important, such as the good of the city? After all, perfect justice comes to sight as utterly selfless. Yet when the just are asked to serve the good of the city, they understand that they are not being exploited in the service of something in which they have no share. Ordinarily, justice obliges us to care not for others as such but for those who belong to the political community to which we belong. Justice presents itself as dedication to a common good from which the just may be expected to benefit along with all the other members of the community. According to the Athenian Stranger, our common mistake is to seek our own good individually, without regard to the good of the whole community. Those who are clear-sighted recognize that the best way to pursue our own, individual good is to advance what is good for the city (*Laws* 831e–32b, 875a–d). But beyond expecting justice to bring them reciprocal benefits from the community, the just regard justice as the virtue of the soul. If justice is the perfection of the soul, then it is manifestly good for the soul and necessary for a complete and happy life. Justice thus comes to sight as having two aspects: In one respect, it demands that we devote ourselves to the good of the city as a whole and that we put aside our thoughts about our individual well-being. Yet in another respect, justice also promises that it will provide us with great good things and especially with what is good for the soul of each citizen. The conviction that justice is good for those who are just is strengthened by the belief that the gods have made laws that command us to be just. As the Athenian Stranger points out, the gods make their laws in the spirit of caring fathers who command the citizen to be just so that he or she may be happy (*Laws* 662d–e, 859a).

This is not to say that morally serious citizens devote themselves to justice simply as a means to their own happiness. They will regard justice as something worth doing for its own sake. At the same time, the just know that justice is somehow good for them, and, without calculating about how it helps them, they expect that it will ultimately provide them with their greatest needs. The Athenian Stranger draws attention to the latter expectation in part because morally serious citizens need to believe that the just life is a happy life if they are to dedicate themselves to such a life. In addition, he emphasizes this expectation because justice itself seems to demand that those who are perfectly just come to enjoy a happy life. Justice presents itself not as the sacrifice or exploitation of those who are just but as the core of the best and most complete way of life.

But even if we associate the just life with a life of happiness, we know that the life of the just citizen is not an easy life. From the start of the dialogue, the Athenian Stranger said that the law seeks to provide citizens with a variety of goods beyond the divine goods. The human goods include wealth with prudence, strength, beauty, and health. Even though the Athenian Stranger begins the dialogue saying that those who have the divine goods will also have the human ones, it is not clear how possessing virtue could guarantee that one will have any of the human goods. Later, he adds that human beings always desire immortality, which we pursue through procreating children or through winning lasting fame and honors (*Laws* 721b–c). Again, it seems possible to have many virtues without also having offspring or eternal glory. Moreover, the just must practice virtues that are very austere. Courage and moderation consist in the exercise of self-command and self-denial. Furthermore, virtuous citizens must devote much of their time to honoring the gods and other higher beings. In the speech that the Athenian Stranger says should be given to the first colonists, he says that citizens who are noble and good will have to make great efforts to honor and serve the gods, as well as the daimonic spirits, the heroes, and their ancestors (*Laws* 716b–c). Because they must neglect or sacrifice so many of their own goods and pleasures in service to these higher beings, noble and good citizens come to deserve happiness from the gods (*Laws* 718a3–6). Thus, those who sacrifice their own goods for the sake of the law will deserve happiness as a compensation for their losses. Correspondingly, these same gods will see to it that those who fail to honor those who deserve to be honored will suffer miserably (*Laws* 717c–d). The just believe that they deserve to be compensated for the losses that they incur for the sake of justice because they believe that justice is the core of a happy life. If justice leads to great hardship, justice itself requires that this hardship be overcome. But how will those who sacrifice their own good for the sake of the city or the law be compensated? And how will the unjust come to suffer for their failure to care for the city or to follow the law?

As the Athenian Stranger notes, the citizen looks first to the laws to supply those things that will bring happiness. Through persuasion and punishment, the laws attempt to guide the citizen to what is best. "If the gods are willing," says the Athenian Stranger, "the laws will make our city blessed and happy" (*Laws* 718b, 858b). In order to supply those things that the city seeks in order to be happy, the gods have established laws. Because the laws are just, they not only seek to secure the blessedness and the happiness of the city but also to provide each citizen with what he or she needs to live happily or well. In order to discern the problem that the laws inevitably face, it is useful to consider an alternative to the rule of law. According to the Athenian Stranger, the gods once arranged for human beings to be ruled directly by daimonic spirits who oversaw the daily lives of every human being. Using these many spirits to watch over each individual, Kronos presided over a race of happy human beings (*Laws* 713c–e). It is because these spirits no longer guide us that we must rely on the rule of law as a second best alternative (*Laws* 713e–14a). The law can replace the direct rule of the daimonic spirits because the law is the expression of intellect, and as such it would care for us in both public and private matters (*Laws* 714a; see 650b, 963b). But it is not immediately clear whether or to what extent the law can provide this care, especially for each individual who lives under the law. As we have noted, divine law places significant burdens on each of the citizens. In order to instill virtues such as courage and moderation, the law requires them to endure great pains and to forgo great pleasures. It enjoins them to make many sacrifices in honor to the gods and to their ancestors. But beyond placing these burdens, the character of law itself prevents it from giving each individual what he or she needs to live happily or well. As we have observed, the difficulty is that the law issues orders in very broad and inflexible terms, with the result that it is not always able to give each citizen what is needed in every circumstance (*Laws* 719d–e, 875c–d; *Minos* 317a; *Statesman* 294b–c). Because the law does not discriminate carefully in attending to the needs of individuals, it cannot be counted on to make sure that every citizen receives all the things that he or she needs to live well or to live happily. And if the law cannot be counted on to provide the just with all the goods that are needed, then the law may not be able to promote a tenable way of life for the virtuous. Moreover, insofar as the law fails to give the just what they need to live well, the law would seem to fall short of being just to those citizens in the fullest sense.

The solution to this problem appears to lie in the gods who established the law in the first place. For if the gods can be counted on to reward the just and to punish the unjust, then whatever shortcomings that may be found in the law can be overcome. Even if citizens are no longer supervised by daimonic spirits as they were in the age of Kronos, they still seem to need divine care. In some respects, the Athenian Stranger has been discouraging citizens from relying on the gods to protect them from all evils. In Book VII, he says that the gods nobly endure great pains and pleasures and expect us to endure them likewise (*Laws* 792c–d). Later, he blames those who run into temples seeking divine help instead of coming to the defense of their cities and their families (*Laws* 814b). Nonetheless, he also directs the citizens' attention to how the god who guides the whole is accompanied by the god Justice, who avenges those who forsake divine law (*Laws* 716a). When the Athenian Stranger discusses punishments for those who defy the law, he affirms that the gods exact retribution on those who commit various crimes (*Laws* 871c, 872e–73a). Further evidence that the morally serious citizen expects the gods to support justice is found in Book X, for it is there that the Athenian Stranger attempts to prove that the gods reward the just and punish the unjust. In Book X, the Athenian Stranger alludes to certain indignant young men who are angry at the gods because they believe that the gods have failed to give justice the support that it needs (*Laws* 899d–900b, 905d). The Athenian Stranger attempts to allay their anger by demonstrating that the gods act directly to make sure that the virtuous are happy and the unjust are miserable. According to Kleinias, it makes no small difference that the Athenian Stranger is able to prove that the gods exercise providence over the just and the unjust. He affirms that if many citizens came to believe that the gods do not exist or that they are indifferent to justice, the law would be undermined (*Laws* 887b–c, 890d). In the *Minos*, Socrates compares divine law to divine music. In making this comparison, Socrates notes that divine music reveals those who are in need of gods (*Minos* 318b). Divine law may also be said to reveal those who are in need of gods, inasmuch as divine law promises those who take it seriously that it will provide them with both the divine and human goods (*Laws* 631b–d). But because of the fundamental limitations of law, divine law in itself cannot provide all those goods to all who are just. Consequently, those who take divine law seriously will tend to look to providential gods to provide them with the goods that they expect from divine law. In this way, divine law can be said to reveal those who are in need of the gods.

But on what basis can the Athenian Stranger prove that the gods exercise such providence? What does reason or intellect tell us about the gods and their relation to those who live under the law? In order to learn whether the perfectly just citizen can expect to be happy, we need to examine the Athenian Stranger's demonstrations regarding divine providence in Book X of the *Laws*.

Natural Theology and Divine Providence

By inquiring into the serious citizen's beliefs about the origins and purposes of divine law, the Athenian Stranger finds that those who believe in divine law expect the gods to support the law so that it can achieve its goals. But what does reason indicate about the kind of support that the gods give to justice and the laws? When discussing penalties for crimes against various forms of sacrilege, the Athenian Stranger points out that there are men who have investigated nature and who have reached the conclusion that the gods do not exist or, if they do exist, do not support justice. And by denying that the gods reward the just or punish the unjust, they threaten the belief in the law itself. According to the Athenian Stranger, those who believe that the gods exist "in the way that the laws say they do" never say impious things nor do illegal acts (*Laws* 885b). But some of those who deny that the gods exercise a just providence over human beings evidently become willing to speak impieties and to do unjust things. In response, the Athenian Stranger offers to provide a rational demonstration that the gods exist, support justice, and punish injustice. Even though Kleinias was previously unaware of the existence of such nonbelievers, he finds their disbelief to be so disturbing and so threatening to the rule of law that he strongly encourages the Athenian Stranger to answer them. "It makes no small difference," he says, whether or not they will be able to answer the atheist's claims. In adding that the Athenian Stranger's refutation of the atheists' arguments would be the "noblest and best prelude on behalf of all the laws" (*Laws* 887b–d), Kleinias suggests that such a demonstration would provide the noblest and best reasons for believing and following the laws.

When the Athenian Stranger begins to describe the atheists whom he has in mind, it quickly becomes clear that he is referring to pre-Socratic philosophers who offer a nonreligious account of the coming into being of the whole. According to the Athenian Stranger, their proof against the gods leads young people to lose respect for law and justice. Yet the Athenian Stranger does not oppose the pre-Socratic philosophers on every point. Instead of arguing for traditional gods such as Zeus or Apollo, he points to problems with the pre-Socratic account of the whole. He suggests that he will show that he can give an even more plausible and better reasoned account that supports the existence of gods who are both providential and unwaveringly just. This ground-breaking natural theology consists of three distinct proofs. The first would demonstrate that a god must exist. The second proof would establish that the gods care for human beings, and the third would argue that the gods who care for us cannot be won over by the unjust but will defend us steadfastly against them.

In undertaking the first proof, the Athenian Stranger takes his bearings from the same starting points as the atheistic natural philosophers. The pre-Socratics offer a materialistic account of the coming into being, endurance, and passing away of the whole. According to the pre-Socratics, everything that exists emerges out of the random motion of matter. They say that everything comes into being through nature, chance, and art (*Laws* 888e). By nature, there exist certain elements that collide randomly with one another to form various composite beings, some of which are living and some of which are not. Human beings use art to imitate or adorn or complement those things that come into being by nature and chance. Some of the arts, such as medicine, farming, and gymnastics, serve natural ends, and they can be worthy of some seriousness (*Laws* 889d). But other arts, like most of the political art, falsify or conceal what is natural (*Laws* 889d–e). Those things that citizens like Kleinias and Megillus take most seriously, such as law, justice, and the gods, are among the arts that are simply conventional and not worthy of serious concern.

As the Athenian Stranger responds to the atheists' thesis, he offers a three-part demonstration. The Athenian Stranger's primary point is that the pre-Socratic philosophers' materialism does not explain the enduring character of things. The materialists say that things come into being as the elements randomly collide. But the Athenian Stranger's comments lead us to ask how it is that they keep growing in certain ways. We are able to recognize that things grow because they grow into things with enduring character (*Laws* 839d). We are able to recognize, for example, that puppies grow into dogs because we know the form of a dog. More generally, we are able to recognize the regularity of heavenly motions because we know the principles of geometry. Our knowledge of bodily things presupposes an intelligence that is not derivative from the material elements (Pangle 1976, 1072–73). Even though this is a powerful objection to pre-Socratic philosophy, the Athenian Stranger does not dwell on it. His reticence may be due to the consideration that if he were to speak at length about the existence of enduring ideas, he would necessarily call into question the powers of the gods. For if everything comes into being, persists, and passes away in accordance with the ideas, then there is a lasting order which the gods do not control. The gods would only manage things with natures that the gods cannot change.

The second part of the first proof concerns the motions that are discernable among the heavenly beings. This proof takes the form of a conversation between the Athenian Stranger who speaks for the three interlocutors and an imagined atheistic natural philosopher. According to the pre-Socratic view, matter is in motion throughout the cosmos. The Athenian Stranger would counter the pre-Socratic philosopher by asking how this motion can be explained. The Athenian Stranger begins this second part of the first demonstration by describing ten different kinds of motion. Of these motions, the final two are the most important for the proof. The first of these is the motion that moves other things but not itself, and the second is the motion that moves both itself and other things as they come into being and pass away (*Laws* 894b). According to the Athenian Stranger, the motion that moves itself and other things is the fundamental motion. It is the first motion both in power and in time, and the cause of all other motions. Looking to the argument made by the materialists, the Athenian Stranger says that most of them say that "all the things that come into being once somehow stood still together" (*Laws* 895a6–b1). If there once was rest, he reasons, then something must have initiated motion. Since there must have been a first motion in order for composite beings to be formed, that first motion is older than anything bodily. And since this first motion is older than body and because it rules body, it is of a higher rank than body. Since we say that things that move themselves are living, this first motion is life itself. And since life is synonymous with soul, the first motion is soul (*Laws* 895c). Consequently, the Athenian Stranger argues that the materialists' account of the whole implies that soul is older than body, that soul rules body, and thus that soul outranks the body.

In addition to its failure to account for the coming into being of intellect, the attempt to provide an entirely materialistic account of the whole falters because it cannot account for the first motion. The materialist could say in response that there is no first motion but instead there is an infinite regress of motions. But such a response leaves the beginnings of the cosmos unexplained. If we say that there is an endless succession of causes, then we say that we do not have a complete account of the whole. If the beginning of motion is obscure, then the materialistic philosopher cannot exclude the possibility that some god is the source of all motion.

In this part of the demonstration, the Athenian Stranger focuses on the character of the soul that initiated subsequent motions. The Athenian Stranger says that whatever is the cause of motion is alive and that whatever has life is soul. He reasons that since soul is the cause of all moving things, soul must be the cause not only of what is good, noble, and just but also of what is evil, base, and unjust. If the same soul would not be the cause of both good and evil, then there must be two souls or two kinds of soul. If the gods are necessarily good, then soul, as such, is not divine. Instead, soul would become godlike only when it is combined with intellect. Insofar as the divine soul is always opposed by the soul that is not divine, the divine is not omnipotent. The Athenian Stranger demonstrates the predominance of the divine kind of soul by pointing out that heavenly bodies have a regular, circular motion.[1] This regularity indicates that the heavenly bodies are moved by a soul that has intellect and that follows principles that are knowable by intellect. As the Athenian Stranger notes, circular motion is an image of the intellect and can be worshiped as a god (*Laws* 898a). There are, however, difficulties with this proof. If the Athenian Stranger has argued that soul is prior to body, he has not proven that all soul is alike. There is no proof that the motion that initiates movement throughout the whole is the same sort of intelligent motion that is able to apprehend motion as such. Thus, the Athenian Stranger has not yet offered a proof that this soul has intellect or a will that is analogous to human will. The Athenian Stranger defines soul in terms of what is common to all souls, but he goes on to attribute to all souls the highest function of the soul, the intellect (Mayhew 2008; Pangle 1976, 1072–76; Stalley 1983, 171–73).

On the basis of the Athenian Stranger's first proof of the existence of a god, it seems that we cannot account for the motions and the endurance of the whole on this basis of materialism alone. The whole is remarkably intelligible, and both heavenly and earthly beings seem to be governed by intelligible principles that are not reducible to the arbitrary mixing of elements. Leaving aside the difficulties with the proofs that we have noted, the Athenian Stranger draws the conclusion that the source of all motion must be a soul that is intelligent and purposive. But even if one accepts such a conclusion, one must recognize that the Athenian Stranger has still not proven the existence of gods like Zeus or Apollo who care about individual human beings, cities, and laws. Nor has he proven the existence of gods who punish the unjust and reward the just. The next two proofs will address these crucial matters.

The Second Proof

The Athenian Stranger's first demonstration in Book X includes a dialogue between himself and a pre-Socratic philosopher. Their greatest disagreement concerns how seriously the philosopher should take the role that soul plays in relation to body and bodily motion. In the second demonstration, the Athenian Stranger converses instead with an imagined interlocutor, an indignant young man who is disturbed by evidence that the gods do not care about human beings at all and thus that the gods fail to support justice. The proof that the gods exercise a just providence rests not on arguments concerning the origins or character of motions but on what the imagined indignant youth believes regarding the gods and their virtues.[2]

In this proof, the Athenian Stranger asks the indignant youth whether or not the gods have courage and intellect (*Laws* 900d). Kleinias is able to speak for the indignant young man because he shares some of the young man's beliefs about the gods and their virtues and concerns. They agree that if the gods have these virtues, then the gods are not soft or careless or lazy (*Laws* 901c, 901e).[3] The Athenian Stranger further asks the indignant young man if the gods know all that human beings may know and if the gods supervise the whole. Speaking again for the indignant youth, Kleinias agrees that if the gods supervise the great things, which are difficult to manage, surely they also supervise the small ones, which can be managed with relative ease. The gods, he concludes, would not neglect the small things out of indolence or ignorance (*Laws* 901a–2b).

Turning his attention to the small things that the gods oversee, the Athenian asks whether human beings are among all living things the most reverent toward the gods (*Laws* 902b). When Kleinias answers on behalf of the indignant youth that they are, the Athenian Stranger argues that all living things are possessions of the gods. Therefore, it follows that the gods who possess all living things surely possess those living things that are most reverent toward the gods. And since the gods care for all of their possessions, they surely care for those possessions that revere them the most. Now, since the gods are the most careful and best supervisors, they presumably work to support justice, making sure that the just are gratified and the unjust are punished. And yet a critical participant could point out that those who own possessions sometimes consume or discard their possessions when they are not needed. How do we know that the gods put each of us to good use? After all, the Athenian Stranger has said that human beings are the playthings of the gods (*Laws* 644d, 803c). If we are the toys of the gods, then we cannot assume that they take us so seriously that they make sure that the just are made happy and the unjust made miserable.

In order to show that the gods truly care for us, the Athenian Stranger likens the gods to experts in various arts. Good doctors, he argues, care for the whole body. If they were to neglect small matters, the whole body would not be healthy (*Laws* 902d). If the gods practice an art whose goal is to care for each of us like a doctor cares for the body of each patient, then it follows that the gods would care for each of the human beings whom they own. The Athenian Stranger also compares the gods to pilots, generals, household managers, and statesmen who will fail if they neglect those things that are few and small (*Laws* 902d–e). Pilots can be expected to care for the vessels and crews that are under their care. But even the best doctors do not exercise great care over every hair on one's head or over every drop of one's blood. Nor do competent generals provide every protection for every soldier under their commands. Just as a doctor is willing to cut or burn certain parts of a patient's body in order to save the patient's life, a general is willing to endanger some soldiers in order to defeat the enemy or to save the army. Even experts in household management who look after all their possessions do not devote much care to things that are of little use to them. Finally, the Athenian Stranger compares the gods to stonemasons who claim that large stones do not lie well without small stones to support them. He says that one must not criticize the gods by saying that they are inferior to mortal craftsmen (*Laws* 902e). But, once again, we must ask whether good stonemasons do not sometimes reject stones that are not suitable to the walls or other structures that they are building.

On the whole, this second demonstration rests on several questionable and unexamined premises. The Athenian Stranger begins from the supposition that the gods own us, that the gods are not only our owners but also expert and virtuous artisans who use us in their arts. But this beginning seems to presume what it sets out to prove. If we begin from the assumption that the gods own us, then we have already granted that the gods take some interest in us. The argument fails to consider the possibility that the gods do not own us because the gods have no use for nor interest in us. We count as possessions only those things that seem good to us (Xenophon *Oeconomicus* 1.7). We might therefore be at the gods' disposal without the gods counting us among their belongings. Now, the fact that we revere the gods may count in our favor, but it also might not. After all, the expert artisan is indifferent to how his implements and other objects that he manages feel about him. Yet even if we grant that the gods own us, consider us valuable, and use us in their art, we do not know that when the gods use us in their art they always do so in a way that results in the happiness of the just and the misery of the unjust. Consequently, it seems that the proof that the gods care about us does not prove that they support the just and oppose the unjust.

The Myth Regarding the Justice of the Gods

The Athenian Stranger evidently recognizes that this demonstration has not proven everything that needs to be proven in order to refute the atheists and to show that the gods support justice, for he says that some "mythical incantations" (*epodoi muthou*) are still needed (*Laws* 903b1–2).[4] It is in this supplementary myth that the Athenian Stranger makes direct statements about how the gods uphold justice. The Athenian Stranger says that the indignant youth has not observed how our lives have a purpose. He says that he who oversees the whole rules it with a view to its safety and virtue (*Laws* 903b). In the whole, each part suffers and contributes what it can. Rulers have been set up to watch over the experience of each part so that there is "perfection to the last detail" (*Laws* 903c1). Everything, he says, comes into being so that the whole may be happy. Addressing the youth, the Athenian Stranger says, "You have come into being for the sake of the whole, not it for the sake of you" (*Laws* 903c). This suggests that if the just suffer, it is because it is somehow better for the cosmos that the just endure some evils. And if the unjust seem to flourish, it is likewise necessary for the good of the whole. But is this just? In order to address this question, the Athenian Stranger also says that everything is put together by the divine artisan so that what has become better goes to a better place while what has become worse goes to a worse one. In this context, he says that everything takes place according to what is fitting for each thing (*Laws* 903d), thus assuring us that each person or thing in the cosmos gets what it deserves. But this once again raises the question why the just sometimes suffer and the unjust sometimes do not.

In order to explain how the gods support the just and punish the unjust, the Athenian Stranger refers to the god who oversees the whole as "our king" (*Laws* 904a). He says that this kingly god recognizes that everything that takes place does so through the soul, that souls have virtues and vices, and that the soul is sempiternal. Moreover, he saw that what is good in the soul is beneficial by nature and that what is bad in the soul is harmful. Thus, he arranged the whole so that virtue will triumph and vice will be defeated. When everything comes into being, it moves to a place that is fitting (*Laws* 903d).

According to these mythic incantations, our wishes are responsible for what kind of person we become. The Athenian Stranger says that our desires and what is in the soul "nearly" determine what sort of person we are or what character we have "for the most part" (*Laws* 904b–c). And without being asked, Kleinias responds that this is likely (*Laws* 904c5). Having argued that we are morally responsible for our actions and dispositions, the Athenian Stranger says that because all things that have souls possess within themselves the cause of their changing or transformation, they are moved according to the "order and law of destiny." This law of destiny states that whenever each individual (voluntarily) becomes unjust, he or she descends to the depths, to places such as the one that the many call "Hades," both when he or she is alive and when the body and soul are separated. When, on the other hand, a soul gets a share of divine virtue, it is carried along a path to a better place. After speaking about those people who gain a share in "divine virtue," the Athenian Stranger quotes Odysseus regarding the slaying of the suitors, saying that "this is the justice of the gods who hold Olympus" (*Laws* 904c–e). Appealing to the indignant young man's desire to see the unjust punished and the just rewarded, he says that according to the law of destiny the vicious soul is moved to dwell among other vicious souls, and in life and in death suffers and does vicious things. Thus, if the unjust do not seem to suffer sufficiently in this life, the god who oversees the whole makes sure that the unjust suffer in the next. The Athenian Stranger says that no one who is unfortunate can boast that he has escaped "the justice of the gods." No matter what, he claims, you will pay the appropriate retribution (*Laws* 905a). The Athenian Stranger tells the indignant youth who doubts that the gods care for human beings that he has failed to recognize how impious people who seem happy make a contribution to the whole. But without knowing this, he says, one could not give a reasoned account (*logon*) of happiness or of an unhappy fortune (*Laws* 905b–c).

These incantations should appeal to those who are indignant at the gods' apparent willingness to allow the just to suffer and the unjust to thrive. As he says at the end of the passage, we would need to know that these things are true if we seek a rational confirmation that the just lead happy lives. Yet there are many questions about the claims made in the incantations. Among the most important is that the Athenian Stranger does not describe in what respect the gods make the whole "good." But failing to provide a single example of how any of the parts relate to the whole leaves it far from clear how it would benefit the whole for a just person to suffer unjustly or how it could help the whole for the unjust to thrive. Moreover, the myth, by itself, does not demonstrate that souls continue to exist after they are separated from the body. The Athenian Stranger says that soul must endure in order for the cosmos to remain in order. But this does not prove that individual souls endure after the death of the individual body. Despite such limits, Kleinias will accept the myth on behalf of the indignant youth because the myth reflects the morally serious citizens' beliefs about the gods and about the relation between justice and happiness. Looking solely at what is said in the myth, it seems that the principal reason for believing that individual souls exist after death is that this would sometimes be necessary if the just are to receive their just rewards and if the unjust are to receive their just punishments.[5]

The Athenian Stranger concludes these mythic incantations by saying that one would have to know that they are true in order to know that the gods make the just happy. He indicates that we need to consider more closely whether these incantations provide a plausible account of how the gods support justice. But before undertaking that investigation, it is useful to complete our summary of the Athenian Stranger's theology in Book X by turning to its third part.

The Third Proof

The third demonstration in Book X shows that the gods who care for their possessions and who reward the just and punish the unjust cannot be won over by the unjust through prayers or sacrifices or other means. In this third proof, the Athenian Stranger's argument is even more vehement and more poetic than the one in the second proof. In this demonstration, the gods are again compared to experts in the arts, as they were in the second. But this time they are also said to be experts who guard their charges against terrible and intractable enemies. He says that the gods are like doctors who fight many diseases in the body and like farmers who plant their crops despite adverse weather during unfavorable seasons. In addition to these examples, he also compares the gods to dogs who guard flocks of sheep from wolves (*Laws* 905e–6a). Throughout this third demonstration, the Athenian Stranger emphasizes that the gods themselves face powerful adversaries who would introduce and perpetuate disorder. In the previous proofs, the gods presided over a beautiful and harmonious whole. In this proof, the Athenian Stranger says that there are more evil things than good in the cosmos. Here, the gods must display an amazing vigilance to confront enemies who wage a deathless battle against the gods, the daimonic spirits, and their possessions (*Laws* 906a). In this battle, he says, the gods, the daimonic spirits, and we human beings are threatened by injustice, hubris, and imprudence, but justice, moderation, and prudence can save us. We see the forces of disorder at work in those who believe that it is possible to get more than their share without paying a penalty. The attempt to get more than one's share is evident in disease in bodies, plagues in seasons, and injustice in cities and regimes (*Laws* 906c). The gods are hard pressed by these dangerous adversaries, and they can be counted upon because they are too noble to betray those over whom they have charge.

As moving as this demonstration may be, questions remain about the care that the gods are able to give to each of us. If the gods are hard pressed to withstand the attacks of their adversaries, they might need to sacrifice some of their possessions to protect the whole. Moreover, the third proof contradicts the claim made in the myth that the whole is a common good in which everything contributes to its harmonious order. For in this proof, injustice is a permanent threat and obstacle to the harmony that the gods seek to establish. Indeed, the unjust sometimes seem to hold their ground, escaping from the punishments that they may be said to deserve.

In the three demonstrations, the Athenian Stranger has shown that the atheistic, pre-Socratic philosophers have not disproved the existence of the gods. Using their premises, he can provide a rational proof that the visible gods exist. The heavenly beings seem to be guided by an intelligent soul. The Athenian Stranger has also argued that if the gods own us, and if the gods are courageous and prudent, then they must be diligent owners who do not neglect us. According to the third proof, they are not only expert artisans but also loyal guardians who would never betray those whom they rule to their mutual enemies. But even if we grant that the gods own us and that the gods have courage, moderation, practical reason, and intellect, we do not find anything in the demonstrations proper that proves that the gods lead every just individual to happiness or that the gods lead every unjust person to misery. The allusions to divine providence regarding the lives of the just and the unjust appear only in the mythic incantations that appear to supplement the reasoned demonstrations concerning the gods. Given the importance of offering a demonstration that the gods support justice directly, why does the Athenian Stranger relegate the claim that the gods reward the virtuous and punish the unjust to a part of the proof that consists in mythical incantations rather than to one of the three actual demonstrations?

Moral Responsibility and Just and Rational Gods

The principal reason why the Athenian Stranger does not supply such arguments in Book X comes to sight when we consider the arguments that he makes in Books V and IX about justice and moral responsibility. Earlier in the dialogue, the Athenian Stranger argued that the unjust should not be blamed for their crimes. At the start of Book V, the Athenian Stranger describes how citizens should honor their own souls. While praising the spirited citizen who helps to punish those who break the law, the Athenian Stranger cautions that "no man is ever voluntarily unjust." The Athenian Stranger reasons that no one wishes to do harm to his own soul (*Laws* 731c). Consequently, no one would knowingly choose to do injustice if he recognized that injustice does the greatest harm to his own soul (*Laws* 731d). Based on this reasoning, the Athenian Stranger concludes that injustice is involuntary. He takes this argument so seriously that he repeats it at the outset of Book IX, where he takes up the penal code for the new colony (*Laws* 860d).

The Athenian Stranger's thinking about the involuntary character of injustice seems to be at odds not only with the myth in Book X but also with the thinking of the ordinary, morally serious citizen who expects the unjust to suffer retribution for their crimes. Bearing this in mind, it may seem that when the Athenian Stranger speaks about the involuntary character of injustice, he is looking at it from the point of view of the Socratic philosopher rather than from that of the morally serious citizen (e.g., Pangle 2009, 459). But the Athenian Stranger's remarks about moral responsibility also follow from the beliefs of someone who regards justice as a virtue and as a great good. As we have noted, the Athenian Stranger has appealed all along to his interlocutors' beliefs that justice is a virtue of the soul and thus a great good for those who are just. The serious citizen does not regard justice merely as a means to his own gratification. He would do what is just even if he had to sacrifice his own good to do so. At the same time, a dedicated citizen also believes that justice is good for him, and he acts justly in the belief that it is necessary for leading a happy life. What is most important, the just citizen believes that the gods have established laws so that the just might be happy. If the just citizen were to reflect on the implications of his belief that justice is a great good, then he should recognize that injustice does not benefit the unjust. Not wishing to harm themselves, the unjust unwittingly bring great harm on themselves. The unjust suffer from opinions that are "diseased" (*Laws* 854b–c). Considering how the unjust suffer because of their crimes, the thoughtful citizen should no longer feel anger at those who are unjust. Following this reasoning, the Athenian Stranger argues that no one deserves to suffer retribution for being unjust. The legislator may need to make the unjust suffer to compensate the victims of crimes for their losses (*Laws* 857a). He says that the legislator should punish criminals because the fear of further punishment can make them more moderate or at least less wicked (*Laws* 854d). But the unjust do not need to pay for having done injustices since injustice harms their own souls and deprives them of happiness. When those who seek retribution say that the unjust should be deprived of those things that make them happy and that the unjust should be made miserable, they implicitly grant that criminals act unjustly in the expectation that doing unjust things will make them happy. Like the unjust, those who call for retribution forget that justice is supposed to be a great good and that injustice is supposed to be a great evil for the unjust. But the Athenian Stranger does not forget the fundamental premise of the just man. He remembers that the gods established the laws for the good of the just citizen. He says that the unjust man is like the man who possesses bad things and that this man "is pitiable in every way, and it is permissible to pity such a man when his illness is curable . . ." (*Laws* 731d). It is true that the Athenian Stranger says that those who are incurably unjust should be put to death, but he says that they should be executed out of pity for their wretchedness rather than out of vengeance (*Laws* 731d).

This reasoning calls into question what the Athenian Stranger says in the mythical incantations regarding the justice of the gods. In the myth, he says that the ostensibly all-powerful god who oversees the whole holds each of us responsible for the sort of person whom we become and for our virtues or vices. This god punishes injustice and rewards virtue by establishing a law of destiny that takes each unjust person to a low, miserable region and each virtuous person to a higher one. This, he says, is the inescapable "justice of the gods." But when reflecting on the claim that justice is good for those who are just and that injustice brings harm to the souls of the unjust, the Athenian Stranger argues that those who are both rational and just must conclude that injustice is involuntary. Because the unjust do not profit from their crimes, the call for retribution is unnecessary and incoherent. The Athenian Stranger's arguments about moral responsibility suggest that gods who are both rational and just would not think it just to inflict additional penalties on the unjust in this life or in the next.

In addition to these arguments, the Athenian Stranger's whole inquiry into the origins and purposes of law calls into question what is said about moral responsibility in the myth regarding the justice of the gods. According to the myth, the god holds us responsible for the kind of people whom we become because our wishes or desires determine our characters. But the Athenian Stranger's inquiry into law shows that law is taken seriously because it is what shapes our wishes and desires and what determines the kind of people whom we become. Throughout the dialogue, the Athenian Stranger describes how the political art can be used to shape the character of those who live under the law (*Laws* 650b). Especially in Book VII, he emphasizes how ostensibly minor habits and beliefs that are acquired in our youth decisively shape the character that we acquire. If law and moral education are as important as citizens such as Kleinias and Megillus claim they are, then the myth regarding the justice of the gods relies on a mistaken view of moral responsibility.

One might say on behalf of the god in the myth that our character is affected not only by law or education but also by what is in the soul by nature. The Athenian Stranger admits in Book II and Book IX that some will not accept what the law intends to teach. Along with law and education, nature, too, determines the kind of people whom we become. But it seems to be as problematic to hold us responsible for our natures as it is to blame us for our upbringing. At the start of Book IX, the Athenian Stranger says that those who have difficulty learning from the laws have "tough" natures (*Laws* 854e; also 875b). When he speaks about those who have good natures, he attributes this not to choice but to a "divine dispensation" (*Laws* 642d–e, 875c). He may mean that the dispensation of intellect or a good nature to some rather than to others can be called a kind of divine providence. But reason suggests that those who receive such a dispensation can have done anything to merit receiving it. More generally, it seems that if we were able to choose our natures, the Athenian Stranger could still point out that insofar as each of us wants to avoid what is harmful and do what is best, no one will want to have a bad nature. Unable to choose either our nurturing or our natures, we seem to be incapable of choosing the wishes and desires that are said to determine our characters by the god in the myth of the gods' justice.

Some might reply to this line of argument that nature may urge us to do what we believe will make us happy. Law may establish habits and may urge us to do what the law praises. But, they say, we are still free to do what is noble. Some act nobly not because they believe that it will make them happy or because the law has disposed them to act nobly but because they wish to do what is noble for its own sake. It may be argued that if some choose to do what is noble, then they do so voluntarily. Thus, when the desire to do what is noble leads us to act justly, our actions are voluntary. Analogously, our decision to disregard what is noble and to act ignobly and unjustly would also seem to be a voluntary act.

Among the witnesses that the Athenian Stranger can bring forward to support the counterargument that we always do what we believe is best and what we believe will make us happy are the myths that are told about the gods. According to those myths, the gods themselves do not believe that those who act nobly care solely about doing what is noble. Otherwise, the gods would not reward those who are virtuous with happiness in this life or in the next (e.g., *Republic* 330d–31a, 363c–e; *Laws* 904c–e). If the gods who are spoken of in these myths thought that those who act nobly sought only to do noble things, then these gods would conclude that the noble things are their own rewards. Moreover, if these gods thought that those who are noble sought only to do what is noble and if these same gods wished to confer some benefit on the noble in the afterlife, then they would give those noble men and women who have died further opportunities to do what is noble in the afterlife. The myths would say that when the virtuous die they are rewarded with fresh opportunities to be courageous, moderate, just, and prudent. And they would say that when those who lack virtue die they are unable to do noble things. But the myths that are ordinarily accepted by citizens such as Kleinias and Megillus claim that those who live unjust lives suffer in the afterlife and that those who live virtuously do not suffer in the afterlife. Even though the Athenian Stranger raises doubts about the coherence and validity of such myths, he could point to them to show that even they support the principle that we always do what we believe will bring us happiness. And insofar as this principle is affirmed, the Athenian Stranger will have strengthened his further claims that no one is voluntarily unjust and that no one deserves to suffer retribution so that he may pay for his injustice.

Following this same reasoning, we must ask if rational and just gods would provide the just with the support that they need to devote themselves to justice. If we begin from the premise that no one is voluntarily unjust, then we must ask why just and rational gods would believe that the just deserve to be rewarded for doing what is just. For if justice is the whole of virtue and the greatest good for the soul, then those who sacrifice other goods for the sake of justice are not sacrificing what is most important to them. No matter what the just may lose in acting justly, they nonetheless acquire the greatest good for the soul. As we have noted, those who are just are not necessarily happy. In order to be happy, they will need not only the divine goods but also the human ones. And they may have fears or hopes that are not fully allayed or gratified by the law. But their unhappiness in itself would not give them grounds for claiming that they deserve further rewards. If they are just, then they should be consoled by the great good that they enjoy. If the gods would not exact retribution on the unjust for mistakenly harming themselves, neither would the gods reward the just for having benefitted themselves by doing what is just and by developing a just disposition. The morally serious citizen believes that justice is the whole of virtue and is thus necessary for happiness. Bearing this in mind, this citizen should recognize that the difference between the just and the unjust citizen is that the former is more clear-sighted or more fortunate than the latter regarding what is best. In light of these considerations, it seems that a rational and just god would conclude that justice does not require either exacting retribution on the unjust or giving rewards to the just. Such a god might urge human beings to be just and to eschew injustice. But it seems that such a god would not give the additional supports to justice that the just often seek and that divine law appears to need to sustain the complete virtue of its citizens.

Involuntary Injustice and the Lack of Self-Control

In Book V and again at the start of Book IX, the Athenian Stranger argues that no one is voluntarily unjust. Yet in some subsequent passages in Book IX, he suggests that under some circumstances injustice can be understood as a voluntary act. If the Athenian Stranger revises his thinking in Book IX because he discerns that some forms of injustice are involuntary, then he may have discovered some reason why we may deserve retributive punishment if we do injustice. In order to learn more precisely what the Athenian Stranger is thinking in Book IX, we need to take a closer look at his arguments regarding moral responsibility in Book IX.

The Athenian Stranger begins Book IX by observing that not everyone will be able to develop the moral virtues that the law tries to teach. Because punishments will be needed, the Athenian Stranger begins to lay out the penal code. At the start, the Athenian Stranger characterizes injustice as a sickness (*Laws* 850d; cf. 720a–e). He says that criminals should be told that they do injustice because of a curse on their families that can be traced back to an ancestor who failed to expiate an ancient crime (*Laws* 854b). The Athenian Stranger recommends that the unjust be punished only to the extent that is needed to deter them from further crimes. A few lines later, he says that they should also be made to pay restitution for any property damage that they cause. Each criminal, he says, should be made to pay double the cost of what he or she has stolen or destroyed (*Laws* 857a). But Kleinias objects to this suggestion. He says that those who steal or damage sacred objects should pay more than those who steal other things (*Laws* 857b), evidently on the grounds that they exhibit great insolence.

In response to this objection, the Athenian Stranger draws out some of the fundamental differences between his understanding of law and that of Kleinias. He begins by reminding Kleinias that they have compared law-givers to doctors who come close to philosophizing as they instruct their patients about the nature of bodies and the course of diseases. He says that if a doctor who practices medicine on the basis of experience rather than reason were to observe how the "philosophic" doctor treats patients, the former would reproach the latter and would say that the sick are being educated rather than doctored (*Laws* 857c–d). At this point, Kleinias agrees with the reproach made by the "practical" doctor and wonders if the laws that they are outlining constitute the education of the citizens rather than lawgiving (*Laws* 857e).

In voicing this objection, Kleinias raises serious doubts about the Athenian Stranger's understanding of the law. He believes that law ought to punish rather than to instruct the wicked. In response to Kleinias's misgivings, the Athenian Stranger appeals to Kleinias's conviction that the gods do not rule us like tyrants who give us written commands and then walk off. Instead, the gods give us laws that would rule us like a caring and intelligent father and mother (*Laws* 859a1–4). He says that the legislator who truly understands the purposes of the laws would show that the laws are coherent (*Laws* 858e7–59a1). Because Kleinias expects law to exact retribution on the unjust rather than to instruct them, Kleinias is not yet a legislator. It is for this reason that the Athenian Stranger says that they are not yet legislators, even though it is likely that they will become legislators (*Laws* 859c).

Having pointed to differences between Kleinias and himself, the Athenian Stranger explores how they understand the nobility of justice. He begins by winning Kleinias's agreement that those whose souls are just are truly noble. When he asks Kleinias if all just things are noble, Kleinias agrees. But the Athenian Stranger observes that they contradict themselves when they say that those who commit grave injustices should suffer shameful penalties (*Laws* 860b). This contradiction or disharmony, he says, is typical of "the many" (*Laws* 860c). They would not contradict themselves, he suggests, were they to say that every legal penalty is somehow noble, in the way that every single thing we endure while undergoing an education is noble. By comparing punishment to education, the Athenian Stranger suggests that injustice is rooted in ignorance about what is best.

After noting this contradiction in Kleinias's understanding of punishment, the Athenian Stranger reaffirms his earlier statement that no one is voluntarily unjust (*Laws* 860d–e). He then suggests that Kleinias and Megillus might object to this thesis, and Kleinias answers that they do, indeed (*Laws* 861a). Rather than try to persuade them to abandon altogether their belief that some are voluntarily unjust, the Athenian Stranger says that he will attempt to draw his own distinction between voluntary and involuntary injustice (*Laws* 860e–61a, 861d). In his first attempt to draw such a distinction, he says that those who do not intend to do harm to others but who do so may be said to inflict an injury, but they do not voluntarily do injustice (*Laws* 862a). Actions are unjust if they are undertaken by someone with an unjust disposition (*Laws* 862b). It follows from this that those whose dispositions are just never do injustices. If they harm others, they inflict injuries. According to the Athenian Stranger, the law should teach and compel the unjust never again to do injustice voluntarily (*Laws* 862d). But this account of the difference between injury and injustice does not make clear how some injustices would be voluntary, since injustice consists in having an unjust disposition, which is not something that we are obviously free to choose for ourselves. Because the Athenian Stranger's first attempt to distinguish between injustice and justice does not suggest that some forms of injustice are voluntary, Kleinias complains that they must say more to clarify the distinction between voluntary and involuntary injustice (*Laws* 863a).

In response to Kleinias's request for a distinction between voluntary and involuntary injustice, the Athenian Stranger offers a second account of the distinction between justice and injustice. In this second account, he identifies injustice with the lack of self-control and justice with self-control. He says that when passions such as anger, envy, pleasure, and fear dominate the soul, then this is injustice. But when the soul is ordered so that the passions obey the opinion about what is best, this is now said to be justice (*Laws* 863e–64a). According to this formulation, it does not matter whether the opinion about what is best is based on an individual's own knowledge of what is best or on a correct opinion that has been established by the law. It does not even matter whether the opinion about what is best is correct or mistaken (*Laws* 864a1–5). Justice consists in the passions submitting to some reasoning or some authoritative opinion about what is best.

By identifying injustice with the passions overcoming either reason or authoritative opinions, the Athenian Stranger raises the possibility that someone can believe that something is best and yet not do it because he or she is overcome by the passions. Since the Athenian Stranger raises this possibility while discussing the distinction between voluntary and involuntary injustice, we might infer that this argument allows that someone could believe that something is unjust and yet could nonetheless choose to do it. But the Athenian Stranger never quite concedes this. When speaking about those who act unjustly out of anger, he says that those who act immediately out of anger do so involuntarily, but those who harbor their anger for a long time before they act are asserted to be "somewhere between voluntariness and involuntariness" (*Laws* 867a, 878b). Why does the Athenian Stranger hesitate to affirm that their actions are voluntary when it is possible for us to do things that are unjust voluntarily?

In order to understand the Athenian Stranger's hesitation, we need to consider what he says about the passions that sometimes overcome a person's beliefs about what is best. According to the Athenian Stranger's earlier remarks about the passions, each of our passions is accompanied by certain beliefs about what is best. In Book I, he says that the passions are imprudent counselors that need to be corrected by reasoning (*Laws* 644c). Again, when describing practical reason in Book III, the Athenian Stranger does not describe the passions as thoughtless drives or instincts that bear no relation to reason. Instead, he compares them to members of a great multitude who meet in an assembly in order to listen to the better part of the soul (*Laws* 689a–c). The image suggests that the reasoning part should rule the passions in a "political" manner, through persuasion rather than through force. The Athenian Stranger says that anger, for example, is "quarrelsome and combative" and that it overcomes us with "unreasoning violence" (*Laws* 864a–b). When he says that anger overcomes us with "unreasoning violence," he means that it pushes aside and disregards the part of the soul that reasons about what is best. But in saying that it is a "quarrelsome and combative" passion, the Athenian Stranger indicates that it is still accompanied by quarrelsome and combative beliefs that supplant our reasoning or calculation about what is best. Even when the passions overcome us, we are not without any opinions at all.

The Athenian Stranger sheds light on how passion "overcomes" the reasoning part of the soul when he reflects on the differences between how we speak about passion and ignorance. While we sometimes say that someone is overcome by passion, we do not say that someone has been overcome by ignorance (*Laws* 863d). The Athenian Stranger points this out not only to show that we tend to identify ourselves with the part of the soul that reasons about what is best but also to note that when strong passions prevail, they override the parts of the soul that reason about what is best. Yet when we suffer from ignorance, we do not say that ignorance has overcome us because ignorance, as such, cannot override or disregard rational knowledge. Thus, if we are overcome by passion, it is because we are not able to consult the part of the soul that reasons about what is best. Instead, we follow the passions and the imprudent beliefs about what is good or bad that accompany the passions. Under the influence of these tyrannical passions and the beliefs that attend them, we are not free to choose what our character will be or whether we will act justly or unjustly.

The Athenian Stranger's remarks about the relation between reason and the passions in Book IX sheds some light on how punishment and, more generally, moral education can aid in the development of practical reason. According to the Athenian Stranger, punishments that deter people from yielding to certain passions can benefit those people by teaching them how to resist their passions (*Laws* 854d–e).[6] Either through moral education or through the threat of punishment, the unreasoning passions can be trained to hold back. When these unreasoning passions are checked, the reasoning part of the soul is able to examine and correct the imprudent beliefs that accompany the passions (*Laws* 644d). As the passions become accustomed to restraint, they can be guided by the beliefs that have been corrected by reasoning (*Laws* 653a–b). As the Athenian Stranger says in Book IX, the "noblest laws" are those that both compel and persuade citizens to hate injustice and to desire, or at least to not hate, justice (*Laws* 862d–e).

But even if the Athenian Stranger believes that education and punishment may help some to restrain their passions and to acquire practical reason, he adds that there are significant obstacles that prevent most citizens from developing that virtue. Important obstacles to moral education include the depth and persistence of passions such as fear and erotic love. In many cases, these passions are so strong that they cannot become accustomed to yielding to reason but must instead always be restrained by habituation and the threat of punishment. Only in rare cases do we find people who are born with natural courage and moderation, and it is these people who can achieve the harmony between passion and reason that is called "virtue" at the start of Book II (*Laws* 635b–c). In addition, the character of the laws that educate and penalize the citizens introduce additional obstacles. As we have seen in our examination of courage and moderation, the divine laws that enjoin citizens to endure pain and to resist pleasure do not readily yield to the discretion of practical reason. For these laws present the passions as intractable enemies who must always be resisted so that the citizen can demonstrate that he or she lives like a higher "race" or "family" of noble, golden, and divine beings. Those who respond to that appeal and who identify virtue with self-command will not readily follow a rational faculty that sometimes determines that it is sometimes prudent to yield to certain pains or to certain pleasures.

To return to the discussion of voluntary and involuntary actions, we should note that in the latter part of Book IX, the Athenian Stranger never grants to Kleinias that people voluntarily do what they know to be harmful to them. He says that some people harbor angry passions for a long time, and that these people appear to act in a way that is "between the voluntary and the involuntary" or that is "more voluntary" than those who act on their passions as soon as they feel them (*Laws* 867a, 878b). Nonetheless, the Athenian Stranger does begin to speak as if he now accepted the conventional view that many injustices are voluntary and deserving of retribution. He suggests that the gods inflict retribution on the unjust for some murders (*Laws* 871c–d, 872e–73a) and endorses laws that would punish whoever or whatever causes death, even if that which causes death is incapable of voluntary choice, such as a beast or a rock (*Laws* 873e–74a). The Athenian Stranger makes these statements not because he has renounced his earlier view that no one is voluntarily unjust. Speaking as a legislator, he instead seeks to win Kleinias's and Megillus's assent to the laws that he is proposing. His goal is not to demonstrate to Kleinias and Megillus that they are ignorant or that their calls for retribution are incoherent. Instead, he wants to learn how far he can go in establishing laws according to what is both rational and just. When Kleinias and Megillus resist, he accommodates the law to their understanding. But he does not modify his guiding principles because these are the principles that Kleinias affirms at the start of the dialogue and that he continues to affirm even when he questions the Athenian Stranger's insight into retribution. For at the very time that Kleinias objects to the Athenian Stranger's claim that no one is voluntarily unjust, he also agrees that divine laws are necessarily coherent and that these laws necessarily aim at leading each citizen to what is best and to happiness (*Laws* 858d–59b). If he were able to think those principles through, he might recognize the disharmony in his own thinking and would concur with the Athenian Stranger about the involuntary character of those who are unjust.

Conclusion

At the beginning of the dialogue, the Athenian Stranger and Kleinias agree that divine law must aim at the whole of virtue and at the civic and individual happiness that should accompany that virtue. In calling the whole of virtue "perfect justice," they say that there is a disposition of the soul that draws upon and directs all the particular virtues to care for the good of the whole city. This disposition is awakened in some by the demanding character of the laws. Despite the burdens that the laws place on the just, the just believe that their virtue will ultimately bring them happiness. In fact, their willingness to bear those burdens helps to per-suade them that they deserve happiness. Insofar as they find that the laws alone do not provide the just with all the goods that they need and deserve, the just look to the gods to reward the just and to punish the unjust. But when we analyze the Athenian Stranger's arguments regarding divine providence, we find that he does not even claim to have proven that the gods always reward the just with happiness or that the gods always punish the unjust with wretchedness. Instead, he makes this claim in the context of the "mythic incantations" that he adds to his proof. These incantations prove to be in tension with what the Athenian Stranger and his interlocu-tors have been saying about the purposes of the law from the beginning of the dialogue. By thinking through the fundamental premise that the gods establish laws because they want what is best for those who live under them, the Athenian Stranger reasons that no one who understood the con-sequences of injustice would willingly be unjust. He further suggests that gods who are altogether rational and just cannot be counted upon to inflict the additional penalties and to proffer the additional rewards that the laws sometimes fail to provide. But if the gods do not give the laws further sup-port, then the laws will not always provide the just with the goods that they need and that they expect from having led virtuous lives. If the Athenian Stranger could show that the gods exercised divine providence on behalf of the law, then he would demonstrate that the laws supply citizens with the goods they need to lead a life of complete virtue and thus that the laws meet their goals. But his reasoning about the gods and moral responsibil-ity suggests that the laws cannot always be counted on to meet those goals. This appears to be an important feature of the instability of the laws that the Athenian Stranger discusses at the end of the dialogue (*Laws* 960d ff.).

Chapter Seven

THE SAVIOR OF DIVINE LAW

In the *Minos,* Socrates wants to know what law is and whether it can be known through reason or through some extra-rational faculty such as divination. While exploring these questions with a nameless Athenian citizen, Socrates argues that law wishes to be the discovery of what is. But instead of disclosing what is just, law seems inevitably to fall short of this goal. Socrates concludes the *Minos* by arguing that a complete inquiry into law must include a serious examination of laws that are said to be divine. He further indicates that the Socratic political philosopher must carry out this inquiry by conversing with those who live under and believe in such laws. The *Laws* begins with the nameless Athenian Stranger asking statesmen from Crete and Sparta about the origins and purposes of their cities' laws. When the Athenian Stranger asks Kleinias if he knows the purposes behind Crete's laws regarding common meals and the training of light infantry, Kleinias tries to show the practical reason behind those laws. And when the Athenian Stranger argues that divine laws should aim at loftier goals, Kleinias agrees and signals that he is open to believing in laws that can be shown to aim at those higher ends. After showing that Megillus shares Kleinias's conviction that divine law must aim at the whole of virtue, civic harmony, and individual happiness, the Athenian Stranger attempts to describe a complete code of law (*Laws* 702c–d, 705d–6a). His initial purpose in laying out such a code of law is to confirm that his interlocutors will accept a code of law that emerges from the philosopher's rational knowledge of the political art. In addition to this, he also wants to examine whether or to what extent any code of law can accomplish the goals of divine law.

Near the end of Book XII, the Athenian Stranger seems to complete his outline of the laws. He has explained how the laws will directly and indirectly promote their own version of the particular virtues. Yet as soon as he finishes elaborating the laws, he says that they are not complete. He says that the laws will be unstable and that they are in need of a savior or safeguard (*soterian ton nomon*) if they are to endure (*Laws* 960d). If a proper savior is not found, the whole regime is at risk (*Laws* 968e–69a). We have already observed some of the manifest shortcomings of the laws. But precisely what is it about the laws that could undermine the whole regime? What would it mean to save the laws? And who can save them?

The Athenian Stranger begins to explain what makes the laws unstable by discussing the role that intellect plays in saving living things. He says that what saves the soul in each living thing is intellect combined with the noblest senses (*Laws* 961d). In the arts, too, it is intelligence associated with each art that mixes with sense perception to accomplish the goal of each art. Thus, he says, doctors, pilots, and generals use intellect to save those things for which they care (*Laws* 961e–62a).

The Athenian Stranger says that in order for a city to be saved, it must have some element that knows the political art, which is to say that it must know what the goal of the city is, how that goal should be obtained, and which laws and which people give the city noble advice (*Laws* 962b). Kleinias correctly surmises that the Athenian Stranger has in mind the Nocturnal Council, a group of citizens who have been specially selected and tasked with the jobs of overseeing the city's program of education and counseling any atheists who have been imprisoned.

The Athenian Stranger says that this council must play an important role because of a problem that confronts every actual city as well as the city in speech that they have just constructed. In actual cities, the laws "wander," meaning that they aim at multiple and disparate goals. The problem before the Athenian Stranger, Kleinias, and Megillus is that their laws, too, seem to lack a foundation or a focus that would prevent the laws from becoming contradictory and unstable (*Laws* 962b–c, 962d–e, 963b).

Upon hearing the Athenian Stranger say that the laws fail to aim at a single goal, Kleinias is surprised. Unlike the Athenian Stranger, Kleinias has not noticed anything problematic or contradictory in the laws. Kleinias responds to the Athenian Stranger by saying that their laws have always aimed at the virtues and above all to promote intellect, which is the leader of the virtues (*Laws* 963a1–9). The Athenian Stranger praises Kleinias's answer but notes that in each of the examples of the arts, intellect always aims at saving something other than itself. Those who have the political art should use intellect to hit some single target that would save the city. But what is the target at which the political art should aim? When Kleinias says that he does not know, the Athenian Stranger indicates that they need to determine how the many different virtues at which their laws have aimed are also "one" (*Laws* 963c9–d2). They need to identify what it is about all of the particular virtues that enables us to speak of them as one thing, as a virtue. Thus, when the Athenian Stranger says that the laws wander and that they fail to aim at a single target, he means that the laws teach a number of particular virtues, but they do not aim at virtue as a whole. Some of the laws that he has described would promote courage, others would promote moderation. Some would aim at awakening a love of perfect justice, while others would prepare the citizen for the arrival of practical reason. While the laws can foster these disparate virtues, they do not promote them in such a way that the particular virtues are able to combine or coalesce into the complete virtue of a human being. The laws do not lead the citizen to a single, coherent life of virtue.

According to the Athenian Stranger, this poses a threat to the laws since it would cause the laws to act "haphazardly," as do the laws of actual cities when they pursue numerous, discrete goals (*Laws* 962b–e). Among the dangers that follow from the laws acting haphazardly is that the laws could make it difficult to promote other virtues. The laws that promote courage can also awaken erotic longings that undermine moderation. And, as we have seen, the laws that promote moderation stand in the way of the full development of practical reason. Furthermore, laws that awaken a strong dedication to justice do not supply all the goods that are needed and expected by those who have virtue as a whole. Moreover, at the beginning of the dialogue, Kleinias was able to identify which code of law is divine by paying attention to which code aims at the whole of virtue. But if the best code of laws fails to aim at such a goal, then we must wonder whether any code of law would be recognizable as a divine code.

In order to illustrate the challenge before them, the Athenian Stranger indicates how the virtues seem to be not one but many. Each of the particular virtues seems to correspond to different dispositions of the soul (*Laws* 963e4–5). According to the Athenian Stranger, courage comes into being prior to and independently of the arrival of reason, for we see courage in animals and small children (*Laws* 963e5–6).[1] While courage can come into being without reason, practical reason (*phronesis*) comes into being only after reason arrives (*Laws* 963e6–8). But if these virtues come into being through such different aspects or parts of the soul, it would seem that each is a different kind of virtue altogether. Comparing courage with practical reason, we note that courage is said to come into being through regular bodily motions and through the physical regimens associated with gymnastic and musical training. But practical reason depends on the arrival of reason, which does not seem to be rooted in bodily motions. It is in light of such differences that Socrates says in the *Republic* that practical reason seems to be the only genuine virtue of the soul. The other virtues, he says, are more akin to virtues of the body (*Republic* 518d–e; cf. *Phaedo* 69b–c).

Having indicated how the particular virtues are many, the Athenian Stranger invites Kleinias to say what makes them one. Before Kleinias can reply, the Athenian Stranger says that they will need to make sure that members of the Nocturnal Council will have the intellect and sense perception that is needed to identify what virtue is and to save the law. For this, the council members will need a "more precise education" than was given to the other citizens (*Laws* 964b–65a). It is here, at the end of the dialogue, that the Athenian Stranger acknowledges that the best moral education that law can provide would not, by itself, promote the intellectual virtues that are needed to save or guard the law.

But how would this new, more precise education be related to the best moral education under the law? How does the latter support the former? In order to get a clearer understanding of the relation between an early, moral education and a higher education, it is useful to compare what the Athenian Stranger recommends with what Socrates endorses in the *Republic*. In Books II and III of the *Republic,* Socrates describes the primary education for young guardians. After laying out the theology that should be taught to small children, he takes up the discussion of how the musical arts should depict heroes and human beings. After sketching the courage, moderation, and self-command that should be celebrated by the early education, Socrates gives great attention to the tunes, rhythms, and harmonious music that the young should hear. Music, he says, has great power to shape the soul, and a good educator must make sure that young people are exposed to only noble presentations of the virtues. The principal goal of this early education seems to be to foster a love of the beauty of virtue, which leads the young to love the correct things even before reason arrives (*Republic* 401d–2a).

This education is supplemented by the education for potential philosophers that is described in Books VI and VII. According to Socrates, the goal of this education is to promote practical reason or more precisely to make practical reason become "useful" or beneficial (*Republic* 518d–e; 530c1). The education begins with the study of mathematics and extends through geometry and astronomy. These subjects have the two-fold benefit of training young people to reason as well as to awaken the intellect to those things that are invisible to the eye but intelligible to the mind. The very peak of the higher education in practical reason comes through dialectics. Dialectics entails using intelligence to apprehend the intelligible things and, what is most important, to know the idea of the good. Only by using intelligence to know the idea of the good is it possible to derive any benefit or profit from anything (*Republic* 505a–b, 505e). In addition, a critical part of the dialectical education comes in an examination of what the well-educated young citizen has learned from the law about what is good as well as what the law has taught about what is noble and what is just (*Republic* 533b8–d1, 534e1–535a1). Socrates says that such an inquiry would begin by asking someone who has been well raised to explain "what is noble." He says that when such a person replies by saying what he has learned from the lawgiver he will find that the argument refutes him many times and in many ways. This person will be reduced "to the opinion that what the law says is no more noble than base, and similarly about the just and the good and most things he held in honor" (*Republic* 538d–e). By reflecting on this experience, the young student may not only lose respect for the authority of the law but also come to doubt that anything is noble and good and just. To prevent young dialecticians from concluding that winning arguments is more important than learning the truth about what is noble, good, and just, educators should make sure that those who undergo this training are mature or, better yet, that those young people who receive the education have the steady and moderate temperaments that we associate with maturity (*Republic* 503c–d). If someone discerns the inadequacy of his beliefs about what is just and noble and good, and if that person has a suitably good nature, then that person's good nature will lead him or her to seek clarity about what is just and noble and good by nature or in truth. This liberation from the legal education concerning the just and the noble and the good is crucial to the "turning around" of the soul, which Socrates calls "education" in Book VII of the Republic (*Republic* 514a, 518d, 521c). In fact, it is a crucial event in the liberation from the cave; it takes place when the prisoner recognizes that the shadows of the cave's walls are merely images of what the law has taught about justice and the noble and the good (*Republic* 517d–e, 521 b).

As we reflect on the two parts of this education, we may wonder why it is important to provide the early, moral training if its teachings are to be questioned and undone by the latter. In order to understand how the moral education contributes to a complete and genuine education, it is helpful to consider some remarks regarding education in Plato's *Seventh Letter*. In that letter, Plato refers to some who are unable to make progress in learning about virtue and vice because they lack a natural attachment to justice and nobility (Plato *Seventh Letter* 344a). Those who lack such an attachment may have difficulty articulating their beliefs about the virtues and may not take to heart the arguments that arise during a dialectical examination. Alcibiades, for example, thinks that he richly deserves to rule in Athens. But he does not take justice seriously enough to be deeply troubled by his own contradictory beliefs about justice (e.g., *Alcibiades Major* 113d–e, 119b–c). Were he to be more deeply concerned with what is just, he might take the trouble to pursue a more coherent account of what is just and noble and good. In light of his negative example, we are able to recognize how an education that promotes moral seriousness might help to prepare some people for the dialectical education that completes education as such.

The moral education in Book VII of the *Laws,* along with the laws themselves, seems able to awaken great moral seriousness among those who are capable of feeling it. The gymnastic and musical training promote a spirited courage and a pride in self-command that would enable many young citizens to combat both pleasure and pain. And this education in Book VII is supplemented by an education in intellectual matters, beginning with the study of numbers, arithmetic, and geometry, and ending in astronomy. This study would awaken the intellect (*Laws* 747b) and would enable the young to recognize the meaning and role of necessity, especially in regard to the motions of the heavenly beings (*Laws* 821a ff.). But there is no education in dialectics that would correspond to the crowning, philosophical education in the *Republic.* The peak of education in Book VII of the *Laws* appears to be the education in hunting, an activity that promotes stamina, resourcefulness, and courage (Morrow 1960, 335). But even if those who learn to hunt must exhibit great ingenuity beyond what they can learn from law, hunting itself does not invite young people to raise fundamental questions about what the law teaches regarding the greatest things.

In order to develop the insight that is needed to discern what virtue is, how it can be taught, and who can teach it (*Laws* 962b), the members of the Nocturnal Council will need an education akin to the dialectical education that is described in Book VII of the *Republic.* The education that the Athenian Stranger says they must receive will consist of three parts. In the first part, the members of the Nocturnal Council must come to study the "idea" of virtue. The Athenian does not introduce the idea of virtue as if it were something unfamiliar to Kleinias and Megillus, such as a perfect or otherworldly being. Instead, he speaks to Kleinias about the form of virtue in familiar terms. Yet this reference to the idea marks an important breakthrough in the dialogue. Up until this time, the Athenian Stranger has not directly questioned what the law teaches about virtue or led his interlocutors to consider the possibility that virtue might be something outside their ordinary understanding. The Athenian Stranger introduces Kleinias to the need to find the idea of virtue by winning Kleinias's agreement that when a craftsman makes artifacts he looks not only to the many particular artifacts that he makes but also to some one thing (*Laws* 965b). For instance, an expert shoemaker considers what a shoe is supposed to look like, its form, and the work that a shoe is supposed to do when he crafts many particular shoes. According to the analogy, the Nocturnal Council would be craftsmen who look to the form of virtue in making many particular virtues.

The problem before them is that they do not yet know the idea of virtue, nor do they know how it is related to the many particular virtues. Their first task will be to learn whether virtue is "one or a whole or both" or "whatever it is according to nature" (*Laws* 965d3–6). If virtue were "one" but not a "whole," this would mean that there is one form of virtue, the idea of virtue, that is virtue in the truest or most complete respect. The many different virtues would be various dispositions of the soul that more or less resemble the form of virtue, but would not be virtues in the strictest sense. The multitude of different virtues would be the images of virtue to which the Athenian Stranger refers in Book II (*Laws* 655b4–5).

If instead virtue were a "whole" but not "one," then the many particular virtues would all be virtues, but they would not be parts of some one greater virtue. They would instead all be examples or instances of virtue, members of the class "virtue," just as many different dogs are members of the class "dog" or many different shapes are members of the class "shape." The idea of virtue would not exist on its own as a self-subsisting being but would be the class characteristics of all the virtues, a kind of pattern that is present in every particular virtue. According to this account of virtue, the different virtues might not be fully compatible with one another. Someone who has, for example, a certain kind of courage might find that it prevents him or her from developing practical reason. And yet all the virtues would share the characters of the class that is called "virtue." Recalling the example of the shoemaker, the shoemaker looks to the form of the shoe in crafting each shoe that he makes, but no one shoe is the shoe itself.

Looking to a third possibility, the Athenian Stranger remarks that if virtue were both "one" and a "whole," this would mean that there is some "virtue as a whole" that is more than the class characteristics of all the virtues. It would be a whole in the sense that it has parts that are the particular virtues. Particular virtues like courage or moderation would not be virtues in themselves or by themselves. But each would contribute to or help constitute some greater virtue that would come to sight as a coherent whole. Were a craftsman to look to a form that is both a whole and one, he would try to imitate some object that has numerous parts and yet that still comes to sight as one, distinct thing.

In order to save the laws, the savior must learn which of these possibilities or some other alternative provides the best account of virtue. The Athenian Stranger does not say which, if any, of these three alternatives he favors. But the Athenian Stranger does say that courage by nature and practical reason differ and that they correspond to different parts of the soul. If this is true, then virtue would seem to comprise different elements, and if there is such a thing as virtue, it would appear to be some sort of whole with parts rather than some undifferentiated thing. Indeed, the possibility that virtue is a whole with many parts would seem to be consistent with the view expressed at the start of the dialogue, according to which there are many particular virtues that culminate or join in something called "virtue as a whole." In this case, the savior would have to figure out not simply what the idea of virtue is but also which versions of the different, particular virtues are truly parts of virtue as a whole. A form of courage, for example, that obstructs the development of other virtues, and thus of virtue as a whole, would not be a virtue in the strict sense but a mere image of that form of courage that is part of virtue as a whole (cf. *Laws* 669a–b). In order for there to be such a thing as virtue as a whole, some version of the particular virtues would have to be shown to contribute to or promote some greater or more complete kind of virtue.

This inquiry into what virtue is would lead members of the Nocturnal Council far beyond the limits of the education that law provides. Yet it is not sufficient to give those members the clarity about virtue that they need to save the laws. The second part of the higher education provides further, essential criteria for learning what virtue is, how it is taught, and who can give noble advice about it. The second part of the education provides further criteria for identifying what virtue is and the nature of the particular virtues. The second part of the education directs students to study what is good and what is noble and to pay special attention to how the good and the noble are both many and one (*Laws* 966a). Upon hearing this, important questions immediately emerge regarding the relation among virtue, the good, and the noble. Ordinarily, virtue is understood to be something good, as was said at the very start of the dialogue (*Laws* 631b–d). But the need for a separate study of the good indicates that virtue is not simply identical to what is good. For whom or in what respect is virtue good? Under some circumstances, could a virtuous disposition of the soul cease to be good? As we have seen, some form or version of the particular virtues might limit or even undermine the development of virtue as a whole. If, on the other hand, virtues are necessarily good, would an ostensibly virtuous disposition of the soul cease to be a virtue if and when it is not good? The Athenian Stranger says that the guardians of the law must study the unity that underlies all things that we regard as good just as they are urged to study the idea of virtue, which is to say that they must seek out the idea of the good.

Along with asking what virtue is and what the good is, they must also examine what is noble. The need for this further study indicates that the noble is distinct from the good. In order to know what virtue is, we need to be clear-sighted about the difference between the good and the noble. If there are good things that are not noble and/or noble things that are not good, what seems to be the difference between these things? The members of the Nocturnal Council will need to ask what it is that moves us when we encounter things that are noble or beautiful but does not move us when we encounter things that are merely useful or beneficial. According to the Athenian Stranger, when the council members consider what is noble, they need to pay special attention to how the noble things come into being "by nature" (*Laws* 966b).[2] By emphasizing the importance of knowing how the noble things emerge naturally, the Athenian Stranger indicates that the guardians of the law should be especially alert to the possibility that some things that seem to be noble by nature are noble merely by custom or law. When the Athenian Stranger says that they will need to look beyond what the law teaches about the noble, he is calling for the dialectical examination of law that is mentioned in the *Republic.*

Turning to the third part of the education, the Athenian Stranger asks whether knowing what pertains to the gods is not one of the noblest things to study (*Laws* 966c). But why would our understanding of virtue depend on our understanding of the gods? After all, at the start of the dialogue, the Athenian Stranger shows us that the serious citizen is able to identify which code of law is divine by noting which one aims at the whole of virtue. But if the serious citizen relies on his knowledge of virtue to recognize the divine, how would learning about the gods inform his understanding of virtue? At the start of his account of the third part of the education, the Athenian Stranger says that members of the Nocturnal Council should think through all the demonstrations regarding the gods. Only those who labor over these matters can become divine and can be qualified to be a guardian of the laws (*Laws* 966c–d). Yet when the Athenian Stranger discusses the demonstrations that should be studied, he does not mention the second or third proofs that he offered in Book X. The second and third proofs do not appear to be part of the higher education. Instead, he confines himself to endorsing the primary proof, which looks at the motions of the heavenly bodies to confirm that those motions are supervised by divine intelligence.

Why would the prospective guardians of the law need to study this proof rather than the proofs that argue that the gods care about human beings and that the gods never cease to protect the just and to oppose the unjust? According to the Athenian Stranger, those who study the priority of soul to body, the origin of motion, and the intelligence that oversees the motions of the heavenly beings will develop a "firm piety" (*Laws* 967d4–8). The statement leaves open the possibility that those who know about the gods only through other sorts of study, including the second and third proofs, may develop a softer piety, a piety that will be soft either in the sense that it is founded on weaker foundations that will cause it to waver or in the sense that it will make those who feel it softer in the soul. In either case, the Athenian Stranger is indicating that those whose fundamental belief about the gods is that they are guided entirely by intellect are better able to understand what virtue is than those who understand the gods principally as beings who reward the just and punish the unjust.

The Athenian Stranger concludes his discussion of the third part of the education by saying that after the members of the Nocturnal Council discern the intelligence that underlies the motions of the heavenly beings, they should find what that orderliness has in common with the orderliness that can be found in music. After considering how this same orderliness is found in the mathematics that underlies the study of both astronomy and music, they should "harmoniously apply" what they have observed to human character (*Laws* 967e3–4). Together with the Muses, the heavenly gods serve as graceful models of orderliness and harmony that should be used to shape the virtues of character.[3]

The Athenian Stranger would teach members of the Nocturnal Council to look to the heavens and to try to instill the orderliness that they find there into their own lives. In saying this, the Athenian Stranger may seem to support those scholars who say that Plato assumes in the *Laws* that the whole is guided by reason (intellect) and that this is a fitting model of conduct for cities and individuals. But if we consider the context, we will note that the Athenian Stranger is saying that the members of the Nocturnal Council should be guided by the divine virtue intellect precisely because they are ignorant about virtue. It is because they cannot assume that they know what it is, how it is taught, and who gives the best advice about it that they must find some way to gain knowledge about these matters. But why should they rely on intellect rather than on some other faculty or source of insight? The members of the Nocturnal Council will not be able to converse directly with a god as Minos and Lycurgus are said to have done. Left to their own resources, they will need to determine what each of the particular virtues is. Like the Socratic philosophers, they will need to scrutinize various opinions about virtue, including those of serious citizens like Kleinias and Megillus and perhaps the opinions of other kinds of people, too. They will have to examine how the particular virtues differ and how they are related to each other and whether or how they relate to virtue as a whole. Beyond this, they will have to consider whether or to what extent virtue as a whole is related to both civic and individual happiness. In order to make these distinctions and to reason about them clearly, they will need to rely on their intellect.

The dialogue has already shown us that the serious citizen will turn to his own intellect to gain a better view of what virtue is and of what divine law aims to accomplish. If we recall how the Athenian Stranger begins the dialogue, we will remember that he shows that citizens like Kleinias resolve problems in their own understanding of divine law through their own reasoning. When confronted with another interpretation or code of divine law, the morally serious citizen must look into his own heart to determine which interpretation or code is truly divine. When he looks within himself, he may find that he does not know precisely what the whole of virtue is. But he knows that whatever virtue may turn out to be, divine law must aim at the whole of virtue and at the civic and individual happiness that would accompany it. Like Kleinias, Megillus too expects virtue to consist in a number of particular virtues that are to be kept separate and distinct. And they both expect that these virtues will not conflict with one another but will culminate in a single, coherent life of complete virtue that is happy and even pleasant. If the members of the Nocturnal Council were to satisfy Kleinias's and Megillus's expectations, they would need to identify the particular virtues, show how they are parts of virtue as a whole, and demonstrate how they bring happiness. At the same time, the council members would need to explore the possibility that virtue is neither a part nor a whole. And they would have to consider the possibility that the many dispositions of the soul that we call "virtues" simply do not share common characteristics. In order to carry out each of these examinations, they will need intellect.

This argument sheds light on why the Athenian Stranger associates divine law with the rule of intellect (*Laws* 714a). Because there are many different versions of the particular virtues, the legislator would need to use intellect to discern and promote each particular virtue in a way that it contributes to virtue as a whole, individual happiness, and civic harmony. Thus, the divine legislator needs to use intellect to make the laws. Insofar as the intellect provides the citizen with knowledge of virtue, it provides the citizen with access to the gods' thinking. To use intellect to discern virtue is to divine what the gods have in mind regarding what the citizen considers to be the most important things (*Laws* 964b, 965e, 968b–c, 969c–d). In this respect, it could be called the divine part of the soul.

The Role of the Nocturnal Council

After offering this sketch of the curriculum of the higher education, the Athenian Stranger says that the education will be adjusted to fit the different natures of the different students (*Laws* 968d–e). In contrast to the education provided by Crete and Sparta, each student would be taken aside and given individual attention (cf. *Laws* 666e–67a). Because there are no fixed rules regarding what takes place at the peak of a genuine, liberal education, the higher education of the Nocturnal Council cannot be described more fully and laws cannot be established for it (*Laws* 968c). Even though the Athenian Stranger cannot lay out any rules for their education, he indicates that it should correspond to the philosophic education that is described in the seventh book of the *Republic*. He says that those members of the Nocturnal Council who absorb the education will have all the virtues, including practical reason and intelligence (*Laws* 962d2–3, 965a). He likens them to philosophers and calls them "perfect guardians" (*Laws* 965a, 969c; cf. *Republic* 414b1).[4]

There is a rich debate about the Nocturnal Council's role in the city. Near the end of the dialogue, the Athenian Stranger says that the city should be "handed over" to the Nocturnal Council (*Laws* 969b, also 968c). Noting the strong resemblance between the council members and the philosophers of the *Republic*, some scholars interpret the line to mean that the Nocturnal Council should rule as guardian-kings in place of the laws (Barker 1960; Klosko 1986; Sabine 1961). Others find this innovation too abrupt and argue that the Council would play an informal role, advising the city about the law, especially regarding education. Rather than replace the laws, they would play an informal, advisory role and would help to adjust the laws whenever changes are needed (Bobonich 2002, 393; Lewis 1998; Morrow 1960; Stalley 1983). According to Lewis, their studies would influence the whole regime and would add a philosophic element to the city's deliberations and discussions (Lewis 1998, 17–20).

To resolve this dispute, it helps to recall why the Nocturnal Council must receive their special education in the first place. The Nocturnal Council is to receive this education not simply because the laws are unstable but because the laws need to be saved. But how precisely would the Nocturnal Council save the laws? In order to answer this, we must consider more carefully what threatens the laws. According to the Athenian Stranger's statements in Book X, the problem with the laws is that they aim at multiple targets. Insofar as the laws are haphazard, they promote disparate and even contradictory dispositions of the soul rather than the complete virtue, individual happiness, and civic harmony that is expected of divine law. By failing to hit such a target, they may produce discord not only in the souls of the individual citizens but also in the city itself. Beyond this, if the laws fail to aim at, let alone to accomplish, the ends that are believed to be the genuine ends of divine law, then the laws would not be recognizable as divine law. Morally serious critics could challenge whether the laws are truly the product of a divine mind. In order to save the laws, the Nocturnal Council may not be able to devise new laws that promote virtue as a whole and that can bring civic and individual happiness. There may be limits to what law can accomplish in teaching moral virtue, and the Athenian Stranger may have shown us all that law can do to promote courage, moderation, and the other particular virtues. What remains for the Nocturnal Council is to interpret and apply the laws in ways that minimize the differences in the virtues that they teach. Because the laws are haphazard, the Nocturnal Council will do all that it can to harmonize the laws and to minimize the discord that will arise from them. It will have to become an interpreter of the law (*Laws* 964b), and it may need great latitude in determining how the laws should be interpreted in general and in particular cases. Consider how the Athenian Stranger is willing to revise the wording of well-known poetry in order to make it conform to what should be said (cf. *Laws* 629a–30c with 660–61a). But if the laws continue to promote versions of the particular virtues that do not culminate in virtue as a whole, then the Nocturnal Council can at least assure the city as a whole that there is a civic body that uses intellect to study the problem of virtue and that uses its knowledge of virtue to interpret and to apply the law. In addition to this, it will need to respond to those morally serious critics who challenge the authority of the law on the grounds that because the laws are haphazard, because the laws do not aim at the whole of virtue, therefore the laws cannot be divine. The members of the Nocturnal Council can respond to morally serious critics of the law by saying that the god establishes the law even though law is an imperfect medium for moral education and for securing justice. If the morally serious critic were to say that it is precisely these imperfections that make it impossible to discern that the laws have a divine origin and that deprive the law of its authority, members of the Nocturnal Council can reply that even if the law is imperfect, it is being interpreted and guided by those who use intellect to inquire into the idea of virtue. Because the guardians of the law seek to share in the divine mind of the lawgiver and because they use their knowledge of virtue to oversee the law, they can vouch for the divine origin or purpose of the laws, even if those laws fall short of their highest objects. Thus, the Nocturnal Council does not replace the rule of law. Nor does it simply give informal advice about it or promote a philosophic understanding among the most influential people in the community. The

Nturnal Council would save the law by strengthening its authority. It would strengthen its authority by showing that the law is interpreted and guided by those who bring intellect to bear on those things that matter most to morally serious citizens.

The drama of the *Laws* helps us to understand the role that the Nocturnal Council would play in the city and its laws. At the end of the dialogue, neither Kleinias nor Megillus claim to know how the many particular virtues are related to virtue as a whole. Both seem to be very much in the dark both about the idea of virtue and about how to save the laws. But both agree emphatically that the Nocturnal Council should receive the education outlined by the Athenian Stranger and should oversee the laws. And both are fully convinced that the laws will not succeed unless the Athenian Stranger joins them in establishing the colony. Kleinias and Megillus trust the Athenian Stranger to interpret and guide divine law because they are persuaded that he knows how to inquire into what virtue is. They would trust the Nocturnal Council to interpret and guide the law because only it would be able to pursue the studies that the Athenian Stranger has outlined to it. Even though Kleinias has supported the Athenian Stranger's arguments regarding divine law all along, he has expressed reservations from time to time (e.g., *Laws* 644d, 661e, 812a, 837e, 842a, 857b, 857e, 861a, 863a). But at the end, he says that they are being led by a god (*Laws* 968b10–c2). In response to Kleinias's strong endorsement of all the Athenian Stranger has said, Megillus refers to Kleinias for the first time as "dear Kleinias" and agrees that the success of the colony depends entirely on giving the Nocturnal Council members their needed education and role in the city and on the Athenian Stranger's agreeing to help establish the laws for the colony (*Laws* 969c–d). These morally serious citizens know that divine law ought to aim at virtue as a whole and at civic and individual happiness. They do not know precisely what the laws should be regarding the education of the Nocturnal Council. Nor do they know what other reforms it might make. But Kleinias and Megillus would accept the divinity of laws that are devised or guided by political philosophers such as the Athenian Stranger. This vindicates the philosopher's attempt to show that by relying on his own reason or expertise in the political art (*Laws* 650b, 837e, 963b), he can establish a code of law that is recognized as divine by those who have been raised believing in the divinity of the law. The laws that he outlines may be imperfect. But when Kleinias and Megillus consider the prudence behind the Athenian Stranger's many proposals about the law and the careful, discerning judgment that the Athenian Stranger has displayed throughout the dialogue, they are able to recognize in him the intellect that they expect to find in a divine lawgiver.

It is possible to question the practicality of the Athenian Stranger's proposal to give the Nocturnal Council a philosophic education and to give it authority over the law. The Nocturnal Council will be composed in large part by elderly citizens who occupy important posts because of their devotion to the law. Following conventional beliefs about the virtues and the gods, they not only may be unable to engage in philosophic examinations of the virtues but also may be hostile to them.[5] It may be for this reason that the Athenian Stranger seems to change the criteria for membership of the council. Early in the discussion he says that it will be composed of elderly civic leaders and the younger men whom they invite to join the council. But as he goes on to describe what the council members must learn, he says that the council should be composed of those with all the virtues (cf. *Laws* 95d–3, 961a–c, 964b). It may be that the Nocturnal Council cannot absorb the education that it needs. It may not be able to accomplish all its goals. But even if it turns out that the Nocturnal Council is unable to do all that needs to be done to save the laws, the Athenian Stranger would still have achieved a great success in the dialogue. For he will have shown that morally serious citizens who have been raised under traditional divine laws can recognize that divine law needs rational guidance from political philosophy.

At the end of the dialogue, both Kleinias and Megillus ask the Athenian Stranger to join them in establishing the new divine laws. But Plato does not provide us with the Athenian Stranger's answer. We do not know if the Athenian Stranger agrees to help establish a code of divine law or, more generally, to implement political reforms. By omitting the Athenian Stranger's response to Kleinias and Megillus, Plato indicates that the dialogue has already achieved its principal objective. The dialogue has shown that the political philosopher can comprehend the law's principles and goals without relying on divination or some other extra-rational faculty. Through both his analysis of law and through the drama of the dialogue, the political philosopher demonstrates that he has insights into the moral matters that are of the gravest concern to those who live under the law. At the same time, the Athenian Stranger demonstrates to Kleinias and Megillus that left to themselves, those who seek to accomplish the ends of divine law would be unable to do so without the rational guidance that political philosophy can supply. In winning their agreement, the Athenian Stranger vindicates the philosophic life before the bar of its most serious critics. Demonstrating that the political philosopher can achieve this success may be even more important to Plato than laying out the practical reforms that are often discussed in the *Laws*.

Conclusion

The *Minos* and the *Laws* show us how Plato demonstrates that the political philosopher has the authority to guide divine law. But these two dialogues by themselves do not complete this demonstration. By showing us how the political philosopher's authority to guide divine law rests on his knowledge of the problem of virtue, these dialogues help us to recognize how Plato's other dialogues contribute to the overall justification of the philosophic life against the charges that defenders of divine law have raised against it. For in those other dialogues, the Platonic Socrates displays his human wisdom regarding what the virtues are, their relation to what is good and to what is noble, and what would constitute the complete virtue of a human being. In addition to showing us how the Platonic political philosopher responds to challenges raised by defenders of divine law, the *Laws* in particular also demonstrates how the political philosopher can play an important role in a city under divine law. For the Athenian Stranger has persuaded Kleinias that the political philosopher is not a threat to the law but a potential ally and perhaps even a savior to the law (*Laws* 967a–d). He has shown that however provocative or disturbing political philosophy may be in its examination of the human things, political philosophy can also play a responsible role in a political community that takes divine law seriously.

Contemporary defenders of political rationalism have had little to say in response to defenders of divine law. The *Minos* and the *Laws* show us how defenders of political rationalism can raise a mutually instructive dialogue with those who argue that divine law should be authoritative in politics and law. The defender of political rationalism who has learned from the *Minos* and the *Laws* would approach proponents of other divine law traditions with the openness exhibited by Socrates and the Athenian Stranger. The contemporary Platonic rationalist would not assume that believers in other forms of divine law have the same beliefs as Kleinias and Megillus have nor even that they come to believe in divine law through the same faculties. Rather, Platonic rationalists would recognize that there is no simple, fixed list of questions or topics that they can pursue in order to quickly plumb the depths of the believer's knowledge. But they might, like the Athenian Stranger, ask their interlocutors about the origins and purposes of their community's laws. If Platonic rationalists ask questions, they must observe whether those whom they question feel compelled to respond. If those who profess belief in divine law do respond, the Platonic rationalists would explore how they know or recognize these things, paying close attention to the extent to which they rely on their own reasoning to discern the answers to those questions or whether their knowledge comes through some other, extra-rational faculty or art. Having studied the *Minos* and the *Laws*, the Platonic rationalist might ask if the goals of divine law include the virtues. But the defender of political rationalism who has learned from Plato must not assume that believers in other faiths will always say that divine law aims at virtue or, if they do, that they will say that it aims at the same virtues as Kleinias and Megillus say it must. Insofar as the code of divine law that is under examination commands us to do what is just, the Platonic rationalist would seek to learn what the law means by justice and how the law would enforce and support it. If divine law seems to promise to make those who follow it happy, then the Platonic rationalist would examine how this is said to take place and the role that divine providence is said to play in the lives of those who live under the law. The Platonic rationalist would also investigate whether divine law aims at some distinctive quality, at some form of piety or holiness, that appears to be altogether distinct from the classical virtues (e.g., *Isaiah* 6:1–7). The Platonic rationalist should also be open to the possibility that divine law will teach that what seem to be virtues to the classical citizen are, in fact, vices (e.g., Augustine *City of God* xix. 25). He or she must also be aware of the possibility that the believer in divine law will deny that the law aims at either civic or individual happiness. At the same time, the defender of political rationalism would be alert to the possibility that the believer's pious reverence is accompanied by the same kind of concern for justice, prudence, and happiness that accompanies Megillus's awe for the laws of Sparta. If the Platonic rationalist finds that the believer harbors such a concern, then he or she would explore how the believer understands the relations among the ends of divine law. This list of questions is obviously not exhaustive. Further, probing, respectful questions would need to be carefully raised and pursued. In the end, Platonic rationalists would have to reflect on whether their interlocutors are troubled by any inconsistencies that may be found in their beliefs about the goals of divine law or whether they are content to live with them. If their interlocutors seem troubled by such inconsistencies, the Platonic rationalist might test whether those who believe in the law are willing to turn to political philosophy for further guidance in interpreting the law. Through this process, the Platonic rationalist would learn whether those who defend other kinds of divine law recognize, explicitly or implicitly, the need to use reason to discern and pursue the goals of divine law.

Read with an eye to the challenges that revealed law poses to the philosophic life, the *Minos* and the *Laws* are models for the defense of political rationalism. They present us with a powerful example of how a political philosopher can establish a respectful and, for that reason, all the more incisive dialogue with defenders of divine law. But the political rationalist who has learned from the *Minos* and the *Laws* should also recognize that what we can learn from studying those works cannot dispose of the need for a thoroughly serious and thoughtful dialogue with those who claim to have their own knowledge of alternative divine law.

NOTES

Introduction

1. As in Christian and Jewish traditions, Islamic scholars take a range of positions on these questions. Instructive readings include Arberry (1957) and Moaddel and Talattof (2002).

2. See, for example, Al-Farabi's *Summary of Plato's Laws,* and Avicenna's remarks in "On the Primary Division of the Rational Sciences," *Metaphysics*, X, and *Tis' Rasail* 85.

1—The *Minos* and the Socratic Examination of Law

1. See Vander Waerdt's discussion of Socrates's reputation in the Hellenistic tradition (Vander Waerdt 1994, 1–4).

2. See, for example, Antiphon fragments 44–61; Empedocles fragments 4, 9, 128, 134, 137; Heraclitus fragments 5, 14, 24, 32, 33, 44, 52, 94, 102, 121, and 128.

3. Plato provides various accounts of the thinking that led to the "Socratic turn" in the *Apology* 20c–23c, *Phaedo* 96a–107b, *Parmenides,* and *Symposium* 201d–12c. On the consistency of the accounts in the *Phaedo* and *Apology,* see Guthrie 1971, 101.

4. The form of a being reflects those characteristics that enable us to recognize that it belongs to a certain class of beings; the form is a cause of the being in that it limits what is and what is not a member of that class (Plato *Phaedo* 100c3–e3; Aristotle *Physics* 196b26–28; Vlastos 1998, 22–24).

5. Socrates says that he examines what is said and looks for the "strongest" account of each of the beings. He says that when he finds something that agrees with that account he calls it "true" (Plato *Phaedo* 100a3–7; cf. *Apology* 21b–d).

6. A helpful account of the persecutions of the ancient Greek philosophers can be found in Ahrensdorf (1994) and Derenne (1976).

7. Lewis discusses its influence among legal scholars (Lewis 2006, 17–19, 38–39).

8. According to Grote (1888), authoritative editions of the dialogues were kept at the Academy so that scholars might distinguish genuine from spurious manuscripts. Copies of those editions were transmitted to the library at Alexandria and used by the great Platonic editors Aristophanes the Grammarian and Thrasyllus. Thrasyllus organized the dialogues into groups of four and in one of these tetralogies, he placed the *Minos* before the *Laws* because he believed that Plato wrote the *Minos* as an introduction to the *Laws*. See Chroust (1965), Phillip (1970), and Pangle (1987).

9. Morrow offers an impressive account of how the *Minos* influenced the ways in which many later Greek and Roman thinkers speak of the historical figure Minos (Morrow 1960, 38–39).

10. Scholars differ regarding whether the style of the *Minos* is worthy of Plato. Lamb complains especially about Socrates's attempt to derive the word for distribution (*nemean*) from the term *nomos* (Lamb 1927, 386, 407). But Morrow says that there is "clearly a Platonic touch in the meaning of *nemean*—"distribute" and "govern"—and its derivative *nomos* (Morrow 1960, 36). Lamb also objects to the phrase "human herd" at 318a and argues that Plato would not use such an inelegant term. But Morrow notes that the term is used in the *Statesman* and the *Laws* and calls it "a favorite of Plato's" (Morrow 1960, 36). Similarly, Pangle observes that England cites the phrase in the *Minos* to resolve a difficulty in the text of the *Laws* (Pangle 1987, 61n13). Shorey seems to differ with himself: he says that the first part of the dialogue is not worthy of Plato, but the last part could not have been written by anyone else (Shorey 1933, 425).

11. For helpful analyses of law in the *Crito* and *Apology*, see Rosano (2000) and Leibowitz (2010) respectively.

12. The external evidence that the *Laws* is Plato's last dialogue comes from Diogenes Laertius, who reports the story that when Plato died, the dialogue was written on wax tablets and that it had to be transcribed onto parchment by Philip of Opus (Diogenes Laertius 3, 37). Looking at the dialogue itself, Stalley says that it seems incomplete because it lacks dramatic polish and clear organization (Stalley 1983).

13. Dionysus of Halicarnassus reports that when Plato died he left a tablet on which he had written several different versions of the first line of the *Republic* (Dionysus of Halicarnassus *On Literary Composition* 25; see also Quintillian *Institutes* VIII, 6: 64). Diogenes Laertius cites two sources who say that Plato continually revised the whole first book of the *Republic* (Diogenes Laertius 3, 37).

14. It is not clear at the outset why Socrates adds the phrase "to us" to the question "what is law?" He may mean to ask what is law to the two of them, what is law to the Athenians, and what is law to us human beings?

15. All citations from the *Minos* are from Burnet's *Platonis Opera* Volume 5, 1967, unless otherwise noted.

16. More recently, John Finnis has argued that in order to find the fullest account of law, one must take one's bearings from those who take law seriously or who regard it as a morally binding rule rather than as a mere statute or edict (Finnis 1980, 3–19).

17. Lewis discounts the difference between the arts of medicine and divination on the grounds that they were "closer in character in antiquity than they are today" (Lewis 2006, 24n22).

18. For example, Cairns 1949; Chroust 1947, 48; Crowe 1977, xi; Grote 1888, 89–92; Jaeger 1947, 369; Lewis 2006, 37–38; Murphy 2005, 41; and Suarez 1944, 22.

19. See Bruell's discussion of what this implies about the relation between a law and a mere decree (Bruell 1999, 9).

20. For a discussion of the *Statesman's* criticism of law, see, e.g., Rowe (2000a) and Stern (1997).

21. Lewis does not think that Socrates refers to Marsyas because he is an expert in an art that makes divine laws that appeal to the pious. Instead of taking

the story as Socrates offers it, he notes that Marsyas had a reputation for lawlessness before he was killed by Apollo for his hubris and that Alcibiades compares Socrates's speeches to Marsyas's music in Plato's *Symposium* (*Symposium* 215c–e). Lewis concludes from this that Socrates alludes to Marsyas in the *Minos* to remind readers that his own philosophic speeches are as lawless and as useless in lawmaking as is the satyr's music (Lewis 2006, 39–40).

22. At the end of the dialogue, Socrates speaks of how one knows how law distributes good to what it is in the soul of each of us, as if each of us shared something in the soul that becomes better or worse (*Minos* 321d6–7). But it is the manifestly great variety of souls that makes law problematic (*Minos* 317d4–5; cf. Plato *Statesman* 294c). Socrates may be suggesting that divine law can accomplish its goals only if everyone has the same kind of soul. But having claimed that the laws of Minos bring about some good in the souls of the citizens, Socrates may mean that there is some common element to every soul that can be influenced or educated by law.

2—The Rational Interpretation of Divine Law

1. Barrett 1958 (79–80). See, e.g., Plutarch "Life of Nicias," *Parallel Lives of Illustrious Greeks and Romans;* Augustine *Confessions* Book VII; Hegel *Lectures on the History of Philosophy* 1. C. 1.

2. Most of the modern commentators on the *Laws* use the word *reason* to translate the Greek "*nous*." While it is understandable that one might use "reason" to refer to the whole range of phenomena that includes *nous, logos, logismos,* and *phronesis,* the need to distinguish *nous* from these other terms should lead one to use a word such as *intellect* to refer specifically to *nous* and terms such as "reason" or "reasoned argument" to refer to *logos.*

3. According to Barker (1960, 302), Bobonich (2002, 94), and Stalley (1983, 28), Plato is so eager to show that the association between reason and law is not his own invention that he mistakenly asserts that the word for law, *nomos,* is derived from *nous,* a word for reason (Plato *Laws* 714a2 and 957c.).

4. Trevor Saunders agrees that Plato "seems simply to assume that knowledge of the higher reality constitutes some sort of control on that of the lower . . ." (Saunders 1992, 468). Following Stalley, he says that the *Laws* is "stuffed" with a "mass of constitutional, administrative, legal, religious, and social detail," but "nowhere does it tell us, in anything but the foggiest terms, how that detail is supposed to relate to metaphysical realities" (Saunders 1992, 469).

5. All citations are from England's edition of the *Laws* (1921) unless otherwise noted.

6. This contrasts not only with Stalley (1983, 29) but also with modern thinkers such as Montesquieu ("Advertisement" *L'esprit des Lois*).

7. Some have noted that the Athenian Stranger does not include piety among the "divine goods" or virtues that are to be brought forth by divine law (Pangle 1988, 386; Zuckert 2009, 143). But in this reading of the dialogue, it appears that the Athenian Stranger begins by establishing the citizen's piety and proceeds to

show that true piety consists in devotion to laws that aim at the particular virtues or at virtue as a whole.

8. In Plato's dialogues, Socrates does not seem to distinguish as sharply as does Aristotle between the realm of practical reason and the realm of intellect. His principal rationale is that practical questions inevitably give rise to questions that require theoretical insight. In the *Laches,* Socrates is asked to give practical advice about the utility of learning the art of fighting in armor. But in order to resolve this, he finds it necessary to ask what courage is and thus to search for the form of courage. In Book VII of the *Republic,* Socrates refers to the education that he would give to the potential philosophers as an education in practical reason (*Republic* 517c, 518e, 521a–b, 530c; also 505a–b).

9. The athlete Crison (*Laws* 840a) is known because of his achievement at the Olympics in 447 B.C.

10. In the *Republic,* Socrates joins the Athenian Stranger in saying that the gods are not the source of evils and that they are the source only of good things (*Republic* 379b–c), thus agreeing that they are not omnipotent beings. As in the *Euthyphro,* these gods would be understood in light of the unchanging ideas (*Republic* 475e–79a, 504e–511e, 534b–c). Moreover, R. E. England suggests that the struggle to which Zuckert alludes is the battle between good and evil, which the Athenian Stranger says at 904b–c is always resolved by the triumph of the good (England 1921b, 500).

11. See Ahrensdorf (1994).

3—The Examination of the Laws of Sparta

1. Pangle translates the passage as saying that there is an "ancient law that seems to be laid down in nature," following Burnet (1906) rather than England (1921a).

2. The other allusion to such a law is made by Callicles, who says that it is a natural law for the strong to take what they can and to dominate the weak (*Gorgias* 483e). While this is the Athenian Stranger's first allusion to some sort of "natural law," it is not the first reference in the dialogue to a link between law and nature. At the start of the dialogue, Kleinias says that the divine lawgiver looked to nature in order to make the laws for Crete. According to Kleinias's original understanding, nature establishes a war among all the cities and gives each city a compelling need to win the war. It is because Kleinias looks to this underlying natural need and to Crete's natural geographic setting that he is able to recognize the prudence of the legislator whose laws are able to meet Crete's fundamental need. Strauss makes the suggestion that later, when the Athenian Stranger takes up the theme of education, the education that is described in the dialogue is analogous to the education that Cyrus receives in the *Cyropaedia* (Strauss 1975, 17). By comparing the education in the *Laws* to the political education that Cyrus receives in the *Cyropaedia* rather than to the philosophic education that Socrates describes in the *Republic,* Strauss suggests that Plato's purpose in the *Laws* is to examine how

non-philosophers understand divine law and to elaborate the best laws for them rather than to revise what he says in the *Republic* about the best or most complete education of a human being. In response to questions about Kleinias's account of the goals of divine law, Kleinias recognizes that divine law must aim at what is best. When confronted with two alternative accounts of divine law, he looks to what he knows about virtue and about how the virtues are ranked in order to identify which laws are divine. This knowledge about the order of the virtues, says the Athenian Stranger, is given by nature (*Laws* 631d1–2). Consequently, it seems Kleinias relies on what he knows about the nature of the virtues in order to recognize not only the virtue of the lawgiver but also the divinity of the law.

3. See Richer and Whitby for discussions of how *aidos* was worshiped as a god in Sparta (Richer 1999, 91–111; Whitby 2001, 101n88). See Thucydides I, 84.3 and Xenophon *Lacedaemonian Constitution* II, 2 and *Symposium* VIII, 35.

4. Strauss seems to doubt Kleinias's reverence for the law not only because of the relative quickness with which the Athenian Stranger is able to persuade him that the laws of Crete are not divine but also because of the existence in Crete of what Strauss calls the "law of laws."

He is referring to the law that states that everyone must declare publicly that the laws of Crete are noble because they are given by the gods. But the same law also says that old men are permitted to criticize the laws privately when no young people are present. Strauss seems to conclude from this that it is an open secret in Crete, at least among the old men, that the laws of Crete are not divine (Strauss 1975, 11, 15, 20).

5. The need to explain what sort of good that justice is reminds one of Glaucon's demand that Socrates show that justice is a good that should be chosen for what it is by itself rather than for any goods that accompany it (*Republic* 357c–58d). This response would not answer Glaucon's demand to be shown how justice is good without regard for its consequences. As Glaucon suggests, it may seem that the just life is not as rewarding as an unjust life in which one cleverly manages to win praise for being just (*Republic* 358b, 361a).

6. It is with respect to this regime that the Athenian Stranger first speaks of the people as the "*demos*" (*Laws* 681c10). Under the rule of law, the people come to sight as a part of the city rather than as children living under the rule of the patriarch.

4—Divine Law and Moral Education

1. Bobonich notes that unlike Socrates in the *Republic*, the Athenian Stranger does not present the soul as having three parts (2002, 43, 218). Whatever the significance may be of the Athenian Stranger's failure to elaborate such a theory, the Athenian Stranger relies on *thumos* to oppose pain and pleasure in his account of virtue in Book VII. See also *Laws* 731b.

2. For an extensive discussion of the role of *thumos* in civic virtue, see Pangle (1976).

3. See Bolotin (1995) for a helpful discussion of this topic in the *Republic*.

5—The Problem of Erotic Love and Practical Reason under Divine Law

1. It is true that Plato's *Symposium* offers arguments in praise of erotic love. Yet the speeches about erotic love are made because no one had ever offered adequate praise to erotic love (*Symposium* 177a–c). In fact, the symposiasts' elaborate praises reflect that lovers are frequently blamed for their excesses (e.g., *Symposium* 182e–83b, 184e–85a, 187d–e). When Socrates praises erotic love in the dialogue, he says that it can lead human beings to what they lack (*Symposium* 200e). But he does not claim that it can lead young people to feel a passionate desire to be citizens or to rule and be ruled with justice.

2. These three means of resisting erotic desire correspond to the three means that the Athenian Stranger said in Book VI control erotic love: fear, law, and true reason (*Laws* 783a; Strauss 1975, 121). His thinking seems to be that reverence for the gods is grounded in fear (*Laws* 646e–47e), that lovers of honor look to the law to establish what is honorable (*Laws* 632a–c), and that those who love the beauty of the soul can reason that gratifying the love of the body can deprive them of the greater satisfaction that is sought from the beauty of the soul (*Laws* 645b). Yet it is striking that when the Athenian Stranger describes how the love of the beauty of the soul overcomes his or her desire for the body, he does not say that he relies solely on reason. Instead, he says that he is able to curb his desires through reverence and awe for the virtues of the beloved (*Laws* 837c–d). This suggests that the love of the beauty of the soul is not rational in every respect. If reason is able to control erotic desire, it may do so by calling into question not only the erotic love of the body but also the erotic love of the soul. See Lutz 1998, 83–110.

3. Plato's philosophers do not draw as sharp a distinction as does Aristotle between the realm of practical reason and that of wisdom (Kochin 2002, 24n43). One can see how they seem to require one another in Plato's *Laches*. In that dialogue, two fathers wish to know how best to educate their sons. They want to know if they should learn the martial art of fighting in armor. In order to answer this, Socrates says that we need to know what courage is. And to learn what courage is, we must also know what is noble, as such, and what is good, as such. Thus, the most practical questions always require theoretical knowledge of the beings.

4. According to Bobonich, Plato's *Laws* marks an important change in Plato's thinking about the inner workings of the self. Unlike the account in the *Republic* and in other earlier dialogues, he says, the *Laws* deny that the various "parts" of the self or of the soul can be associated with beliefs of their own. There is no reasoning with or persuading the passions. Bobonich acknowledges that when the Stranger calls pain and pleasure "imprudent counselors" he contradicts this thesis. But Bobonich attempts to set aside this passage by saying that it is immediately "rejected as unclear" (2002, 540n78). However, the image is not said to be unclear by the Athenian Stranger but by Kleinias and Megillus (*Laws* 644d4–6). Having been educated by the rule of law, they do not recognize the account of self-rule described by the first image but can accept the "myth of virtue" which accords with their own notions of virtuous self-rule. It is only after the Athenian Stranger substitutes a different description of self-rule that the Cretan and Spartan citizens recognize what he is discussing.

5. The difference between the initial image and the later myth is usually ignored by scholars (e.g., Bobonich 2002; England 1921a, 255; Morrow 1960, 564; and Stalley 1983). Nightingale (1999), however, observes that the first refers to an individual who is ruled by his own reasoning while the latter refers to a whole city that is ruled by law.

6. Bobonich observes that he experiences an intensified sense of self (2002, 274).

6—Perfect Justice and Divine Providence

1. According to Robert Mayhew, "Plato denies the retrograde motion of the planets" in saying that they always follow the same paths and that they do not follow "many paths but only one path" (Mayhew 2008, 147). But the Athenian Stranger may be aware of efforts to account for the retrograde motions of the planets by hypothesizing that the planets move with the circular motions of multiple spheres that move in different directions and at different speeds. See G. E. R. Lloyd (1974), 88–90.

2. In commenting on this passage, Mayhew notes that the Athenian Stranger lists three of the four cardinal virtues but omits justice. Mayhew says that "scholars who seek esoteric readings of the text could have a field day here (and I leave them to it). Plato surely believes that the gods are just; in fact, it is a crucial part of his argument against traditional theism" (Mayhew 2008, 159–60). But we do not need to develop esoteric readings to account for the omission of justice from the start of the argument. Because the Athenian Stranger is trying to provide the indignant youth with a coherent and convincing proof that the gods care about justice, he recognizes that he cannot begin such a proof by positing that they are just.

3. Mayhew very reasonably wonders why the Athenian Stranger concludes that the gods possess the virtues that they demand of us. Mayhew points out that "one could argue that the gods may not admire laziness in humans, and may even command humans not to be lazy, but that they themselves could nevertheless be lazy." Mayhew claims that Plato reasons this way because Plato assumes that "the gods are consistent" and/or "what is good applies to all moral agents" (Mayhew 2008, 161). But instead of tracing the argument to Plato's carelessness, it is more plausible to attribute it to Plato's desire to bring to light how the morally serious citizen thinks about the gods. The reason why the indignant are angry about the gods is that they believe that the gods should be consistent even though they are not. The indignant say that the gods tell us to be just even though they do not pay attention to justice themselves. The Athenian Stranger's strategy in the argument is to appeal to the indignant young man's convictions about the gods. The Athenian Stranger draws on the young man's belief that the gods have numerous virtues. If the gods are what gods are supposed to be, then their virtues do not allow them to be as negligent in regard to us as the indignant youth believes them to be.

4. Bobonich says that the mythic incantations are extensions of the Athenian Stranger's rational argument (2000, 385). But Mayhew joins Dodd in arguing that the mythic incantations are not in themselves "rational" even though they "serve rational ends" (Mayhew 2008, 170; Dodd 1957, 212). According to Strauss, there is a long-standing tradition that holds that the Athenian Stranger's account of

divine providence emerges not from "theoretical philosophy" but from "political" concerns (Strauss 2004, 536). Strauss finds evidence of this tradition in Alexander of Aphrodisias, Galen, Al-Farabi, and Maimonides (Strauss 2004, 542–45).

5. According to Stalley, the myth denies that the god exacts retributive justice on the wicked. He understands it to mean that those who are bad naturally and inevitably live bad lives. But this, he says, cannot be proven and must be taken as a matter of faith. Yet he allows that 904c–d uses conventional language of "rewards in heaven and of punishments in Hades." More generally, he says that Plato "quite illegitimately takes it for granted that, 'because of our common origin,' what is good for the universe as a whole must be good for us as individuals (903c)—a line of argument pervasive in Plato's thought though nonetheless fallacious" (Stalley 1983, 176–77). Stalley does not allow for the possibility that Plato, or rather, his "spokesmen," sometimes say things in order to show us what is persuasive to their interlocutors and to invite us to scrutinize what his interlocutors "take for granted." In this case, the Athenian Stranger makes a point of placing this purportedly pervasive line of argument among the mythic incantations that are meant to persuade an indignant youth to believe that the gods care for human beings.

6. Pangle (1988, 499); see also Aristotle *Nichomachean Ethics* 1104b.

7—The Savior of Divine Law

1. The Athenian Stranger's discussion of courage may seem surprising in that it alludes to a version of courage that develops not through law but through nature. Up until now, he has spoken chiefly about the virtues that are cultivated through law and through moral education. He has argued that human beings are born with an innate fearfulness (*Laws* 791b) and has shown us how this fearfulness is used by the Spartans to build fear and reverence for the law. He has also shown how this fear should be combated by those who provide a correct education or the best education under law. But according to this passage in Book XII, at least some small children acquire a kind of courage without training and cultivation. One might think these children would not need laws or education to maintain and exercise it. But since the Athenian Stranger speaks about this sort of courage as a kind of courage that is a concern of the lawgiver, he suggests that it, too, needs some sort of cultivation. Even natural courage should be guided so that it is consistent with the development of other virtues, especially the intellectual virtues of practical reason and intellect.

2. The Athenian Stranger has provided an example of what it means to take one's bearings by nature by showing the inadequacy of Kleinias's original account of the goals of divine law (*Laws* 625c, 626a, 627d, 631d).

3. Morrow suggests that Plato follows the Pythagoreans in believing that mathematical harmonies pervade the cosmos (Morrow 1960, 506).

4. Stalley notes that the education in the *Laws* falls short of the one in the *Republic* because it mentions neither a separate philosophic way of life nor the

altogether separate forms. The philosophers in the *Republic* study "all reality" while the students in the *Laws* focus only on how to give moral and political guidance (Stalley 1983, 135–36). But the Nocturnal Councilors' education does contain an individualized, critical examination of what the law teaches that is analogous to the dialectical criticism of law in the *Republic* as well as a version of the theoretical life that comes from studying the orderly motions of the heavens, mathematics, and music.

5. For a more developed argument along these lines, see Zuckert 2009, 138–46.

MODERN WORKS CITED

Ahrensdorf, Peter. 1994. "The Question of Historical Context and the Study of Plato." *Polity* 27:113–35.

Arberry, A. J. 1957. *Reason and Revelation in Islam.* London: George Allen & Unwin.

Barker, Ernest. 1960. *Greek Political Theory.* London: Methuen.

Barrett, William. 1958. *Irrational Man.* Garden City, NY: Doubleday.

Benardete, Seth. 2000. *Plato's Laws.* Chicago: University of Chicago Press.

Best, Judith. 1980. "What Is Law? The Minos Reconsidered." *Interpretation* 8 (May):102–13.

Bobonich, Christopher. 2000. "Reading the *Laws.*" In *Form and Argument in Late Plato.* Edited by Christopher Gill and Mary Margaret McCabe. Oxford: Oxford University Press.

———. 2002. *Plato's Utopia Recast.* Oxford: Oxford University Press.

———. 2008. "Plato's Politics." In *Oxford Handbook of Plato.* Edited by Gail Fine. Oxford: Oxford University Press.

Bolotin, David. 1995. "The Critique of Homer and the Homeric Heroes in Plato's *Republic.*" In *Political Philosophy and the Human Soul.* Edited by Michael Palmer and Thomas L. Pangle. Lanham, MD: Rowman and Littlefield. 83–94.

Brisson, Luc, and Samuel Scolnicov, eds. 2003. *Plato's Laws: From Theory into Practice: Proceedings of the 6th Symposium Platonicum.* St. Augustin, Germany: Academia Verlag.

Bruell, Christopher. 1999. *On the Socratic Education.* Lanham, MD: Rowman and Littlefield.

Burges, George. 1891. "Introduction: The *Minos.*" In *Plato.* London: G. Bell & Sons.

Burnet, John. 1906. *Platonis Opera.* Oxford: Oxford University Press.

Cairns, Huntington. 1949. *Legal Philosophy from Plato to Hegel.* Baltimore: Johns Hopkins University Press.

Chroust, Anton Hermann. 1947. "An Anonymous Treatise on Law." *Notre Dame Lawyer* 23:48.

———. 1965. "The Organization of the Corpus Platonicum in Antiquity." *Hermes* 93:34–46.

Cobb, William. 1988. "Plato's *Minos.*" *Ancient Philosophy* 8:187–207.

Cohen, David. 1993. "Law, Autonomy, and Political Community in Plato's *Laws.*" *Classical Philology* 88:301–17.

Crowe, M. B. 1977. *The Changing Profile of the Natural Law.* The Hague: Martinus Nijhoff.

Derenne, Eudore. 1976. *Les Procès D'Impiété.* New York: Arno Press.

Diamond, Eli. 2002. "Understanding and Individuality in the Three Cities: An Interpretation of *Plato's Laws.*" *Animus* 7:2–27.

Dodd, E. R. 1957. *The Greeks and the Irrational*. Boston: Beacon Press.

England, E. B., ed. 1921a. *The Laws of Plato*. Volume One. London: Manchester.

———, ed. 1921b. *The Laws of Plato*. Volume Two. London: Manchester.

Finnis, John. 1980. *Natural Law and Natural Rights*. Oxford: Oxford University Press.

Fustel de Coulanges, Numa Denis. 1984. *La Cité Antique*. Paris: Flammarion.

Gill, Christopher, and Mary Margaret McCabe. 2000. *Form and Argument in Late Plato*. Oxford: Oxford University Press.

Grote, George. 1888. *Plato, and the Other Companions of Socrates*. London: John Murray.

Guthrie, W. K. C. 1971. *Socrates*. London: Cambridge University Press.

Hathaway, R. F., and L. D. Houlgate. 1969. "The Platonic *Minos* and the Classical Theory of Natural Law." *American Journal of Jurisprudence* 14:105–24.

Hodkinson, Stephen, and Anton Powell. 1999. *Sparta: New Perspectives*. London: Duckworth.

Irwin, Terence. 1979. *Plato's Moral Theory*. Oxford: Oxford University Press.

Jaeger, Werner. 1947. "Praise of Law." In *Interpretations of Modern Legal Philosophy*. Edited by Paul Sayre. New York: Oxford University Press.

Kahn, Charles H. 1998. *Plato and the Socratic Dialogue*. Cambridge: Cambridge University Press.

Kelly, John M. 1992. *A Short History of Western Legal Theory*. Oxford: Oxford University Press.

Klosko, George. 1986. *The Development of Plato's Political Theory*. New York: Methuen.

Kochin, Michael. 2002. *Gender and Rhetoric in Plato's Political Thought*. Cambridge: Cambridge University Press.

Kraut, Richard. 1984. *Socrates and the State*. Princeton: Princeton University Press.

———, ed. 1992. *Cambridge Companion to Plato*. Cambridge: Cambridge University Press.

Laks, Andre. 1990. "Legislation and Demiurgy: On the relation between Plato's *Republic* and *Laws*." *Classical Antiquity* 9:209–29.

———. 1991. "L'Utopie legislative de Platon." *Revue philosophique de La France et de l'etranger*. 115:417–28.

———. 2005. "Plato's Laws." In *Cambridge History of Greek and Roman Political Thought*. Edited by Christopher Rowe, Malcolm Schofield, et al. Cambridge: Cambridge University Press.

Lamb, W. R. M. 1927. "Introduction." In *Plato VIII*. London: Loeb.

Lane, Melissa. 2000. "Socrates and Plato: An Introduction." In *The Cambridge History of Greek and Roman Political Thought*. Edited by Christopher Rowe and Malcolm Schofield. Cambridge: Cambridge University Press.

Leibowitz, David. 2010. *The Ironic Defense of Socrates: Plato's Apology*. Cambridge: Cambridge University Press.

Lewis, V. Bradley. 1998. "The Nocturnal Council and Platonic Political Philosophy." *History of Political Thought* 19:1–20.

———. 2006. "Plato's *Minos*: The Political and Philosophical Context of the Problem of Natural Right." *The Review of Metaphysics* 60:17–53.

Lloyd, G. E. R. 1974. *Early Greek Science*. New York: W.W. Norton & Company.

Lutz, Mark J. 1998. *Socrates' Education to Virtue*. Albany: State University of New York Press.

Mayhew, Robert, ed. and trans. 2008. *Plato Laws 10*. Oxford: Oxford University Press.

Meier, Heinrich. 2006. *Leo Strauss and the Theological-Political Problem*. Cambridge: Cambridge University Press.

Moaddel, Mansoor, and Kamran Talattof, eds. 2002. *Modernist and Fundamentalist Debates in Islam*. New York: Palgrave MacMillan.

Morrow, Glenn. 1960. *Plato's Cretan City*. Princeton: Princeton University Press.

Muller, C. W. 1975. *Die Kurzdialoge der Appendix Platonica*. Munich: W. Fink.

Mulroy, David. 2007. "The Concealed Artistry of the *Minos* and the *Hipparchus*." *Transactions of the American Philological Association* 137:115–31.

Murphy, James. 2005. *The Philosophy of Positive Law: Foundations of Jurisprudence*. New Haven: Yale University Press.

Nelson, Alan Jean, ed. 2005. *A Companion to Rationalism*. Oxford: Blackwell.

Nightingale, Andrea Wilson. 1999. "Plato's Lawcode in Context: Rule by Written Law in Athens and Magnesia." *The Classical Quarterly* 49:100–122.

Otto, Rudolph. 1958. *The Idea of the Holy*. Translated by John W. Henry. Oxford: Oxford University Press.

Pangle, Lorraine. 2009. "Moral and Criminal Responsibility in Plato's *Laws*." *American Political Science Review* 103:456–73.

Pangle, Thomas. 1976. "The Political Psychology of Religion in Plato's *Laws*." *The American Political Science Review* 70:1059–77.

———. 1988. "Interpretive Essay." In *The Laws of Plato*. Edited by Thomas Pangle. Chicago: University of Chicago Press. 375–510.

———, ed. and trans. 1987. "The *Minos*." In *The Roots of Political Philosophy*. Ithaca, NY: Cornell University Press.

Parens, Joshua. 1995. *Metaphysics as Rhetoric*. Albany: State University of New York Press.

Penner, Terry. 1992. "Socrates and the Early Dialogues." In *The Cambridge Companion to Plato*. Edited by Richard Kraut. Cambridge: Cambridge University Press.

———. 2000. "Socrates." In *The Cambridge History of Greek and Roman Political Thought*. Edited by Christopher Rowe, Malcolm Schofield, et al. Cambridge: Cambridge University Press.

Phillip, J. A. 1970. "The Platonic Corpus." *Phoenix* 24:296–308.

Raz, Joseph. 1986. *The Morality of Freedom*. Oxford: Oxford University Press.

Richer, Nicolas. 1999. "*Aidos* at Sparta." In *Sparta: New Perspectives*. Edited by Stephen Hodkinson and Anton Powell. London: Duckworth Press.

Rorty, Richard. 1982. *Consequences of Pragmatism*. Minneapolis: University of Minnesota Press.

Rosano, Michael J. 2000. "Citizenship and Socrates in Plato's *Crito*." *Review of Politics* Vol. 62, No. 3:451–77.

Rowe, Christopher. 2000a. "The *Politicus* and Other Dialogues." In *The Cambridge History of Greek and Roman Political Thought*. Cambridge: Cambridge University Press.

———. 2000b. "The *Cleitophon* and *Minos*." In *The Cambridge History of Greek and Roman Political Thought*. Cambridge: Cambridge University Press.

Rowe, Christopher, and Malcolm Schofield, eds. 2005. *The Cambridge History of Greek and Roman Political Thought*. Cambridge: Cambridge University Press.

Sabine, George. 1961. *A History of Political Theory*. London: Harrap.

Saunders, Trevor. 1970. *The Laws* by Plato. New York: Penguin Books.

———. 1992. "Plato's Later Political Theory." In *Cambridge Companion to Plato*. Edited by Richard Kraut. Cambridge: Cambridge University Press.

Schofield, Malcolm. 2003. "Religion and Philosophy in the *Laws*." In *Plato's Laws: From Theory to Practice*. Edited by Samuel Scolnicov and Luc Brisson. St. Augustin, Germany: Academia Verlag.

Shorey, Paul. 1933. *What Plato Said*. Chicago: University of Chicago Press.

Sinclair, T. A. 1952. *A History of Greek Political Thought*. London: Routledge & Kegan Paul.

Stalley, R. F. 1983. *An Introduction to Plato's Laws*. New York: Hackett.

———. 1994. "Persuasion in Plato's *Laws*." *History of Political Thought* Vol XV:157–77.

Stern, Paul. 1997. "The Rule of Wisdom and the Rule of Law in Plato's *Statesman*." *American Political Science Review* Vol. 91, 2:264–76.

Strauss, Leo. 1975. *The Argument and the Action of Plato's Laws*. Chicago: the University of Chicago Press.

———. 1987. "On the *Minos*." In *The Roots of Political Philosophy*. Edited by Thomas Pangle. Ithaca, NY: Cornell University Press.

———. 2004. "The Place of the Doctrine of Providence According to Maimonides." *Review of Metaphysics* Vol. 57, 3:537–49.

———. 2006. "Reason and Revelation (1948)." In *Leo Strauss and the Theological-Political Problem*. Edited by Heinrich Meier. Cambridge: Cambridge University Press.

Suarez, Francisco. 1944. *Three Selections from the Works of Suarez*. Oxford: Clarendon Press.

Vander Waerdt, Paul, ed. 1994. *The Socratic Movement*. Ithaca, NY: Cornell University Press.

Vlastos, Gregory. 1991. *Socrates, Ironist and Moral Philosopher*. Ithaca, NY: Cornell University Press.

———. 1998. "Reason and Causes in the Phaedo." In *Plato: Critical Assessments Volume 3*. Edited by Nicholas D. Smith. New York: Routledge Press.

Weinreb, Lloyd L. 1987. *Natural Law and Justice*. Cambridge, MA: Harvard University Press.

Whitby, Michael. 2001. *Sparta*. New York: Routledge Press.

Zuckert, Catherine. 2004. "Plato's *Laws*: Postlude or Prelude to Socratic Political Philosophy?" *The Journal of Politics* 66:374–95.

———. 2009. *Plato's Philosophers: The Coherence of the Dialogues*. Chicago: The University of Chicago Press.

INDEX